LIBERTY AND SLAVERY

CONFLICTING WORLDS

New Dimensions of the American Civil War

T. Michael Parrish, Series Editor

LIBERTY

—AND—

SLAVERY

EUROPEAN SEPARATISTS, SOUTHERN SECESSION, AND THE AMERICAN CIVIL WAR

NIELS EICHHORN

LOUISIANA STATE UNIVERSITY PRESS

BATON ROUGE

Published by Louisiana State University Press
Manufactured in the United States of America
First printing

Designer: Barbara Neely Bourgoyne
Typeface: Ingeborg
Printer and binder: LSI

Library of Congress Cataloging-in-Publication Data
Names: Eichhorn, Niels, 1984– author.
Title: Liberty and slavery : European separatists, southern secession, and the
    American Civil War / Niels Eichhorn.
Description: Baton Rouge : Louisiana State University Press, [2019] | Series:
    Conflicting worlds : new dimensions of the American Civil War | Includes
    bibliographical references and index.
Identifiers: LCCN 2019005203 | ISBN 978-0-8071-7167-7 (cloth : alk. paper) |
    ISBN 978-0-8071-7181-3 (pdf) | ISBN 978-0-8071-7182-0 (epub)
Subjects: LCSH: Separatist movements—History—19th century. | Europe—
    History—Autonomy and independence movements. | Secession—Southern
    States. | Forty—Eighters (American immigrants) | United States—History—
    Civil War, 1861–1865—Participation, Foreign. | United States—History—Civil
    War, 1861–1865—Causes. | Liberty—History—19th century. | Antislavery
    movements—History—19th century. | Europe—Emigration and immigration—
    History—19th century. | United States—Emigration and immigration—
    History—19th century.
Classification: LCC D359.7 .E53 2019 | DDC 973.7/13—dc23

To Stephanie

CONTENTS

ACKNOWLEDGMENTS

Liberty and Slavery had a long and at times crooked route to navigate. I hardly imagined becoming a Civil War historian when I first got a peek at the conflict, in the late 1990s, watching the movie *Gettysburg* at home in Germany. While I got interested, many people along the way helped steer me away from the military and toward the transnational aspects of the war.

Much of my thanks belongs to Terry Beckenbaugh and Judy Gentry, who took an interested ESOL student under their wings. Terry got me interested in the relations between the German states and the United States during the Civil War, where I discovered Rudolph Schleiden, a figure that greatly intrigued me. I only later discovered that we both are from the same region and that I was in part doing a local history of my home region by studying him. During Terry's brief mentorship, I had not yet asked how a revolutionary from 1848 translated his experiences into the Civil War era. Judy humored my interest in the diplomatic side of the Civil War, dramatically advanced my understanding of the subject, and pushed me as a writer and historian. I am extremely thankful to have had these two wonderful teachers in my early career.

However, much of the credit for the transnational nature of *Liberty and Slavery* goes to Dan Sutherland and Laurence Hare. Dan's mentorship and Laurence's intellectual challenges dramatically transformed what I had envisioned as a study chronicling Schleiden's life into a project that looked at a few individuals from the Schleswig-Holstein uprising of 1848 as they translated their revolutionary experiences into the sectionally torn United States. The interlibrary loan staff at the University of Arkansas was just amazing in obtaining all my requests for rare, old German publications, which they at times got from as far away as Denmark. However, I have to especially thank Dan for his patience.

Although the subject was interesting as a project, I quickly determined to make major changes and to expand my focus beyond Schleswig-Holstein and look at other secessionist movements. Again the interlibrary loan staff, both at the University of Arkansas and at Middle Georgia State College (later University), were extremely helpful in obtaining rare works on Irish, Polish, and Hungarian history. My editor at LSU Press, Mike Parrish, was always a great help when I had questions about structure or direction. It has been a great pleasure working with LSU Press on this project.

I also wish to thank the staff at the Schleswig-Holsteinische Landesbibliothek in Kiel, the Staatsarchiv Bremen, and the library at the Christian Albrecht Universität in Kiel. They were extremely helpful in working with my often limited amount of time and the vast pile of documents I wished to consult. The secretary in Bremen, especially, was extremely helpful in making sure that I could take along, in person, as many copies as possible, to cut down on mailing costs.

At the same time, my many friends and colleagues deserve thanks for their support and conversations at conferences, especially Bob May, Paul Quigley, Brian Schoen, Pat Kelly, Duncan Campbell, Phil Myers, and David Schieffler. Of great help was the Virginia Sesquicentennial conference at George Mason and the Forty-Eighter conference at Wartburg College, where I presented on and got some good feedback for this project. Special thanks goes to Enrico Dal Lago and Daniel Nagel, who read the entire manuscript and provided extremely helpful feedback to strengthen the work.

However, my greatest thanks goes to my family. My mother, who was torn from us too early by cancer, in August 2017, supported the crazy history undertaking of her son financially and morally in its early stages, both during research trips in Germany and at my U.S. universities. Even more, my wonderful wife, Steph, and the many furries she brought into our lives, by choice or accidentally, and who frequently reminded me of having to take breaks, have been incredibly important to keep me going to complete this project. It is to my love that *Liberty and Slavery* is dedicated.

LIBERTY AND SLAVERY

INTRODUCTION

The Separatist Atlantic World

A single section governed by the will of the numerical majority, has now, in fact, the control of the Government and the entire powers of the system. What was once a constitutional federal republic, is now converted, in reality, into one as absolute as that of the Autocrat of Russia, and as despotic in its tendency as any absolute government that ever existed.

—JOHN C. CALHOUN, *The Papers of John C. Calhoun*

On October 26, 1863, the Hungarian refugee Emeric Szabad, serving with the Third Corps of the Union Army of the Potomac, left camp for a reconnaissance ride along the Rappahannock River in northern Virginia. As Szabad's horse trotted through the night, he had an unfortunate encounter with Confederate pickets. While his companion escaped, Szabad did not. A Confederate officer questioned the Hungarian.

"On being asked what state I belonged to, I replied, 'Hungary,'" Szabad confessed in his diary. "This word filled my captain with a sort of astonishment; he found it incomprehensible, how a Hungarian could fight with the d—d Yankees against the Southern people who were fighting for what Hungarians had fought for in 1848." Szabad explained, "I came to America to fight for the Union, the destruction of which would cause joy to none but tyrants and despots."[1] To Szabad, the inquiry by the Confederate officer had a straightforward answer.

Historians have not adequately asked the Confederate's question when dealing with European separatist migrants. After all, the Civil War was only the latest iteration of a series of conflicts between nationalities in 1830 and 1848 to bring about independence from enslavement and oppression. If European migrants had feared enslavement in Europe, they frequently interpreted the southern defense of constitutional rights as originating from an aristocratic minority intent on forcing its will on the country as a whole. Others identified the southern desire for self-determination in the face of an oppressive, imperial Union with their own separatist struggle in Europe. Their separatist background and the way in which they interpreted the sectional struggle influenced the decision of European separatist migrants from the failed 1830 and 1848 uprisings to side with either the Union or the Confederacy.

Usually, Europeans who participated in the revolutions of 1848 are seen as staunch defenders of the ideals of democracy and nationalism. As one conference program described them, "The 'Forty-Eighters' were a relatively small number of individuals who emigrated from Europe in the late 1840s and early 1850s after fighting unsuccessfully with both pen and sword for liberty, democracy, and national unity."[2] Such a view is simplistic, since only a small group embraced democracy. If European revolutionaries supported independence, liberty, liberalism, republicanism, or democratic governments, why would some support an oppressive, slaveholding minority? How could revolutionaries such as the Irish, who had shown a love for liberty and anger at British subjugation, support an oppressive institution such as slavery?

These questions are not new. Members of the founding generation in the United States, including Thomas Jefferson and George Washington, struggled with being both slaveholders and proponents of liberty. As drafter of the Declaration of Independence, Jefferson enshrined the idea that "all men are created equal." Nevertheless, Jefferson was a slaveholder, with as many as two hundred slaves working on his plantation in Albemarle County, Virginia. Even though he supported emancipation, he wished to educate slaves and to return them to Africa.

In fact, Jefferson and Virginia represented racial social organization like nowhere else. During its colonial period, Virginia had created a racial dichotomy to define a person's status and ameliorate socioeconomic difference in white society. By making slaves the oppressed social underclass, Virginia's planter elite merged poor and rich white interests and temporarily eliminated the danger of the lower strata rising against the elite. Southern republicans claimed that slavery reminded white people about the preciousness of freedom. Rich planters only reluctantly extended to the lower strata of society the right to vote, to avoid challenges to the planters' hold on power.[3] However, new enlightened and revolutionary ideas caused dilemmas for slaveholders.

Slavery did not necessarily mean the permanent chattel bondage of a human being; some people considered themselves slaves because they lacked political, social, and/or economic rights. One could suffer from tyrannical rule as an individual or as a people without being owned. In the Declaration of Independence, Jefferson called on people "to alter or to abolish" destructive, oppressive, or despotic forms of government. He asserted the right and duty of oppressed people to rise up. In their arguments against the perceived oppressive policies of the British mother country, the revolutionaries relied on the political language of England's Glorious Revolution of 1688 to 1689.[4]

The Glorious Revolution laid an important foundation for the development of liberal nation-states. During the rebellion, opponents of King James II feared religious and political oppression—or as they termed it, slavery. Willem III van Oranje, in his declaration of October 1688, justified his assumption of government in England by saying, "We may prevent all those miseries, which must needs follow upon the nations being kept under arbitrary government and slavery." Colley Cibber, a critic of King James II, argued that the old king's intention was "to drive all England into popery and slavery."[5]

Obviously, neither Willem nor Cibber feared that the English people would face literal enslavement like African chattel, but, for them, the lack of political, economic, and social liberties degraded them into a state of slavery. Terms associated with slavery or abolition appeared frequently in the literature of political reform movements as they questioned tyrannical rulers.

The French Revolution provided a new language for revolutionaries, as they demanded constitutional governments, though few were ready to embrace democratic institutions outright, in light of the disastrous outcome of the Reign of Terror. Nevertheless, the desire for more representative governments and for monarchies reined in by constitutions grew. In addition, the advancing French armies and the repressive policies of the Congress of Vienna system led oppressed nationalities and ethnic groups to demand independent nation-states. Calls to end oppression and create nation-states remained restricted to elite groups, which had to imagine a community of shared interests, cultures, and traditions before a successful rebellion could materialize.[6]

In 1807, German intellectual Johann Gottlieb Fichte elaborated on a universal but ethnically based nationalism. After a lengthy explanation of the Roman past, he argued, "It is they whom we must thank—we, the immediate heirs of their soil, their language, and their way of thinking—for being Germans still, for being still borne along on the stream of original and independent life. It is they whom we must thank for everything that we have been as a nation since those days, and to them we shall be indebted for everything that we shall be in the future, unless things come to an end with us now and the last drop of blood inherited from them has dried up in our veins."[7] Fichte made the lasting connection between a people and the land they lived on—ethnic nationalism. However, even an ethnic nationalism needed imagining. At the same time, Fichte did not attach a political ideology to nationalism.

Fichte's suggestions of blood ties between people and soil found many converts, much to the displeasure of the reactionary authorities, who desired to protect the political and national status quo. In 1820, the archconservative framer of the new Europe, Klemens Wenzel Lothar, Fürst von Metternich-Winneburg zu Beilstein, provided a counterargument. He explained, "The first principle to be followed by the monarchs, united as they are by the coincidence of their desires and opinions, should be that of maintaining the stability of political institutions against the disorganised excitement which has taken possession of men's minds; the immutability of principles against the madness of their interpretation; and respect for laws actually in force against a desire for their destruction." Metternich did not tolerate liberal or national challenges. However, like his liberal nationalist rivals, Metternich's vision was universal. "In short," Metternich wrote, "let the great monarchs strengthen their union, and prove to the world that if it exists, it is beneficent, and ensures the political peace of Europe."[8] Metternich's views were out of touch with the new nineteenth-century reality.

Building on nationalist thinkers, Giuseppe Mazzini emphasized historical achievements, cultural ties, shared traditions, and common language to call on the Italian people to unified and to create a republican nation-state. To Mazzini, national and political revolution went hand in hand. In his criticism of cautious revolutionaries, Mazzini argued, "They do not understand that, after many centuries of slavery, a nation can only be generated through virtue, or through death." Obviously, Italians were not in a state of chattel slavery, but foreign rule kept Italy oppressed and fragmented. Italy needed liberation, emancipation from oppression. "Without liberty there is no true society," Mazzini wrote, "because any association between free men and slaves is impossible."[9]

In contrast to his predecessors, Mazzini added a political vision to his national one. He dismissed monarchy, which no longer maintained "a bond of unity and authority in the state." Mazzini believed in the inevitability of a liberal Italian nation-state. "Republican—because theoretically every nation is destined by the law of God and humanity, to form a free and equal community of brothers," he wrote, "and the republican is the only form of government that insures this future. Because all true sovereignty resides essentially in the nation, the sole progressive and continuous interpreter of the supreme moral law."[10] Mazzini's message was universal, but cautious with regard to democratic reforms.

The early nineteenth century witnessed a clash of visions between reactionary monarchical principles and liberal nationalism. Many liberals and nationalists across Europe embraced aspects of Mazzini's vision. The present study explores perceptions of political, social, economic, and national oppression or enslavement.

The middle decades of the nineteenth century witnessed a series of major political and national revolutions, which sent a flood of political migrants across the Atlantic Ocean.[11] Around 1830, political and nationalist rebellions swept across the European continent. However, these events paled in comparison with those of 1848, when literally the entire continent suffered from political and national revolutions.

Faced with defeat, hundreds of revolutionaries arrived in the United States, where they contributed to the growing sectional conflict.

Among these migrants, historians have often focused on the so-called Forty-Eighters from the German states. However, scholars present a superficial and flawed understanding of the events in Europe. Some revolutions indeed aimed for national unity, such as that of the liberal German nation-state. However, not all Forty-Eighters favored unification. Some demanded separation from an oppressive state. In addition, the ideological spectrum was incredibly diverse, with conservatives, monarchists, liberals, democrats, republicans, socialists, communists, Marxists, and various shades thereof vying for influence. Grouping Karl Daniel Adolph Douai, the Thuringian socialist who participated in the Saxe-Altenburg uprisings; Friedrich Franz Karl Hecker, a future Union general who was part of the radical movement in Baden; Johann August Ernst von Willich, an early communist thinker and Prussian noble who fought alongside Hecker; and Carl Schurz, a Prussian Rhineland radical who supported the creation of a republican-based German nation-state, into one large liberal, liberty-embracing group of German national unifiers and unquestioned Union supporters is problematic. Historians have only recently started to take into consideration the European background of Forty-Eighters.[12]

Despite addressing Forty-Eighter studies, the present book embraces a transnational methodology. Civil War historians such as Don Doyle, Andre Fleche, and Paul Quigley have inaugurated a new transnational framework to understand how people in the United States looked to Europe for inspiration as both northern and southern sections formulated their national identities. Fleche asserts that radical thinkers on both sides of the Atlantic took inspiration from one another. The conflict in North America had broad implications for the political and national development of the world. Fleche and Quigley focus on the formation of a national identity in the United States. Others, such as Enrico Dal Lago, have used a comparative methodology to better understand what the United States and European countries went through in their nation-defining conflicts or to compare radical thinkers like Mazzini and William Lloyd Garrison.[13]

Even in its infancy, transnational scholarship has shown the importance of a wider perspective on the Civil War era to understanding
why the disagreements between the two factions culminated in such
a devastating war.

More importantly, transnational scholarship challenges perceptions of U.S. exceptionalism. To some, the United States is a special
place because of its unique birth as a free and democratic nation with
an abundance of natural resources. On the other hand, the United
States is negatively unique with its acceptance of violence, racism
toward nonwhite people, and overbearing attitude. However, for
decades, Ian Tyrrell has reminded historians that the United States
was deeply connected with the world through the exchange of goods,
ideas, and people. Regarding the Civil War, he argues, "Not only have
Americans wrongly treated the war as unique. Foreigners did likewise
at the time." Although Tyrrell's list of similarities is extensive, ranging
from casualty figures to military modernization, national unification,
economic relations, and emancipation, there is one missing aspect:
secession. Taking a more ambiguous stance, James McPherson claims
that the southern states were not exceptional. The industrializing
North was the exception in the world. The debate continues, with
some historians still focused on how the United States influenced "European institutions, religions, mores, and political philosophies."[14]
Placing the Civil War in a transnational context demonstrates that
neither secession nor the southern political system was exceptional.

Challenging exceptionalism narratives by building on Forty-Eighter
and transnational scholarship, this study looks at European separatist revolutionaries, whose primary goal in Europe was to break
away from oppressive states. Separatism was not a new, nineteenth-
century ism. The independence movements in the Americas were
separatist in nature. Broadly defined, secession is the breaking of
one people away from an existing state and the creation of a new
state. As Jean-Pierre Cabestan and Aleksandar Pavković define it,
"Separatism is based on a political objective that aims to reduce the
political and other powers of the central government of a state over
a particular territory and to transfer those powers to the population
or elites representing the population of the territory in question."[15]

As is true of many studies on secession/separatism and nationalism, Cabestan and Pavković unfortunately focus on the twentieth century in Europe.

Successful secession achieves independence. Threats of or the use of force were often necessary to accomplish secessionist goals. The de facto creation of a new state required the establishment of government institutions. Secessionist nation-states had to determine how to deal with ethnic or national minorities who did not wish to be part of the newly emerging state. The concept of self-determination, which underlay secession/separatism, emerged during the eighteenth century and drew inspiration from theories of national identity.

Furthermore, secessionists tended to seek redress for their grievances within the established political system and turned to violence only as a last resort. Secessionists often lacked the political, military, and economic structures needed to defend themselves. Regardless of the reasons and intentions of separatists, unless the state constitution permitted secession, the step was illegal. The formal right of self-determination is a recent development; nevertheless, people have long claimed the right to overthrow oppressive rulers.[16]

In contrast to historians of the twentieth century, Don Doyle explains that *secessio* was a peaceful Roman plebeian protest of temporary withdrawal. In the nineteenth century, with the rise of liberal politics and nationalism, Doyle argues, separatism became more prominent. He defines "secession [as coming] to mean a more permanent separation, usually from a nation-state or other political alliance, though it was also used to describe withdrawal from a church or other nonpolitical organization." He furthers his definition by stating, "When a territory and its inhabitants *secede,* however, they not only withdraw their allegiance to the nation but also—and here is the rub—separate from it, abolish the former government, and set up a new independent state." Separatism was permanent when successful. In his definition, Doyle embraces the assumption that nations are an artificial creation, an "imagined community."[17]

The concept of an imagined national community has gained favor over Fichte's nineteenth-century notion of an ethnic nationalism. However, the old dichotomy between ethnic and civic nationalism is no longer valid. Nationalism studies frequently ignore the Americas, despite the many similarities between the formation of European and American nation-states. Without a coherent ethnic identity, nationalism in the United States relied on the ideals of the founding generation. Nineteenth-century political elites had to reach out to apolitical peasants and workers, who cared primarily about their economic status, to artificially create nation-states. Michael Mann claims, "As states transformed first into national states, then into nation-states, classes became caged, unintentionally "naturalized" and politicized.[18]

Nationalism could invoke emotional or irrational fears shaped either over a prolonged period of nation-state creation or for short-term goals. While the formation of nation-states often involved the creation of large new entities, regionalism and local identities were the framework around which these states emerged. Furthermore, war was an effective means to instill a national identity.[19] Considering the multiple factors underlying nation-states, a dichotomy of civic and ethnic nation-state is too simplistic. Separatists had to contend with religion, language, ethnic/racial origins, economic development, political institutions, and war as they molded national identities.

Therefore, this work defines separatism as a national identity grounded in a shared heritage and political history, which was at odds with the larger state's national identity. As a result, separatists searched for freedom from national and political oppression. In their quest for liberation, separatist-minded communities adopted identities based on a shared culture, history, religion, political institutions, language, and way of life. National identity did not require but benefitted from ethnic ties. With two different nationalities at odds and one being in political control, the weaker group demanded national and constitutional protection. When attempts to gain greater political freedom and autonomy failed, separatists embraced rebellion and independence. Importantly, separatism was both nationalist and political.

Historians have overlooked the separatist rebellions in Poland, Hungary, Ireland, and Schleswig-Holstein and the migration experiences of separatists from these regions. Military or Forty-Eighter studies usually ignore the political, ideological, and national origins of their subjects. A study of these four groups not only places the secession crisis in the United States in a broader, transnational nineteenth-century separatist context but also shows that European separatists had a difficult decision to make when the war in the United States started. They came to the United States with heavy ideological baggage.

The Irish, who are often seen as either refugees of the famine or as important contributors to the armies during the American Civil War, had the shortest rebellion of 1848. Lasting only six days, young Irish radicals unsuccessfully tried to separate their homeland from British political oppression. At the same time, the Hungarians made a case against Austrian-Habsburg oppression. However, Austrian and Russian gun barrels blasted Hungarian independence desires into oblivion. The longest uprising of 1848 was the unsuccessful and complicated separatist attempt by German residents in the Dano-German borderland of Schleswig-Holstein. Even Poland briefly rebelled, but utterly failed, against the conservative eastern powers. All uprisings sent waves of separatist-minded political refugees across the Atlantic to the United States.

Separatists of the 1848 revolution were a large group but only the second group of secessionists to come to the United States. Already in 1830, Europe had suffered from a series of political and national rebellions. With Greece and France leading the way, Poland struggled to shed Russian despotism. The ill-prepared Poles fought an unsuccessful, almost yearlong war against Russia. Faced with death, many Poles sought exile. The so-called Novembrists or *Dreissiger*, refugees of the political upheavals of the 1830s, were not numerous; many of them remained in Europe, awaiting their second chance.[20] Both Novembrists and Forty-Eighters made important contributions and looked back at their revolutionary experiences when another separatist revolution approached, in the United States in 1860.

One goal of this study is to show that separatism/secessionism was a widespread phenomenon during the early and mid-nineteenth century. Historians have done little comparative work with regard to separatist uprisings during the nineteenth century. Don Doyle, in his edited volume on separatism, only includes the United States and Texas/Yucatan as examples of nineteenth-century separatism. Most works on secession focus on the twentieth century.[21] However, there are many similarities among the uprisings in Poland in 1830; in Ireland, Poland, Schleswig-Holstein, and Hungary in 1848; and in the southern

Confederacy in 1860 to 1861. In all five regions, people argued against a constitutional or even imperial oppression of their nationality by what they perceived as a foreign power. They shared the perception that their rights, if not already violated, were in danger of violation and needed defending, by separation if necessary. The initial push was to remedy the legal oppression by requesting autonomy. When those moderate demands failed, extremists gained the upper hand and pushed for independence.

The vast majority of European separatist refugees who resided in the United States at the start of the Civil War sympathized with the Union and fought the southern slavocracy, though there were notable exceptions, such as Irish and Polish exiles who supported the Confederacy. The major question of this work is why revolutionary separatists, who shared experiences similar to those of the Confederacy, decided to fight against a fellow separatist uprising.

Most historians have argued that the Forty-Eighters' abhorrence of slavery, or their residency in the northern states, kept them away from the Confederacy.[22] However, this generalization fails when one considers that some Forty-Eighters did fight for the southern states and that European separatist migrants did not universally oppose slavery. The other often-used explanation—that most Forty-Eighters resided in the north and by default of geography sided with the Union—does not consider the many people who crossed the sectional divide to fight with the section of their choice rather than their residence. The story of European revolutionaries in the United States, as told so far, is too simple and needs to take into consideration the complexities faced by separatist migrants.

In contrast to previous scholarship, this book takes a different point of origin. Where Forty-Eighter or transnational histories usually start with the arrival of immigrants in the United States, thus ignoring their political, social, or economic backgrounds, this study explores their crucial European political roots, which explains not only the ideological baggage they carried with them but also their decision to side with either the Union or the Confederacy. Furthermore, thinking in comparative terms about separatist movements around the Atlantic World between 1830 and 1865 requires detailed introductions to all five regions and uprisings. Such an undertaking faces the dilemma that contemporaries did not leave detailed accounts of their activities in Europe and the United States. For example, Irish patriot Patrick Cleburne's life in Arkansas and the Confederate Army is well documented, but little is known about his Irish upbringing.

This study relies on the stories of a number of influential leaders from Poland, Hungary, Schleswig-Holstein, and Ireland. Few Polish Novembrists migrated to the United States. The stories of Adam Gurowski, the Polish revolutionary turned U.S. State Department employee, and of Kacper Tochman and Ignatius Szymański, both of whom fought for the Confederacy, illustrate the tensions within the Polish community. Polish Forty-Eighters like Włodzimierz Krzyżanowski and Joseph Kargé had no love for the Confederacy.

Only a small number of Hungarian Forty-Eighters came to the United States. Union military leaders such as Alexander Asbóth and Charles Zagonyi illustrate the firm Hungarian commitment to the Union. Similarly, Schleswig-Holstein German separatists, such as radical nationalists Theodor Olshausen and Hans Reimer Claussen and the moderate liberal nationalist Rudolph Schleiden, favored the Union.

Finally, the stories of Irish Forty-Eighters John Mitchel, Thomas Francis Meagher, and Patrick Cleburne indicate how deeply divided the Irish community was when faced with sectionalism. This relatively small group of separatist revolutionaries personalizes the decisions made by separatist-minded nationalists in the United States.

Following these individuals from revolution to revolution, this study will progress chronologically. Starting with the first set of separatist revolutions, in 1830, each of the five regions—Hungary, Ireland, Poland, Schleswig-Holstein, and the U.S. South—struggled against oppressive overlords. Ireland, Poland, and South Carolina challenged authority, but the other two regions remained calm. None of the five regions had yet developed a coherent national identity. The revolutionary-minded separatists shared a growing perception that they were enslaved people who needed liberation. The calls for emancipation were loudest in Hungary, Ireland, and Poland. Where Ireland was successful with Catholic emancipation, Poland failed dismally to regain its independence. Finally, U.S. southern separatists discovered the need for unity during the Nullification Crisis. All separatist-minded revolutionaries demanded liberal, republican, and/or democratic political changes, shying away from universal manhood suffrage.

In 1848, separatist uprisings occurred in Hungary, Ireland, Poland, and Schleswig-Holstein. However, a new cast of revolutionary leaders had emerged with radical demands. The Irish and the Schleswig-Holstein Germans no longer perceived themselves as enslaved people and instead embraced constitutional, political arguments against their oppressors. In the eastern parts of Europe, separatist leaders continued to argue against their enslavement. Many radical-minded revolutionaries questioned their own governments' policies, demanding democratic reforms. Despite the almost universal disintegration of Europe, however, separatist demands for national independence and political reform faced insurmountable barricades. Moreover, such separatist challenges did not occur only in Europe; in the course of the Free Soil revolt of 1848, the United States once more faced the specter of southern secession. Thus, all five regions experienced some form of revolutionary challenge, the justifications and arguments differing only slightly, and there was a widespread perception of oppression and of a need for independence.

Failure forced many separatists into exile in the United States, infusing their revolutionary views and language into the growing sectional divide. European migrants took diverse paths to reach the promised land of freedom. They found their new residence politically, economically, and socially challenging. Even more, European separatist migrants faced an all too familiar situation. The expansion of slavery and the growing and vocal extremism on both sides took their political toll. Both North and South claimed to represent the ideal of the Declaration of Independence, embracing liberty, equality, and democracy. As tensions increased, separatist Novembrists and Forty-Eighters found themselves leading their respective immigrant communities. Slavery was an important issue, and some Europeans questioned southern slaveholding practices as well as the moral and social impact of slavery on southern society. Translating their experiences to the United States, European separatists could support either an imperially oppressed southern minority or a northern majority upholding constitutional law.

With separatism a reality, European separatists had to decide, based on their experiences, whether to support fellow separatists or oppose southern separatism. If they had perceived of themselves as enslaved people, separatists were especially likely to see the conflict through the prism of an oppressive, aristocratic minority enslaving the country and destroying the constitutional system of government. However, the ambiguity of political arguments allowed others to see an oppressive North intent on enslaving southerners. At the same time, another revolutionary legacy reappeared among these radicals. As Union and Confederate authorities infringed upon civil liberties, separatists questioned their governments once again. Only the highest principles of liberal, republican, and/or democratic government received support, and any violations were fought to the utmost. For many, the Civil War was a second chance.

Despite their work in the United States, many separatists remained at heart loyal to their home nation and desired nothing less than independence. Having failed in 1830, 1848, and 1861, separatists received one last chance to challenge their overlords, in the 1860s and 1870s. Some separatists returned to Europe at the end of the Civil War and supported their own nations' second attempt to gain independence. They were always separatist nationalists, even if they stood against southern separatism. Separatist challenges in Ireland, Poland, and Schleswig-Holstein in the 1860s and 1870s again failed. However, Hungary and the U.S. South gained autonomy, leaving both regions in charge of their own social, economic, and political destiny. At the same time, new class identities replaced national ones. Defeat overshadowed mid-nineteenth-century separatism as powerful new nation-state empires emerged.

Separatism was a universal experience across the Atlantic World during the middle decades of the nineteenth century. As nationalism created identities and constitutions reined in monarchical powers, people searched for their place in the world of liberal nationalism. When nationalities realized their separateness and the oppression of both their nationality and their political rights, demands for independence appeared. Some separatists accepted small and incremental changes; many demanded autonomy and independence. From Charleston to Pest and from Warsaw to Galway, separatists looked to each other for inspiration.

Southern secession in 1861 was just the latest manifestation. However, for European separatist migrants, who had failed in their own independence struggles in 1830 or 1848, southern secession was a dilemma. European separatists who had feared enslavement in Europe frequently looked to a southern minority forcing its will on, enslaving, the United States. Some migrants sympathized with the desire of southerners to claim self-determination, continue a democratic legacy, and escape an oppressive, imperial Union. However, the vast majority of European migrants supported the Union against an aristocratic-looking minority intent on destroying or at least dominating the United States, eliminating the beacon many European separatists had looked to for help and inspiration during their own rebellions. Their European background and interpretation of the sectional struggle influenced their decision to side with Union or Confederacy.

1

THE REVOLUTIONS OF 1830

"Brave Belgians, you gloriously defeated. Know how to enjoy the victory. Your cowardly enemies shall be astonished. Do not waste a moment. . . . Freedom for all! Equality before the supreme power: the nation; before his will: the law. You crushed despotism; your faith is in the power that you have created; you will protect yourselves against anarchy and its fatal consequences. The Belgians should shake their enemies."[1] With these words, Louis Joseph Antoine de Potter, a prominent Belgian pamphleteer and thinker, announced Belgium's independence from the Netherlands, on September 28, 1830. He asked his fellow countrymen to focus on the struggle for freedom and to oust the oppressive Dutch. Belgians should not accept defeat, he argued, and should use the overconfidence of their enemy to push for independence.

The Belgian nation demanded freedom and a new political system. Belgians used the national and political arguments of previous revolutions to justify their own bid for independence. The French Revolution of 1789 laid the foundation for liberalism, republicanism, and nationalism. Since all three required time to mature and spread among people, the desire for liberal nation-states remained restricted to the upper intellectual strata. Students and professors believed that a constitutional government built by a people with a shared ethnic, cultural, or historical identity provided a stronger basis for a state than did monarchy. The imagined community these thinkers envisioned was slow to form, and few were prepared to challenge the reactionary order in 1830. Nevertheless, challenges appeared when Belgium, Greece, Ireland, Poland, Rio Grande do Sul, Texas, Yucatan, and many other parts of the Atlantic region rose up to demand the restoration of constitutional rights and redress for other specific grievances.[2] When governments and kings ignored, refused, or brushed aside those requests, conflict followed and calls for independence appeared.

The first separatist challenge came in Greece. After more than three hundred years of Ottoman rule, the Greek elite perceived the religious differences between themselves and their Islamic overlords, the heavy burden of taxation, and the legal oppression as significant enough to demand autonomy. The rebellion started in 1821. Faced with an impossible military situation, the Ottoman sultan enlisted the help of his vassal Muhammad Ali, the pasha of Egypt, whose involvement elevated the conflict from a domestic uprising to an international conflict. As a result, Russia and Great Britain offered their good office. After the unfortunate incident in the Bay of Navarino, the European powers actively supported the Greek cause, which allowed Greece to claim its independence in 1832, a separatist success.[3]

Inspiration for other uprisings came not only from Greece but also from France. In the 1820s, Charles X had restored the Catholic Church to a place of prominence, reimbursed French nobles who had lost property in the process of the French Revolution, and embraced a reactionary political agenda. On March 17, 1830, the chamber of deputies passed a motion of no confidence against the Jules Auguste Armand Marie de Polignac ministry. In response, the king dissolved the chamber and called for new elections. Making matters worse, on April 30, Charles X dismissed the national guard, a popular military organization among the middle strata. The king issued Les Ordonnances de Saint-Cloud on July 25, 1830, severely restricting the freedom of the press, limiting the electoral franchise, and reducing the power of the chamber of deputies.

On the following day, Paris disintegrated into barricade fighting. The Trois Glorieuses, or the three days of violence, forced Charles X into exile. At the Hôtel de Ville, moderate liberals worked feverishly to counterbalance the perceived despotism emanating from monarchy, mob, and democratic government. The leaders adopted a limited republican–monarchical system of government, which embraced aspects of democracy but remained conservative. Louis-Philippe of the House of Orléans became the new constitutional monarch.[4] The revolution sent shockwaves through Europe.

In other parts of the Atlantic World, revolutionaries demanded the creation of nation-states. These new nation-states could embrace constitutional monarchy or radical forms of government. Inspired by France, the people in the southern parts of the Netherlands rose up against the oppressive Dutch king, Willem I. Industrial entrepreneurs perceived the Dutch free trade policy as detrimental. Furthermore, there were the cultural and linguistic differences. On the evening of August 25, 1830, the Théâtre Royal de la Monnaie in Brussels performed Daniel Auber's *La muette de Portici*, a play infused with the spirit of rebellion, nationalism, and romanticism. Inspired, the people of Brussels started a separatist uprising. By October 1830, Charles Latour Rogier's revolutionary government had drafted a constitution and declared Belgium independent. With European assistance, Belgium defeated the Netherlands and found in Leopold of Saxe-Coburg a constitutional monarch.[5]

History, culture, and traditions provided a foundation for an emerging national identity. Oppression gave rise to political and national demands. The American and French revolutions provided inspiration for republican forms of government and confirmed the right of people to rebel. The disparity in nation-state development undermined separatist rebellions. Only Poland violently challenged its oppressors. Irish leaders successfully overcame religious and some political oppression without resorting to violence. Hungarians and Schleswig-Holstein Germans lacked the leadership and national consciousness to start a rebellion in 1830. In South Carolina, leaders were ready to challenge the government over tariff policies, but they had no support. In all five regions, leaders demanded an end to their enslavement and oppression.

———

Despite a proud history, the Poles lacked a coherent national identity. Divided between Austria, Prussia, and Russia, Poland disappeared in the late 1700s. After a brief reappearance during the Napoleonic Wars, the Congress of Vienna awarded Poland to Russia. The tsar ruled his new realm in personal union as king of Poland. While the tsar created the Polish chancery in Saint Petersburg, Poland had an elected diet with biennial meetings. By the late 1820s, anti-Russianism materialized during the meetings of the Polish diet. Young nationalists, especially students and journalists, cheered speakers who demanded a redefinition of the relationship between Poland and Russia. In response, the tsar and his first minister, Karl Robert Nesselrode, closed the meetings to the public, further alienating young nationalists.

Among members of the military, especially, nationalism found many recruits. Inspired by Mazzini's Young Italy movement and the secret Carbonari, Major Waleryan Łukasiński of the Fourth Infantry Regiment and staff officer Lieutenant Colonel Ignacy Pantaleon Prądzyński tried, but failed, to create a similar secret organization. The conspiratorial organization of young subalterns of the Warsaw garrison and cadets at the local military academy was more successful.[6]

European revolutionaries such as Harro Paul Harring took an interest in Polish independence. Harring, who had already participated in the Greek uprising, summarized the Polish situation in a poem. He argued that "as long as the slaves do not break the chains" the power of despotism prevailed and there was no "golden light" of freedom. Harring assumed that freedom could not prevail where a "slave/servant" loved his master; the more love, the more the master beats him.[7] Harring concluded his recollections of the Polish insurrection, "To the happy satisfaction of mankind, in retrospect of the great of past time, the great of lost civilizations will feel strengthened and revived in the knowledge of the inhuman strength of the Poles, in their divine ordained struggle for rights and freedom, against the shame and dishonor of slavery." Although the term "slave" derived from the often-enslaved Slavic people, Harring meant a state of political slavery. This perception of enslavement, tyranny, and despotism set the tone for separatist movements.

On November 29, 1830, Józef Wysocki, an officer in the Fourth Infantry Regiment, and his coconspirators attacked Belvedere Palace. Though they failed to capture the Russian governor, Duke Constantine, the widespread resentment against Russian rule allowed the uprising to succeed, even if some segments looked more like a plundering mob. Surprised by the rebellion, Constantine ordered the Polish troops from the outlying provinces to cordon off Warsaw. However, with orders from both the revolutionary administrative council and the grand duke, confused officers refused to implement Constantine's orders. Stalemated, the administrative council and Constantine agreed to a temporary settlement, preventing Russian troops from attacking Warsaw.[8]

Poland immediately faced a political crisis. Political revolutions face the danger not only of the established order regaining power but also of fringe groups, especially republicans and democrats, trying to implement their agendas. In Poland, radicals successfully but temporarily added Wladyslaw Tomasz Rawicz-Ostrowski, Gustaw Małachowski, and Joachim Lelewel to the governing council and demanded independence. For the moment, moderates checked those demands. When the well-respected Józef Grzegorz Chłopicki threatened to resign in protest, radicals accepted that Poland was not yet ready for independence or democracy.[9] Political division complicated the revolution.

At the same time, negotiations with the tsar went nowhere because the ruler refused to make constitutional concessions. With neither side willing to fire the first shots, Polish radicals questioned Chłopicki's leadership. The government appointed Michał Gedeon Radziwiłł to command the Polish forces, hoping to silence the radicals. On January 25, 1831, the parliament debated the negotiations in Saint Petersburg. Radicals reacted angrily and forced moderates to surrender the initiative. Poland ousted the tsar and took steps toward independence. The new motto was "Die rather than submit." Privately, Adam Jerzy Czartoryski asserted, "The nation, carried away by an irresistible torrent, has expressed loudly and unanimously its determination to defend itself; and if ever there were a moment when the destiny of countries depended upon their own exertions, and not upon accidental circumstances, such was the present condition of Poland. The nation ought to enjoy with moderation the liberty she has conquered. . . . Union must be considered as the foundation of all national happiness."[10] With independence, the diet reorganized as a constitutional assembly. With Russia unrepentant and a growing radical political movement, Poland took its first fateful steps as an independent nation-state.

Once Poland had declared independence, Nicholas I ordered his armies to attack. In the Battle of Białołęka (February 24 and 25, 1831), many young Poles got their first taste of combat. Lieutenant Gacpar Tochman fought heroically and earned an Order Wojenny Virtuti Militari (Medal for Military Virtue). His contemporary Ignatius Szymański fought with Harro Harring in Adam Woroniecki's lancer unit. In the Battle of Olszynka Grochowska (February 23 to 25, 1831), the Poles defeated the numerically superior Russian army, but it was a Pyrrhic victory. The Poles could ill afford more than seven thousand casualties. Jan Zygmunt Skrzynecki assumed command of the Polish armies, replacing Chłopicki and Radziwiłł. The military situation caused new protests; among the protesters was the young Adam Gurowski.[11]

The continued political infighting and military setbacks disillusioned many Poles. By February 28, 1831, the diet could not muster a quorum, which made the conduct of political business and war impossible. The small Polish army could not police the state and fight the superior Russians. Skrzynecki's defeat of a Russian advance guard on April 1 provided the government some breathing space. Ten days later, he defeated a Russian army in the Battle of Iganie. At the same time, another Polish army, under Józef Dwernicki, retreated into Austrian territory and a third army invaded Lithuania. The successes were short-lived, and in the Battle of Ostrołęka, on May 26, the Russians won.[12] The Polish uprising was in its final stage.

Czartoryski appealed to the Polish people in Lithuania with a carefully drafted proclamation, asking them to join the struggle for independence. He appealed to his "brethren and fellow-citizens": "United as we are hand and heart, we will henceforth proceed in concert to accomplish the difficult, perilous, but just and sacred work—the restoration of our country." The Polish leader argued that the Russian tsar would not "regard us as Poles bowed down with injuries—as citizens of a free and independent country—and would treat with us only as slaves who had rebelled against Russia." He argued that the partition of Poland was illegal and that, therefore, the Polish people "deserve to be a free Nation." Czartoryski asked for a "general rising to hail you as members of the free and independent nations of Europe."[13]

By summer, Poland faced disaster. Henryk Dembiński assumed

command of the Polish armies. On July 21, Russian troops crossed the strategically important Vistula and marched on the weakly defended Warsaw, where political upheaval, mob unrest, and political murders undermined the government. On August 6, almost eighty thousand Russians approached the outskirts of the Polish capital. When the two commanding officers met, the Russian accused the Poles of being rebels, which the Polish commander refuted. Nevertheless, the two officers agreed to a temporary armistice. Because the diet found the Russian demands offensive, however, it declined to authorize negotiations. Jan Stefan Krukowiecki negotiated on his own initiative. By November 1, 1831, the tsar had reestablished his authority over Poland. Without an amnesty, many Polish leaders went into exile.[14] Polish separatism had failed.

The suffering of the Polish people attracted attention. In the United States, the *Buffalo Journal and General Advertiser* wrote, "Let the shoulders of our nation be opened for receiving these gallant tatters from the Russian massacres as befits a free and great people who are indebted to the forefathers of those who now expect protection against despotic governments of terror." Similarly, a correspondent from the *Times* of London reported from the Prussian-Polish frontier. As the remnants of the Polish army and government crossed the border, an elderly gentleman explained, "Do you imagine that it is not painful to us to take refuge in a country whose Sovereigns were so long vassals to the crown of Poland? Had we to do with the Emperor of Russia alone, and had we not been convinced that all our representations against the willful tyranny of his brother were disregarded, we should never have begun the revolution."[15] Russian enslavement continued.

Lelewel summarized Poland's struggle for independence best. Toward the end of his work on Polish history, he wrote, "From the Tagus to the Volga Delta, in France and in Turkey, in Germany as in Greece and Russia, everywhere is the spirit of change, which calls for the improvement and freedom/liberty of the people. . . . Poland had made social improvement before its partition. Once the other European people have successfully gained their freedom, Poland too will rise up and emerge honorable and unharmed from all its social reforms."[16] While the removal of oppressive political chains was important, there was a need for social change. The Polish people were not alone in their separatist struggle against enslavement.

In contrast to the unsuccessful Polish uprising, the Irish found redress for their limited set of demands. Ireland came under foreign rule in 1536, during the reign of Henry VIII, who completed what the Normans had started two centuries earlier. The island's inhabitants were reduced to second-class citizenship as colonial subjects. Oppression was based not only on ethnic differences but also on religion. Religious dissenters and Catholics were excluded from the electoral franchise during the so-called Age of Oligarchy (1688–1830).

In 1798, two years after a failed invasion of Ireland by French forces, the Irish rebelled against the imposition of martial law. The British authorities brutally suppressed the insurgency. Just as British forces gained the upper hand, French troops arrived to support the remaining rebels, but the English swiftly defeated the enemy. To prevent future rebellion, the Act of Union of 1800/1801 abolished the Irish parliament, giving greater authority to the London authorities. The political union maintained the inferior status of Catholics and accelerated the demands for self-government, autonomy, and independence on the part of the Irish.[17]

The leader of the 1798 rebellion, Theobald Wolfe Tone, explained the Irish subordination. "England, by dissolving that Irish government, *has fully confirmed the charges adducted against it,*" he claimed, "and till the abuses which it supported, and which have survived its fall, are corrected,—till that monopoly is removed by which all the rights and powers of citizenship and sovereignty are usurped by a favoured minority, whilst the remainder of the population groans in slavery,—Ireland, either under a separate and national administration . . . will ever remain in an unnatural state of anarchy and misery." He repeatedly asserted that England kept the people of Ireland in a state of slavery, referring to the total political, social, and economic subjugation of the Irish. He concluded, "The people show no symptoms of attachment or loyalty to their new masters:—and for what should they be loyal? For six hundred years of slavery, misrule, and persecution!" He nevertheless cautioned that, although a republican government would serve Ireland well, he was unsure if such a system was best.[18]

After Wolfe Tone's defeat, new leaders with less militarist agendas emerged. Daniel O'Connell had supported the British effort to repulse the French invasion. By September 1810, he started his attack on the Test Act, which prohibited Catholics from holding office. In his opposition, O'Connell mimicked Wolfe Tone. He explained that the repeal of the union between Britain and Ireland was essential because, by creation of the union, "ignorance, incapacity, and profligacy obtained certain promotion—and our ill-fated but beloved country was degraded to her utmost limits before she was transfixed in slavery."[19] Like his famous Irish predecessor, O'Connell perceived the need to break the chains of enslavement.

O'Connell's moment came in 1828, when he won the County Clare by-election. However, as a Catholic, he could not take the Oath of Supremacy. Prime Minister Arthur Wellesley, the Duke of Wellington, and Home Secretary Sir Robert Peel faced a political crisis. They could not deny O'Connell his seat. Therefore, they proposed the Catholic Relief Act. The repeal of the Test and Corporation acts followed, eliminating religion as a barrier to office holding. The Catholic middle class embraced the opportunity. At the same time, property qualifications for voting increased in Ireland, undermining the growing spirit of democracy.

In the aftermath of Catholic emancipation, O'Connell focused on the repeal of the Act of Union. He also aimed to broaden his appeal. As the "Liberator," O'Connell fought not only political oppression but also the institution of chattel slavery, a decision that was unpopular with Irish migrants in the United States. He claimed, "Of all men living, an American citizen who is the owner of slaves is the most despicable." He argued that the holding of slaves made the people in the United States "traitors to the cause of human liberty, and foul detractors of the democratic principle."[20] O'Connell controversially opposed slavery both at home and abroad. Slavery in any form did not fit into O'Connell's liberal, constitutional system of government.

Many young nationalists, who eventually demanded additional reforms, were still too young to challenge O'Connell in the 1830s. On

November 3, 1815, John Mitchel was born into a Presbyterian minister's family in Dungiven. Mitchel and his father sympathized with the plight of the Catholic inhabitants of Ireland. They embraced Wolfe Tone's nonsectarian Irish vision. In February 1836, Mitchel graduated from Trinity College and failed in a few professions, including banking, before turning to law.[21]

Thomas Francis Meagher, born on August 23, 1823, grew up in a Catholic family with Canadian commercial ties. At age seven, Meagher paid little attention to Catholic emancipation. When he was eleven, he enrolled in the Jesuit-run Clongowes Wood College, focusing on English composition and rhetoric, which laid the foundation for his future as a spokesperson of Irish nationalism. After Clongowes Wood, Meagher attended Stonyhurst College in England.[22]

In contrast to the more politically savvy Irishmen, Patrick R. Cleburne was an average Irishman without political ambitions. Born into a Protestant family, Cleburne saw the light of day on March 16, 1828. Raised by his father and his father's new nineteen-year-old wife, Cleburne grew up on an estate near Cork. Despite the high cost of maintaining the home, Cleburne's father provided his sons with a basic education.[23]

For Ireland, Catholic emancipation was a successful first step toward autonomy. With the ability to finally hold office, Irish leaders focused on the repeal of the political union between Ireland and England. Irish revolutionaries such as Tone and O'Connell called for an end of their enslavement at the hands of the English. However, religious emancipation was only the first step, and younger members of the Irish nationalist movement grew up to challenge the political elite and its cautious approach. At least Ireland had success; most regions were not ready for outright rebellion.

In the Dano-German borderland on the Jutland peninsula, the German inhabitants of the duchies of Schleswig and Holstein had accumulated their own set of grievances. However, they were not yet ready to openly challenge their Danish duke/king. German nationalism was still in its infancy during the 1820s and 1830s. There were few intellectual leaders to take up arms.

In the eighth century, Danes, Franks, and Slavs had battled one another for control of Jutland. In order to stop incursions from the south, the Danes constructed a defensive perimeter, the Danevirke/ Dannewerk, which eventually became a symbolic divider between Danish and German residents.[24] During the Middle Ages, the duchies were fragmented into a number of small, independent fiefs. In 1460, the Danish king Christian I established a permanent claim to the duchies of Schleswig and Holstein, ruling them in personal union as duke. In the Treaty of Ripe, the king also agreed to maintain the duchies "up ewig ungedeelt" (forever undivided). German nationalists used the treaty to argue for the inseparable relationship of Schleswig and Holstein. Therefore, the Danish king could not integrate one duchy into the Danish kingdom. Neither could a German nation-state integrate only one of the duchies.

Over the next three centuries, the Schleswig-Holstein question became increasingly more complicated. The Danish ruling dynasty, the House of Oldenburg, established family branches and granted them territory in the kingdom and duchies. These branch families developed their own claims to parts of the kingdom and the duchies. As a result, claims to Denmark's throne and the duchies resided with the House of Oldenburg and its branches, the Swedish monarchy and the Russian tsars. As in other parts of Europe, royal succession questions created major challenges. Furthermore, the Danish decision to side with Napoleon Bonaparte brought hardship and destruction to Danish subjects, even in the German duchies.[25]

As national identities took shape in the early nineteenth century, Friedrich Christoph Dahlmann, in his Waterloo speech of 1815, called for German unity. He wished to use the energy employed to fight Napoleon to bring about a German nation-state. "The secret of the art of revolutionary warfare is exposed," he declared. "'The universal legacy of the French Revolution' was defeated with its own weapons."[26] His argument for unity among the "German tribes," as he phrased it, built on their shared interest in liberty, justice, and traditionalism. He wished the German people to embrace freedom and oust slavery/servitude from the German lands. In relation to the duchies, he claimed both Holstein and Schleswig for the German Bund. Nevertheless, the search for a German identity was a slow process.

Without a German national uprising in 1830, nationalist thinkers voiced their anger in writing. On November 5, 1830, Uwe Jens Lornsen, a German residing in Schleswig, published a pamphlet dealing with the constitutional question of the duchies. Lornsen had worked for the Danish government and understood Danish administrative inefficiency. He asked the king to call a provisional state diet to represent the entire population. He did not ask for democratic elections or a republic. His suggestions included taxes approved by the state diets and a consolidated administration of the duchies. He wanted to replace the *helstat* (one unified state) with a dual-state solution. A modern, efficient state and economy required a separation of the duchies from Denmark. He especially complained about the foreigners who ruled over the duchies but who had little knowledge about them.

However, his thoughts were not restricted to just an administrative revision. In contrast to later nationalists, he wanted to maintain the unity of the duchies, which he emphasized by using the word "Schleswigholstein" rather than the more common Schleswig-Holstein. Denmark had tried to "fuse the people" and undermine the people's German national identity over the previous decades. He assumed that freedom from Denmark would increase the prosperity of the duchies and remove the "shackles" that retarded commerce and economy.[27] Lornsen built on the ideas of other nationalist writers, but there was no uprising in Schleswig-Holstein, and Lornsen had to flee the country.

German nationalism was underdeveloped in Schleswig-Holstein, and most future nationalists had only just entered university during the upheavals of 1830. The future separatist leader Theodor Olshausen, born on June 19, 1802, received his initial schooling at the *Gelehrtenschule* in Glückstadt and the gymnasium in Eutin. Instead of a religious education, Olshausen pursued a law degree at the University of Kiel. He transferred to the University of Jena in 1820, where his participation in a liberal- and nationalist-minded *Burschenschaft* (fraternity) placed him in conflict with the reactionary authorities. Olshausen spent the next few years in exile, first in Paris, then in Switzerland as a mathematics teacher, and eventually as editor of the *Neue Augsburger Zeitung* in Bavaria. In early July 1828, he returned home, finished his law degree, and accepted editorship of the

Correspondenz-Blatt in Kiel, where he promoted the Holstein cause for autonomy.[28]

In contrast, Hans Reimer Claussen was born on February 23, 1804, in Fedderingen, near Heide, in Dithmarschen. After attending the *Gelehrtenschule* in Meldorf, Claussen studied law at the University of Kiel, from 1824 to 1829, and embraced a legal career. He had little interest in the political situation in Holstein or in the national demands of the German people.[29]

Finally, born on July 22, 1815, Rudolph Matthias Jacob Schleiden grew up on the manor of Ascheberg, near Plön, in Holstein, where he learned to resent the heavy tax burden and the preferential treatment of Danish peasants.[30] Schleiden was, at fifteen, far too young to assume a revolutionary role in 1830.

With many young separatist nationalist minds still formulating their ideology in 1830, the Dano-German borderland lacked a cadre of revolutionaries who could use Lornsen's ideas and bring about a separation of the duchies from the Danish crown. At the same time, German nationalist thinkers perceived of their oppression as slavery and called for the formation of a German identity. In the duchies, nationalists did not perceive of their status as enslavement. The duchies relied on their historic identity as independent entities governed in personal union by the Danish king/duke. They employed overwhelmingly constitutional arguments to describe their status as oppressed people. Since the duchies were technically independent, their demand for independence from oppression represented a puzzling paradox for outsiders.

———

Similar to other oppressed people, the Magyar suffered from subjugation by the Austro-Habsburg dynasty. The Kingdom of Hungary emerged during the reign of István (Stephen) I. Its throne was known as *Magyar Szent Korona* (the Crown of Saint Stephen). Located in Eastern Europe, Hungary faced constant attacks, and by the early 1500s the Ottoman Empire had conquered large parts of Hungary. The crown of Hungary passed into the hands of the Habsburg dynasty in 1526. The Habsburgs governed the country in personal union for the next four centuries, accepting a separate coronation ceremony based on Hungarian traditions.

The proud Hungarians felt neglected by their rulers. Hungary was economically, culturally, and socially backward. Nationalist reformers demanded the abolition of serfdom and the creation of a modern industrial economy. Nationalists like István Széchenyi and Lajos Kossuth understood that Hungarian independence was only possible if the country modernized, industrialized, and improved its transportation networks. Furthermore, Hungarians suffered from serfdom, an institution similar to slavery. Though the growing sense of national distinctiveness and demands for reforms remained restricted to the Hungarian elite, the Natio Hungarica, pride in Hungarian language, music, dances, and clothing style emerged, along with the composition of the Hungarian national anthem. Alongside this national awakening was the incorporation of Magyar as the language of education.[31]

When the Hungarian assembly came together, in 1825, conflicts immediately emerged between the liberal nationalists and their conservative counterparts. Some reformers envisioned the aristocracy taking the lead in the restructuring of the Hungarian state. István Széchenyi wanted to improve the banking and transportation system of Hungary to escape Austrian enslavement. He called on the Hungarian people to establish credit. He concluded, "But, most important, dear reader, we are not permitted to dream as long as our poverty keeps us enslaved in ignorance, prejudices, and wrong opinions. Money and real wealth will not come to us as long as our fatherland lacks credit." Furthermore, Széchenyi claimed that only when people shed the "burden of slavery and destroy their chains" was freedom possible. In contrast to moderate reformers, who desired to maintain the union between Austria and Hungary, radicals supported a separatist ideology and demanded at least autonomy in economic and political questions. They hoped for complete independence from Austria. The radicals desired a middle class–based political organization. They gained strength and their proposals found widespread sympathy. Conservatives preferred to maintain the status quo.[32]

During the 1825 session of the assembly, Miklós Wesselényi de Hadad questioned Austrian oppression. "The government sucks out the marrow of nine millions of men (the peasantry)," Wesselényi said. "It will not allow us nobles to better their condition by legislative means; but retaining them in their present state, it only waits its own time to exasperate them against us,—then it will come forward to rescue us. But wo [sic] to us! From freemen we shall be degraded to the state of slaves."[33] Wesselényi did not mean slavery as practiced in the United States but a state of oppression without legal or constitutional rights. The Habsburgs were the oppressive masters and Hungarians the slaves.

Over time, István Széchenyi had to make way for younger radicals. Among them, Lajos Kossuth gained notoriety. He repeatedly spoke up against Austrian rule. He established an anti-Austrian newspaper in Pest, which gained him the attention of the reactionary authorities. In May 1837, the Austrians arrested Kossuth, charging him with "disloyalty and sedition." Kossuth emerged from the botched trial as a national hero. In January 1841, Kossuth took over *Pesti Hírlap* and turned the paper into the mouthpiece of radical reforms.[34]

While Kossuth and Széchenyi fought political battles, many future separatists were not yet ready to assume leadership positions. Alexander Sándor Asbóth was born on December 18, 1811, in Keszthely, on the southeastern side of Lake Balaton. Asbóth's father was an agriculture expert, and he opposed his son's desire to join the Austrian army. Instead, Asbóth studied engineering at the *Bergakademie* (mining school) in Selmecbánya. Some biographers have claimed that Asbóth received an engineering degree from the Institutum Geometricum at Pest. Asbóth worked as a civil engineer after graduation. Although Asbóth's graduation date is unknown, he remained politically uninvolved in the 1830s.[35]

Charles Zagonyi, even younger than Asbóth, was born on October 19, 1822, in Szinérváralja. (Some historians claim he was born in 1826 in the Szatmár region.) Very little is known about his early life, including his education and profession.[36]

Even though the Hungarians did not rise up in 1830, they looked to the West, especially the United States, for inspiration. Even in small Hungarian villages, some people toasted Daniel Webster and Millard Fillmore. The United States could teach Hungary many lessons. In 1834, Sándor Farkas Bölöni published his observations after visiting the United States. Széchenyi commented, "I thank the Almighty for the birth of this book; its beneficial effect on our country can not be estimated." Miklós Wesselényi wrote enthusiastically that "the young giant of human rights and freedom," the United States, was an attractive symbol because it was superior in "civic equality, the political system and the pleasant social conditions."[37] The United States and its political leaders were examples the Hungarians wished to mimic.

The Hungarian nationalists perceived themselves as enslaved people, and they vocally opposed Austrian oppression. Therefore, demands for liberation grew. Many Hungarians desired emancipation and independence. The Hungarian moderate and radical separatist nationalists prepared their arguments, but they were not yet ready for an all-out challenge to the Austrian monarchy.

———

Separatism was not solely a European problem. The United States, created out of thirteen independent British colonies, struggled with its identity. The Declaration of Independence and the Constitution provided a basis for a national identity. Even as some politicians thought of the United States as a unified whole, however, many southerners continued to view the country as a confederation of sovereign states. In their interpretation, the states had voluntarily joined that confederation, and they could similarly leave. In addition, the original republican government, with property qualifications, gave way to democracy. As the United States turned fifty, many in the southern states started to perceive of their section, state, and region as oppressed by the northern states–dominated federal government. In contrast to their European separatist counterparts, southern separatists had to express their anger at northern oppression without questioning the oppressive institution on which southern society and economy rested.

During the first decades of the country's existence, there was much talk about secession, as New England, southern, and western interests collided. The sectional differences manifested during the Quasi-War (1798–1800), when the Federalist party implemented the Alien and Sedition Acts, which undermined freedom of speech. In response, Thomas Jefferson penned the first states' rights manifesto, arguing that states were "not united on the principle of unlimited submission to their general government" and, therefore, that a law like the Sedition Act, "which does abridge the freedom of the press, is not law, but is altogether void, and of no force." Jefferson concluded that "these and successive acts . . . unless arrested at the threshold, necessarily drive these States into revolution and blood and will furnish new calumnies against republican governments, . . . [and] that it would be a dangerous delusion were a confidence in the men of our choice to silence our fears for the safety of our rights: that confidence is everywhere the parent of despotism."[38] With the Kentucky Resolution, Jefferson laid the foundation for states to nullify federal laws.

Northerners were just as adamant about protecting their regional interests and rights. When the country stumbled into the War of 1812, New England merchants had already suffered extensively from the detrimental trade policies instituted by southern presidents. New England's support for the war was limited. Calls for secession increased in the course of the war, culminating with the Hartford Convention. Fearing minority status and oppression at the hands of southern and western interests, New England Federalists contemplated secession. To them, the War of 1812 was "needless and unwise." James Madison, who had established states' rights with the Virginia Resolution, opposed New England mimicking him.[39] New England retained a memory of its own secession attempt, and abolitionists eventually argued for northern secession to escape the morally degraded southern slaveholding states.

By the late 1820s, southerners had developed a separate identity for their section and intended to protect their rights against what they felt was a northern campaign of oppression. The admission of Missouri increased antagonistic perceptions on both sides of the Mason–Dixon Line. Both North and South feared that the other side undermined the principles of Union. While there was a slim chance of a separation of the South in 1820, some worried about the direction of the sectional conflict. Sectional differences increased, with political instability mounting in the aftermath of the 1824 election and with the rise of Andrew Jackson. Jackson had indicated his support for recent tariff changes to appease southerners who perceived the tariff as detrimental to their region and a ploy of hostile northerners.[40]

Furthermore, Jackson brought a renewed spirit of democratization to the United States. Sectional fears had grown with the emergence of radical abolitionists like William L. Garrison and the vivid memory of the events in the French colony of Saint-Domingue. The perception of oppression in the southern states was mirrored by a northern perception that, with the Three-Fifths Compromise, the southern states had a proportionally higher representation in the House of Representatives. There were serious misunderstandings between the sections.

As tensions increased, South Carolina became the hotbed of secession. South Carolina's elite behaved like aristocrats and democrats at the same time. "South Carolina masters flashed signs of uncertainty, fear, inferiority complex," writes historian William W. Freehling. "The next moment, the same people emitted signals of cockiness, fearlessness, felt superiority." The state's economy relied heavily on slave-grown products, including short staple cotton, Sea Island cotton, and rice. Slaves constituted as much as 85 percent of the population. James Hammond summed up the political situation in South Carolina: "The government of So. Carolina is that of an aristocracy. . . . The South Carolina 'legislature' . . . has all power. The Executive has none. The people have none beyond electing members of the legislature, a power very negligently exercised from time immemorial."[41] Regardless, South Carolina was democratic, since the people elected their leaders.

Southern politicians and economists had developed theories about the effects of tariffs. Since tariffs protected northern manufacturing, southern states feared higher prices for commodities imported from Europe. A tariff of 40 percent, according to southerners, meant price increases of 40 percent. The theory became known as "forty bales," because "the manufacturer actually invades your barns, and plunders you of 40 out of every 100 bales that you produce," explained a contemporary. The tariff was only a scapegoat for structural problems within the South. Population growth and soil depletion, as well as a rise in cotton production, had reduced profits. In South Carolina, people came to believe that "tariffs supposedly robbed and depopulated Mother Carolina," using a state-centered national identity.[42] The "Tariff of Abominations" of 1828 increased the perception of a North strangling the South economically.

Vice President John C. Calhoun, upon request, anonymously published the "South Carolina Exposition and Protest," outlining his perceptions about the tariff and the right of a state to nullify a federal law. Basing his argument on the assumption that Congress had only the rights enumerated in the Constitution, which did not include protection of industry, Calhoun concluded that the tariffs were illegal. Calhoun relied on arguments made by Thomas Jefferson and James Madison. Since the tariff created a majority oppressing a minority, the only solution was to nullify the law in question and thus prevent its enforcement. Calhoun continued by outlining a final remedy in case the government did not address the grievances: "With these views the committee are solemnly of impression if the system be persevered in," he wrote, "after due forbearance on the part of the State, that it will be her sacred duty to interpose her veto; a duty to herself, to the Union, to present, and to future generations, and to the cause of liberty over the world, to arrest the progress of a power, which, if not arrested, must in its consequences, corrupt the public morals, and destroy the liberty of the country." Calhoun thought that, with nullification, the "concurring majority" would overcome the oppression of the "absolute majority."[43] He avoided discussion of slavery, tyranny, and oppression, though they were all on his mind as he addressed the tariff issue. North and South had opposing interpretations of the Constitution, republicanism, and democracy.

Tensions between states' rights advocates and unionists grew. Congress passed the Tariff of 1832, which cut the rates back to an average of 25 percent, except for tariffs on woolen, cotton, and iron goods, which remained at 50 percent. Therefore, South Carolina's main complaint remained valid. In response, South Carolina's governor, James Hamilton Jr., called for nullification of the new tariff, which he connected with renewed proposals for monetary support for the American Colonization Society and fears of "a tyrannical congressional majority . . . oppress[ing] all South Carolinians." Hamilton and the nullifiers desired a two-third majority in favor of nullification and, for reasons of legitimacy, a convention was required to nullify the offending tariff. "Once South Carolina won the principle that one state dominated by one elite could veto any national law," historian Freehling writes bluntly, "the Forty Bale robber would be routed, a potential northern–Upper South majority for federal colonizing of blacks aborted, patriarchal republicanism resurrected, King Numbers dethroned, elitist domination consolidated over masses white and black." Nullification of the tariff would undermine the federal budget and reduce federal power. If Jackson used coercion tactics, separation followed naturally.[44]

In the fall of 1832, South Carolinians elected delegates for a nullification convention. To Unionists, nullification was the worst possible outcome, and they made comparisons to oppressive aristocracies. "The lordly planter only swear more, about 'plunder, robbery and protection,'" one Unionist wrote. Revolution and submission were prominent fears in the state. Once the people had spoken, the convention nullified the tariffs of 1828 and 1832. For Governor Robert Y. Hayne, nullification required the preparation of the militia to "suppress insurrection, repel invasion, or support the civil authorities." At the same time, the Unionists perceived the nullifiers' actions as tyrannical.[45] South Carolina had started a separatist revolution to protect democracy as interpreted by members of South Carolina's elite.

Angrily, Jackson supposedly fumed, "I will hang the first man of them I can get my hands on to the first tree I can find." Some people in South Carolina believed Jackson's threat was a bluff and that he was not ready to fire the aggressor's first shot. Jackson tried to appease the nullifiers by asking Congress for additional tariff reductions, but he also prepared for conflict. He instructed the revenue cutter and other federal employees in Charleston to relocate to Fort Moultrie. Here, under the protection of the federal garrison, they were to enforce federal law and collect tariffs at sea. Jackson hoped that South Carolina would challenge the measures.

On December 10, 1832, Jackson publicly reacted to nullification. The president explained that the government had the constitutional right to pass tariffs. However, secession was unconstitutional and revolutionary. Even if South Carolina could claim a moral high ground, it still lacked legitimacy. Jackson had to act immediately to forestall nullification, or secession could follow. Other southern states worried about the implications of nullification and urged South Carolina to aim for a compromise.[46]

With Jackson preparing to use force and South Carolina isolated, the nullifiers searched for a compromise. Calhoun, now in the U.S. Senate, cautioned his supporters that secession was "the most fatal of all steps" and should only happen "in the last extremity."[47] As Congress searched for a compromise solution, the nullifiers in South Carolina suspended their rebellion. The Verplanck Bill, which lowered tariff rates to 20 percent over the coming years, was well within the demands of the nullifiers and could provide a compromise.

With adjournment looming on March 4, 1833, however, the lame duck Congress was not in a mood for compromise. Time had run out, and the issue could not wait until December. In order to accomplish a compromise, Calhoun joined forces with Kentucky's Henry Clay, who had already gained fame during the Missouri Compromise of 1820. The two southerners held opposing views on the tariff but, after a series of secret meetings, Calhoun had to surrender his isolated position. Even as the nullifiers accepted the compromise tariff, they nullified the Force Bill. Southern nullification had lost.

At the same time, political challenges to the planter aristocracy grew. In Virginia, the slaveholding interests of the Tidewater planter elite and the yeomanry of the western districts clashed at the state's constitutional convention. Despite their minority status within the state, Tidewater planters controlled the legislature and exposed themselves to accusations of overseeing an undemocratic government. Planters such as Benjamin Leigh believed that the elite had a duty to govern and that only they had the leisure to engage in meaningful study of political subjects. While he was cautious to not equate chattel slaves with white yeomen in the western parts of the state, Leigh did suggest that westerners would always have to work hard for their daily subsistence and he asked, therefore, whether "those who are obliged to depend on their daily labor for daily subsistence, can, or do ever enter into political affairs?"[48] Like his Tidewater colleagues, Leigh believed that the wealthy elite was to lead the people and to avoid majority oppression of the minority.

The challengers countered with their own invocation of slavery and oppression. Phillip Doddridge argued against the control of slaveholders, claiming, "I may still live in the west; may pursue my own business and obey my own inclinations, but so long as you hold political dominion over me, I am a slave." He wondered how a majority of people, equal to one another in "intelligence and virtue," could be forced to follow a minority. Doddridge wondered, "Do I misrepresent or exaggerate when I say your doctrine makes me a slave?"[49] A white southerner could use slavery to describe political oppression, if that oppression emanated from the slaveholding elite.

The South had not seceded, because of internal disunity, but a powerful separatist southern identity emerged around the contested interpretations of southern rights and democratic-republicanism. Both needed protection from outside aggressors. South Carolina's fire-eaters had failed to gain outside support from the other southern states to make their rebellion a success. At the same time, southern arguments against outside oppression mimicked claims by European separatist. Secessionists, especially those of the planter elite, avoided using slavery to justify separatism because the institution of chattel slavery loomed large in their identity. Western Virginia farmers had no such burden, however, and they challenged their political enslavement and oppression by the slaveholding planter aristocracy. The conflict between northern unionists and southern secessionists had only just started. Robert Barnwell Rhett expressed the feeling among separatists in the South: "Until this Government is made a limited Government . . . there is no liberty—no security for the South."[50]

———

In 1830, separatist movements challenged oppressive overlords. In justifying their rebellion, European and North American separatists employed a strikingly similar set of arguments. To them, the oppressor undermined the rights and freedoms of nationality. Separatist movements frequently perceived of themselves as enslaved people. Unique among the separatist movements, the southern states held human slaves and did not refer to their oppressed status as "enslavement." Separatist movements built on the ideas of liberal nationalism and supported the creation of new nation-states.

Separatist rebellions in 1830 were part of a larger set of challenges to the established status quo. While Ireland, Poland, and South Carolina revolted against their oppressors, Schleswig-Holstein and Hungary were not ready. Poland and South Carolina lacked support and faced domestic dissent, prematurely ending their separatist challenges. Furthermore, Poland suffered from political division as radicals undermined the provisional government and the conduct of the war. In South Carolina, or in the South more generally, the same problem existed. Separatist desires for independence continued to grow as perceptions of oppression increased. Separatist-minded leaders continued to plan for rebellion. They got their next chance eighteen years in the future.

2

1848 IN THE NORTH ATLANTIC
REVOLUTIONARY WORLD

"C'est un point essentiel pour hâter l'émancipation de ce pays" (This is an essential point to hasten the emancipation of this country), said Adam J. Czajkowski, and his call for emancipation was a common rallying cry during the "springtime of people," as were "liberty, democracy, and national unity."[1] However, the principles of emancipation, liberty, democracy, and national unity did not apply universally. In France, demands for political and social reform predominated. In Austria-Hungary and Schleswig-Holstein, promoters of national unity and separation appealed to different ethnic groups. Similarly, the political demands of middle class, university-educated literati differed dramatically from the socioeconomic demands of oppressed and landless serfs. Leaders disagreed about the political identity and size of new unified or separatist states. Political ideologies, from communism to democracy, vied for inclusion in new constitutions. A new generation of separatists called for extensive political reforms and independence. Young nationalists in Ireland, Hungary, and Schleswig-Holstein had refined their political ideology to incorporate separatist, democratic, and sectarian identities.

The 1848 story usually starts with France, where politicians called for republican reforms. Whereas historians once limited their narratives to France, Germany, Italy, and Austria-Hungary, however, modern scholarship includes nationalism, separatism, and communism in the Rhineland; Sicily; Wallachia and Moldova; Poland; the Low Countries; and Scandinavia. In addition, transnational narratives incorporate the political struggles in Argentina, Brazil, Chile, Peru, and the United States. Nonetheless, despite the growing understanding of how widespread the 1848 uprisings were, unification and liberal political narratives continue to predominate. Separatists in 1848 disagreed with unification demands and desired to break away from oppressive states. At the same time, they quarreled about what form of government to support; democracy and communism remained fringe movements.[2]

Separatist uprisings formed a crucial part of the 1848 revolutions, with the shortest one in Ireland and the longest rebellion in Schleswig-Holstein, demanding independence. Historians have pushed the chronological start back to 1847, with the Swiss and Sicilian rebellions, but the Polish free city of Cracow had voiced political and national demands as early as 1846. As in 1830, however, the Poles failed to overcome Austrian, Prussian, and Russian resistance. After their failure, many Poles joined the Hungarian uprising, which initially embraced autonomy within the realm of the Habsburg monarchy. As the monarchy refused to provide Hungary with concessions and ethnic minorities resisted, radicals gained influence and declared independence from Austria. The Austrians used their military power to subdue the rebellion. Similarly, the Danes could rely on international support to suppress their rebellious Schleswig-Holstein German subjects. Insisting on independence, Germans had long resisted incorporation of Schleswig by Denmark.

In all three of these cases, political demands were secondary to national demands. In contrast, Irish revolutionaries had long-standing political differences with the English mother country and demanded the restoration of their own parliament. The British failure to provide adequate relief during the famine increased desires for independence. While the older, Catholic-centered group supported the political process, younger nationalists desired independence, through violence if necessary. Likewise, sectional differences and the expansion of slavery renewed demands for secession in the United States but faltered with the Compromise of 1850. In 1848, separatists with their radicalized and forceful language unsuccessfully struggled for independence and republican governments.

In 1846, the Polish residents of Poznań, Cracow, and Galicia challenged their oppressive lords. The four-year-long rebellion demanded social change, including freeing the peasantry from servile duties. At the same time, demands for a Polish nation-state continued. In February 1846, the Prussian authorities arrested Ludwik Mierosławski and 254 Polish coconspirators in Poznań and West Prussia. In Galicia, Polish peasants rebelled against their oppressive lords, causing the death of more than a thousand Polish aristocrats. In Cracow, Jan Tysowski successfully ousted the small Austrian garrison but received only limited support from the peasantry and the mine workers in Wieliczka. Polish desires for independence died when an Austrian occupation force arrived in November 1846.[3]

In Prussia, Polish aspirations for an independent state lingered. Polish nationalists struggled for independence, taking over local governments in Poznań and Galicia. In Poznań, Joseph Kargé and Włodzimierz Bonawentura Krzyżanowski militarily defended their home. Austria and Prussia maintained a friendly demeanor toward the Polish nationalists but prepared their armies to end Polish separatism. In May 1848, the Prussian army ended all thoughts of Polish independence.[4] The national desires of the Polish people had failed once more. Nevertheless, Polish exiles fought in many of the European revolutionary engagements of 1848, including the separatist struggle of the Hungarians.

Poland's downfall was the German preoccupation with the contentious Schleswig-Holstein question. In 1848, the German population in the Dano-German borderland of Schleswig-Holstein challenged what they perceived as repressive Danish attempts to undermine the unity between the two duchies. For the next three years, young radicals frequently voiced their opinions demanding implementation of at least republican, if not democratic, political institutions. Regardless of political orientation, German nationalists desired independence.

The radical "Neuholsteiner" Hans R. Claussen and Theodor Olshausen, who wanted Holstein and Schleswig separated, continued to dismiss the concept of "up ewig ungedeelt" (forever undivided). Nevertheless, they desired the unification of the German states, Holstein's inclusion in the new entity, and democratic reforms. As a democrat, Claussen criticized the governing, privileged order, which prevented the establishment of an efficient political and impartial legal system.

He called for Holstein's diet to consist only of members elected by enfranchised voters, including women. Passage of laws should require a two-third majority. Public and press should have access to the meetings. Like most republicans, Claussen feared both aristocratic privilege and mob rule.[5]

Meanwhile, Olshausen propagated German separatist nationalism and protested Danish tax laws. In his *Correspondenz-Blatt*, he established Holstein's national identity, and the lack thereof in Schleswig. As early as 1839, Olshausen explained the national and political divisions between Germans and Danes, with both sides demanding language supremacy because neither wanted "to turn home into a foreign environment." At the same time, he stated, German not only was the language of instruction but also was superior. In an emotional diatribe, Olshausen claimed that Denmark was intellectually, philosophically, and theologically underdeveloped. The article concluded, "The Democratic element in Schleswig cannot be allowed to force the German education system into a Danish one and thus lower its standards."[6] By the mid-1840s, the Neuholsteiners had established themselves as leading secessionists, with a republican, even democratic, agenda.

Danish nationalists pursued their own agenda of territorial expansion and domestic political reform. In particular, the nationalist Eider-Danish party demanded the extension of the kingdom all the way to the Eider, which was the southern border of Schleswig, and the use of Danish as Schleswig's official language. In October 1844, the mayor of Copenhagen, Tage Algreen-Ussing, called Denmark, including the duchies, an indivisible empire. Algreen-Ussing raised the possibility of incorporating Schleswig. For the moment, moderates maintained the upper hand and silenced such extremism. To defuse the issue, the Danish king issued a royal patent, in March 1844, allowing members of the Schleswig diet to deliver their speeches in Danish.

In July 1846, the Danish king tried to reduce apprehensions on both sides with an open letter to the Prince of Augustenburg, addressing the contentious succession question. The letter started with the controversial claim that Schleswig was historically part of Denmark. The king elaborated on the provision that the king/duke "should succeed to both territories undivided." Despite the Augustenburg family paying homage to the Danish king in 1721 and lodging a reservation in 1806 about the succession question, the Danish king denied them any right to the duchies.[7] Instead of clarifying the succession question, the king's letter increased tensions.

On January 20, 1848, Christian VIII died and the duties of state fell to Frederik VII. The nationalist Faedreland Partei sought to influence the new king to incorporate Schleswig. For a week, Frederik resisted Danish nationalist pressures, ultimately accepting the need for a new constitution, which granted limited autonomy to the various parts of the kingdom and left the common diet with limited lawmaking power. Danish nationalists worried about the power German subjects might exercise under the new constitution. Similarly, nationalists in the duchies greeted the proposed constitution with suspicion.[8] Suspicions and mistrust escalated long-standing nationalist tensions.

When news of the events in Paris arrived, Copenhagen was already abuzz over the new constitution and the call for a joint meeting of the diets of Schleswig and Holstein in Kiel. With a radical separatist majority, the meeting called on the people to reject all attempts to tie Schleswig-Holstein, or only Schleswig, closer to Denmark. Another meeting, in Rendsburg, called for a united diet of Schleswig and Holstein to debate a constitution for the duchies and the inclusion of Schleswig in the German Bund. A five-man deputation consisting of Olshausen, Claussen, Lucius Carl von Neergaard-Oevelgönne, Jacob Guido Theodor Gülich, and Casper Engel submitted these demands to Copenhagen, where, on March 7, Lauritz Nicolai Hvidt, Orla Lehmann, and Anton Frederik Tscherning called a meeting of the Faedrelands Partei to coordinate policy.[9] With tensions at fever pitch, demands for political and national change grew.

On March 21, Frederik VII unintentionally set in motion the revolution. He asked his ministers to incorporate Schleswig into Denmark. The entire ministry resigned in protest. Some Germans contemplated outright rebellion. The moderate Schleiden cautioned, "Only once a clear intrusion in the independence of the duchies had occurred would the time have come for action." Nationalists awaited apprehensively the formation of a new cabinet. At the same time, the delegation from the duchies faced an angry Danish mob instigated by rumors that the duchies were already in insurrection. Uncertain about decisions in Copenhagen, leaders in the duchies decided to form a provisional government. Wilhelm Hartwig Beseler, Jürgen Bremer, Friedrich Graf von Reventlow-Preetz, Martin Thorsen Schmidt, Theodor Olshausen, and Friedrich von Nör ruled the duchies until their "unfree sovereign," whom the people in Copenhagen had forced to take a hostile position toward the duchies, regained his political independence. On the afternoon of March 24, Denmark announced the incorporation of Schleswig, causing an exodus of German nationalists from Copenhagen.[10] From a Danish perspective, the Schleswig-Holstein Germans were separatists; German nationalists claimed they only defended their legal rights.

Addressing the rebellion, the king issued a royal declaration to calm tensions and to guarantee Holstein's status in the German Bund. He promised freedom of the press and electoral reforms. The king even granted the duchy its own civil administration, military organization, and financial responsibilities. However, he referred to Schleswig as "our duchy of Schleswig." The king emphasized his desire to strengthen the ties between Denmark and Schleswig, a serious blunder.[11] The proclamation was unacceptable to German nationalists.

Since the duchies were in a state of open rebellion and the Danish army was preparing to invade, the duchies needed military assistance. The provisional government explained that Denmark attacked the independence and sovereignty of the duchies. Regarding Schleswig, the government proclaimed, "If Denmark wished, against all legal precedents and by use of force, to turn Schleswig into a part of the Danish state, this would create an eternal cause for conflict. The German population would, aided by the powerful German neighbors, continuously attempt to free/emancipate themselves from foreign rule and not rest until that was accomplished."[12]

The German states came to the assistance of their German brethren, which escalated a regional and domestic crisis into an international conflict. At the German Bundestag in Frankfurt, Schleswig-Holstein's representative, Schleiden, joined the Vor-Parlament and asked for Schleswig's inclusion into the German Bund and for military support. The request for inclusion found widespread support but unintentionally jump-started the debate over Germany's future size. Meanwhile, on March 28, 1848, the Danish foreign minister conferred with the British and Russian representatives, blaming Prussia's proclamation of March 23 for the escalation.[13] The duchies and their allies faced international pressure.

Across the German lands, radical demands for republican and democratic reforms increased. Claussen questioned the political power of the privileged order. He called for an independent and democratic Schleswig-Holstein within a unified Germany. He frequently clarified that his support for a German republic did not mean statelessness, anarchy, or worker-run governments. He desired a government where the rulers were legally held to the same standards as the ruled. The United States and its federal system should serve as a model for a German executive and state organization, he claimed. At the same time, Claussen demanded an honorable resolution to the Schleswig-Holstein conflict and restoration of the unity between the duchies. He personally would not accept "peace at any price."[14] However, Schleswig-Holstein's radicals had little influence on the developments.

The Danish army's invasion started with a diversionary landing at Holdnaes, east of Flensburg, and the defeat of the disorganized Schleswig-Holstein army at Bov/Bau on April 9. German military assistance was unable to arrive soon enough to "liberate their German brethren in the duchies from foreign oppression." When the armies of General Friedrich Heinrich Ernst Graf von Wrangel defeated the Danish troops on the heights west of Sonderburg/Sønderborg near Düppel/Dybbøl and advanced into Denmark, international pressure increased for Prussia to withdraw from Danish territory. On July 2, Albert Graf von Pourtalès, who was supposed to represent Prussia in Constantinople, and his Danish counterpart Knuth, under the supervision of the Swedish foreign minister Friherre Gustaf Nils Algernon Adolf Stierneld and cabinet secretary Christoffer Rutger Ludvig Manderström, signed a six-month cease-fire agreement, which the duchies opposed.[15]

In the duchies, radicals continued their uncompromising opposition to a peace without independence. On July 8, 1848, the radical Friedrich Hedde voiced his opposition to the humiliating cease-fire, especially the provisions regarding the withdrawal of German troops from the duchies, the payment for damages done in Jutland, and the replacement of the provisional government. Paradoxically, the victor in this cease-fire, he marveled, was bowing to the defeated. "As a result of such a humiliating cease-fire," he declared, "an even more humiliating peace will probably grow out of it." Hedde worried about the freedom of the people under arbitrary Danish involvement in the domestic affairs of the duchies. He finally emphasized the sovereignty of the people and their desire to protect the honor and laws of the German nation. The only people that Schleswig-Holstein could trust were Germans. "On our own power and the German people must we rely," Hedde insisted. "Otherwise, at the end, we have suffered through the revolution and war without victory or honor."[16] Unfortunately, an honorable peace was increasingly unlikely.

Radicals like Olshausen and Claussen questioned the provisional government's legitimacy. In mid-August, Olshausen tendered his resignation, jump-starting a debate over the direction of the uprising. Radicals voiced demands for republican and democratic reforms to grant the provisional government the consent of the governed. Claussen spoke of the "revolution" that had given the provisional government its right to exist. Conservative members challenged Claussen's use of the term "revolution." To the conservatives, all actions by the provisional government were in the name of the duke and therefore legitimate.[17] Radical opposition continued to grow, but moderates were able to keep them in check for the moment.

With the end of the cease-fire, Wilhelm Hartwig Beseler and Friedrich Graf von Reventlow-Preetz assumed power—the Statthalterschaft. On April 3, Danish troops crossed the border into northern Schleswig. On the following day, the Danish navy sent a seven-ship fleet against Eckernförde, with disastrous results. Having defeated the advancing Danes, the Schleswig-Holstein army and its German allies advanced into Denmark. General von Bülow's army laid siege to Fredericia on May 7, 1849. However, with no naval force to cut off access from the sea, Danish reinforcements poured into the city. After two months under siege, the Danes broke out and forced the Schleswig-Holstein army into full retreat. On July 8, two days after the siege of Fredericia ended, Graf von Schleinitz, Prussia's new foreign minister, and Holger Christian von Reedtz, the Danish minister in Berlin, agreed to the withdrawal of all German troops from the duchies. With the revolutionary government in Frankfurt disintegrating, "the duchies lost their most important moral support," Schleiden observed.[18] The radicals mounted another attack on the Statthalterschaft.

On November 1, 1849, the radicals again demanded political reforms and that the Statthalterschaft do something about the "anarchical" situation in Schleswig. At the same time, the duchies unsuccessfully approached Denmark about peace terms. As negotiations commenced in Berlin and London, the Statthalterschaft was under pressure to continue the war and improve accountability. In the face of foreign and domestic pressure, the Statthalterschaft buckled and key ministers resigned. Even worse, the two armies met again, on July 25, in the Battle of Idstedt, the largest land battle in the Nordic countries, with about 26,800 Schleswig-Holstein German and 37,500 Danish soldiers involved. Schleswig-Holstein's army suffered a resounding defeat.

With the army falling apart and small excursions against Mysunde and Friedrichstadt unsuccessful, General Karl Wilhelm Freiherr von Willisen resigned. By late 1850, the German states wanted to put the regrettable Schleswig-Holstein episode behind them. On January 6, 1851, generals Wilhelm von Thümen and Alexander Graf von Mensdorff arrived to take over the government. Their request gave the impression that the people had risen up against their lord, which the Statthalterschaft vehemently denied.[19] The duchies had failed.

The Statthalterschaft briefly contemplated a two-front war, but with victory against the Danes unlikely and most of the officers reluctant to engage the Austrian, Prussian, and other German troops, the cause was lost. On February 1, 1851, the Statthalterschaft relinquished power. The first Schleswig-Holstein war was over. Negotiations commenced, culminating in the Protocol of London of 1852, signed by Prussia, Great Britain, Denmark, Sweden, and Russia. In the protocol, Denmark promised to maintain Schleswig's independence and to provide a constitution for the duchies.[20] Unfortunately, the return to the prewar status quo satisfied nobody and only increased the bitterness on both sides of the nationality divide. The Schleswig-Holstein question remained unresolved.

The German separatists in the Dano-German borderland had failed to accomplish their goal. The longest of the 1848 uprisings had ended. With three stages of conflict and two prolonged armistices, the Schleswig-Holstein war was just as difficult as the succession and nationality questions causing it. The German radicals in Schleswig-Holstein remained true to the language first used by Uwe Jens Lornsen in 1830. They continued to describe Danish oppression in constitutional and legal terms, which allowed them to legitimize the uprising. Throughout, moderates struggled with radical demands for independence, democratic reforms, and republicanism, which undermine their chance of success.

As Germans and Danes fought in Schleswig-Holstein, Germans and Hungarians engaged in a similar separatist struggle. By 1848, Hungarian demands for political reform and autonomy appeared in the meetings of the Hungarian diet. Like other uprisings, the Hungarians fought against "the complete subjugation of Hungary." In addition, the Hungarians explained, "Far from being a rebellion, [their uprising] was simply an act of self-defense." On March 3, 1848, Lajos Kossuth, whose radical supporters had increased their influence, spoke up in parliament, calling for autonomy in military, administrative, and parliamentary matters.[21]

Young Hungarian radicals in the streets of Pest called for liberal reforms, such as freedom of the press, trial by jury, civil and religious equality, the end of political prosecutions, and the establishment of a national guard. Their demands concluded with the French Revolution–inspired call for "Equality, Liberty, Fraternity!" Only half of the twelve demands related to national questions; the rest were social. The protests, supposedly well controlled by Kossuth, brought twenty thousand people into the streets and left the conservative forces, which had only seven thousand unreliable Italian soldiers available, immobilized. The palatine of Hungary, Stefan Franz Viktor, Erzherzog von Österreich, outmaneuvered the Vienna government and obtained from Emperor Ferdinand I complete acceptance of all Hungarian demands. Lajos Batthyány de Németújvár became prime minister of Hungary.[22]

Batthyány called on the people to "maintain peace and order." The Hungarian parliament liberalized the press, emancipated Jews, created a national guard, and extended the right to vote, but it did not grant universal suffrage. Radicals demanded more reforms and professed their loyalty to the monarchy. On March 15, in a proclamation calling for the establishment of a national guard, the radicals closed with "Long live the king! Constitutional reform, liberty, equality, peace, and order!" Kossuth explained in the legislature: "This nation possesses liberty and all its members want to be free. Just as the word 'nation' cannot be arrogated by one caste, it cannot be arrogated by one city either. Fifteen million Hungarians together make the fatherland and the nation."[23] As radicals and moderates battled, social and ethnic groups challenged Magyar power.

The Hungarian revolutionary government considered worker demands for an end of guild laws and for improving the position of journeymen. The government did abolish feudalism in Hungary, but the peasantry remained landless. In addition, the government had to address the pleas of ethnic minorities. Croats, Serbs, and Romanians, in particular, had national ambitions of their own, desiring separation from Hungarian oppression. The Austrian appointment of Josip Jelačić Bužimski as *ban* (governor) of Croatia, a province of Hungary, without consulting the Hungarian government, was troubling. The Hungarians faced a Croatian separatist challenge as moderates and radicals battled each other over domestic policies and separation from Austria.[24]

By the summer, the reactionary forces had had enough with revolution. Encouraged by the violent suppression of the Prague uprising, Vienna's appeasement policy ended with the appointment of Alfred Candidus Ferdinand, Fürst zu Windisch-Graetz. In Transylvania, Magyars and Romanians engaged in brutal guerrilla warfare. The Serbs in Hungary fought the Hungarian authorities. Finally, the Croats demanded liberal reforms, an end to feudalism, and autonomy within the Hungarian kingdom.[25] Hungary faced powerful enemies everywhere, many with similar demands. Ironically, Hungary wanted to escape Austrian oppression as much as minorities wanted to leave Hungary.

In June 1848, Ferdinand I reaffirmed the relationship between

Austria and Hungary and discredited Hungarian perception of Austrian oppression. He argued, "Both your nationality and your municipal rights are enlarged, and secured against any encroachment; as not only the use of your native language is lawfully guaranteed to you forever in your schools and churches, but it is likewise introduced in the public assemblies." Like his Danish counterpart, Ferdinand was angry when his subjects did not greet his conciliatory gestures with "thankfulness, love and loyalty, which they owe to ourselves" but by unfolding "the standard of fanatical distrust." Most importantly, the king challenged, "He who revolts against the law, revolts against our royal throne, which rests upon the law." In addition, the king dismissed the concerns about the appointment of Jelačić. He closed by appealing to the people's loyalty: "Listen to the well-wishing voice of your king addressing you, as many as still are his faithful Croats and Sclavonians."[26]

On July 8, the king followed up with a speech to the Hungarian diet. He dismissed all arguments that Austria intended to destroy Hungarian autonomy. "Croatia rose in undisguised sedition; in the districts of the Lower Danube, bands of armed rebels have broken the peace of the country," the king argued. "The assembled representatives of the nation will regard it as their first and chief duty to provide all the means required to restore the troubled tranquility of the country, to preserve the integrity of the Hungarian realm." Some Hungarian nationalists took offense when the king stated his desire to maintain "the integrity and inviolability of his crown against all attacks from without." At the same time, the king closed with another appeal to Hungarian loyalty.[27]

With the reaction gaining strength, Hungary prepared for the military onslaught that Windisch-Graetz and Johann Josef Wenzel Anton Franz Karl, Graf Radetzky von Radetz had already unleashed in other parts of the empire. Since Batthyány was not an inspiring, revolutionary, and charismatic leader, radicals such as Sándor Petőfi demanded political changes but not the end of monarchy. Even as the moderate leadership maintained control, questions arose about the loyalty of the troops stationed in Hungary and the need to train *honvéd* (national guard) units. German officers had to decide whether they should serve the Habsburgs or the Hungarian government. As minister of finance, Kossuth had the impossible task of finding money to pay for 200,000 Hungarian soldiers.[28] Hungary never had the troops to challenge Austria.

In late August, tensions escalated. Austria ordered Jelačić to subdue the Hungarians. Meanwhile, the Hungarians demanded the resettling of the king to Buda-Pest and the calling off of Jelačić: "In the names of the United States of Hungary and Transylvania, we appear before your Majesty" to defend against Jelačić's Croatian army. The Hungarians argued, "Now several parts of the kingdom are disturbed by a rebellion, whose leaders plainly assert that they rise in the interest of the reigning house, and are rebels in your Majesty's name, against the freedom and independence, which your Majesty lawfully guaranteed to the Hungarian nation. One part of the Hungarian army sheds its blood in Italy, for the interests of the monarchy, and reaps there, on every battle-field, laurels of triumph; while another part of the same army is being instigated to refuse obedience to the legal government of the kingdom." In their opposition to the Croatians, the Hungarians explained, "A rebellion from Croatia threatens Hungary with hostile invasion, and, without any cause, has occupied the Hungarian port of Fiume, and the Sclavonian counties." The Hungarians closed with a strong affirmation of their loyalty.[29] As the Hungarian-Croatian civil war started, the irony of the Hungarian conflict emerged: Austria had to accept Hungarian secession, but Croatian secession from Hungary was not acceptable.

Increasingly, Kossuth's radicals and Batthyány's moderates disagreed. The radicalization of the uprising concerned Batthyány, who wished to rein in Kossuth's followers. Undeterred, Kossuth appealed to the Hungarian people: "If the Hungarian race proves so cowardly as not to disperse the Croatian and Servian invaders," then they did not understand that their struggle was for "Freedom or death!" Foreshadowing his eventual embrace of independence, Kossuth wondered whether Jelačić's invasion provided the reason why Hungary needed to gain its independence. He closed with a cry for help: "All hail! To Hungary, for her freedom, happiness and fame." By mid-September, Batthyány had resigned, opening the door to more radical policies with Kossuth as his successor.[30]

On September 11, 1848, Jelačić invaded Hungary to restore the proper relationship between Austria and Hungary. Kossuth ordered the residents of Buda-Pest to construct fortifications. On September 29, the inexperienced Hungarian and Croatian armies met in battle near Pákozd. Jelačić lost and withdrew. Despite the defeat, Austria insisted that the "Hungarian Kingdom separate from the Austrian Empire was a political impossibility." While Windisch-Graetz stormed revolutionary Vienna, an Austro-Croatian army defeated the Hungarians. The new emperor, Franz Josef, promulgated a new constitution on March 4, 1849. Hungary was part of the Austrian Empire, temporarily ending any chances for autonomy or independence.[31]

The war escalated as Hungary faced new enemies. In Transylvania, Hungarian troops under Józef Zachariasz Bem, a veteran of the Polish uprising of 1830, held off loyal Austrian troops, Romanian nationalists, and Russian soldiers. Fighting alongside Bem was the young cavalry lieutenant Charles Zagonyi. In the west, with the retreating Hungarian army leaving Buda-Pest exposed, the government relocated to Debrecen. Having assumed power, Kossuth frequently ignored the minister of war, adding confusion to Hungarian politics. Furthermore, he felt threatened by the rise of Arthur Görgey de Görgő et Toporcz, one of Hungary's few successful generals. Avoiding Görgey, Kossuth disastrously appointed Henryk Dembiński, another veteran of the Polish revolutionary of 1830, to command all Hungarian armies.[32]

The Battle of Kápolna altered the dynamics of the war. After the battle, Kossuth paid homage to the fallen soldiers. "Accept the bloody offering which has been presented to Thee, and let it propitiate Thy favor to our land," he said. "Consecrate this spot by Thy grace, that the ashes of my brethren who have fallen in this sacred cause may rest undisturbed in hallowed repose. . . . Bless our effort to promote that liberty of which Thine own spirit is the essence; for to Thee, in the name of the whole people, I ascribe all honor and praise." With the officers turning against Dembiński, Kossuth once more avoided Görgey and appointed Antal Vetter. Once Vetter had embarrassed himself, Kossuth finally appointed Görgey.[33] Despite Görgey's victories and Hungarian sacrifices, the downward trajectory continued.

On April 19, 1849, Kossuth outmaneuvered moderates and declared Hungarian independence. The Hungarian Declaration Relative to the Separation of Hungary from Austria started with the relatively familiar phrase "We, the legally constituted representatives of the Hungarian nation, assembled in Diet, do by these presents solemnly proclaim, in the maintenance of the inalienable natural rights of Hungary, with all its dependencies, to occupy the position of an independent European state." Like other separatist declarations, the Hungarians laid out their grievances. Most importantly, the declaration charged, "The House of Austria has publicly used every effort to deprive the country of its legitimate independence and constitution, designing to reduce it to a level with the other provinces long since deprived of all freedom, and to unite all in a common link of slavery."[34] Only independence could end Hungary's enslavement and oppression at the hand of the Austrians.

The Hungarians took up arms to defend themselves against "systemized tyranny." The struggles to maintain the constitutional rights of Hungary required defensive, military measures, the declaration explained, but those had been "laid down . . . as soon as the king by new compact and fresh oaths has guaranteed the duration of its rights and liberty." They emphasized once more that the Austrians had oppressed Hungary for more than three hundred years. Nevertheless, "the Hungarian nation has all along respected the tie by which it was united to this dynasty; and in now decreeing its expulsion from the throne, it acts under the natural law of self-preservation." Therefore, Hungary had not only a natural but also divine blessing for its revolution. The list of grievances was long and included "alliances with the enemies . . . robbers, or partisan chieftains, . . . attempts to annihilate the independence of the country, . . . attacking with an armed force the people who have committed no act of revolt," and violating the integrity of the country.[35] Hungary had to separate from the Habsburg Empire to escape oppression.

Furthermore, the declaration explained, the German people of Austria did not offend the Hungarians; the Habsburg dynasty was the enemy. "The House of Lorraine-Hapsburg is unexampled in the compass of its perjuries, and has committed every one of these crimes against the nation," stated the declaration, in "its determination to extinguish the independence of Hungary." The Hungarians desired additional rights, but the Austrians would not listen. The declaration boldly asserted that Hungary and Transylvania "formed a separate, independent kingdom" and that "its independence, self-government, constitution, and privileges shall remain inviolate and especially guaranteed." Austrian despotism had forced Hungary into unwanted wars. In its zealousness, Austria had tried to dismember Hungary. The Hungarians claimed, "Croatia and Slavonia were chosen to begin this rebellion, because, in those countries, the inhuman policy of Prince Metternich had, with a view to the weakening of all parties, for years cherished hatred against the Hungarian nation." Besides the continued demands for financial, commercial, and military independence, the Hungarians demanded the integrity of Hungary, Transylvania, and all other provinces, which should remain united, and that Hungary should remain an "independent, sovereign state." The House of Habsburg-Lorraine had violated the Hungarian rights for the last time. As a result, Hungary took its place among the "free and independent states" of Europe.[36]

The Hungarian government, military leadership, and Kossuth continued to quarrel, teetering on the verge of a coup d'état. With Görgey's continued successes, Kossuth rewarded him with the ministry of war. Serving in the ministry was Lieutenant Colonel Asbóth, who was one of Kossuth's most loyal advisers. Realizing that the war was in the last stretch and victory was imminent, Austria appointed Julius Jakob Freiherr von Haynau, well known for his brutality, to command all Austrian forces. Over the next two months, Haynau defeated the numerically superior Hungarians in a series of battles. With invasion forces on Hungarian soil, Kossuth requested supreme command of the army, causing renewed conflict between himself, the cabinet, and Görgey. To improve morale, Kossuth appealed to the loyalty of the officers. He asked them, "In the name of liberty and the people, I summon you by your patriotism . . . to preserve the union, which in the present dangerous moment, can alone save our country, and indeed the liberty of Europe, and to co-operate now, as you did formerly, for the salvation of our country and of liberty."[37] However, words do not win wars against superior armies.

With the Russo-Austrian advance, defeat looming, and no mercy from the Austrians, Hungarian officers wished to surrender to the Russians. Despite the desolate situation, Kossuth did not trust Görgey, who was willing to surrender if Hungary remained an autonomous region in the Habsburg Empire. In contrast, Haynau announced his intention "to carry my victorious arms onward in pursuit, and to annihilation of a rebellious enemy." In order to stop the Hungarian soldiers from fighting, he warned, "They, too, deceived by the leaders of the rebellion, made themselves accomplices to treason. Their fate will show you whether or not I know how to pity rebellious subjects."[38]

On August 11, Kossuth accepted the consequence of Hungarian defeat, resigned from all positions, and allowed Görgey to take over. In a proclamation to the Hungarian people, Kossuth explained his decision: "The salvation of the national existence, and the protection of its fortune, lies in the hands of the leaders of the army." He accepted that Hungarian independence had to follow military victory. Kossuth asked of Görgey, "May he love his country with that disinterested love which I bear it! May his endeavors to reconquer the independence and happiness of the nation be crowned with greater success than mine were!"

In contrast, Görgey sought peace at all costs and offered an unconditional surrender to the Russians. He knew that "the policy of Europe compelled his majesty, the Czar of Russia, to league with Austria for our overthrow, and for the termination of our war for the Hungarian constitution." The Hungarian desired to prevent further bloodshed and appealed to the Russians: "Since I am too weak to defend my peaceable fellow-citizens, I will, at least, liberate them from the miseries of war. I make an unconditional surrender. . . . I place my reliance on the well-known generosity of his majesty, the Czar, trusting that he will consider the case of numbers of my brave comrades."

On August 13, the Hungarian army surrendered. The surrender allowed the Austrians to abandon their conciliatory policy. While all soldiers and low-ranking noncommissioned officers received an amnesty, military courts determined whether ranking officers had committed treason. Over the next few months, 4,628 Hungarians were put on trial. Many served prison sentences or were executed, including the "Thirteen Martyrs of Arad," who included Vetter and Görgey.[39]

On August 17, Kossuth and many loyal followers, including Asbóth, left Hungary for the Ottoman Empire. Before his departure,

Kossuth issued a farewell address to the Hungary people. "How many streams of blood have run, as proofs," he wrote, "how the Hungarian loves his father-land, and how he can *die* for it! And yet hast thou, beloved father-land, become a slave! Thy beloved sons are chained and dragged away like slaves, destined to fetter again every thing that is holy." To Kossuth, Austria still enslaved and oppressed the Hungarians. He also pointed to Görgey's treason. "Thy sentence of death, beloved father-land, was written by him," Kossuth wrote, "whose love to his country I never questioned for a moment." He questioned the general's loyalty and called him a traitor, concluding, "Curse him, people of the Magyars! Curse the heart, which did not dry up, when it attempted to nourish him with the moisture of life! . . . The God of liberty will never blot you out from His memory. . . . You may still be proud, for the lion of Europe had to be aroused to conquer the rebels!"[40]

Kossuth's words present a microcosm of separatism in this era. The Hungarians had many grievances against the Habsburg dynasty. When, in 1848, the opportunity arose, the Hungarians demanded autonomy. Their demands were partially answered, but by granting special privileges to the Croatians, the Austrians caused a civil war in Hungary. As the uprising continued and radicalized, the Hungarian demands shifted from autonomy to independence. Kossuth invoked slavery and oppression to justify secession. The result was a war for independence that pitched Hungary against an Austro-Russian alliance. Hungarian independence was doomed.

―――――

The Irish uprising, induced by the Great Famine, was the shortest, worst-planned, and most poorly executed of all the rebellions in 1848. Today, historians often derogatorily dismiss the incident as the "Battle of Widow McCormack's Cabbage Patch." The British government's mismanagement of the famine relief and the continued lack of adequate political representation gave rise to a belligerent young group of nationalists who opposed Daniel O'Connell's Catholic identity politics. British oppression had to end, and Irish independence—at least political, if not national—was the only acceptable outcome.

After Catholic emancipation, support for Daniel O'Connell, who was often called the "Liberator," waned, and the political landscape in Ireland shifted. Many young intellectuals demanded nondenominational education and an end to the Church of Ireland's stranglehold. They wished to reform the Irish Poor Law to provide better assistance to the 2.3 million poverty-stricken Irish peasants. Young politicians felt that Ireland was still a colony. In October 1842, Thomas Davis, Blake Dillon, and Charles G. Duffy published the first edition of the *Nation*, which called for Irish independence.[41] The movement attracted many young radical minds.

By the early 1840s, O'Connell was staging peaceful mass meetings so that the people could voice their opposition to British oppression. John Mitchel took advantage of the opportunity to voice his contempt: "England declared that if all Ireland demanded that measure, England would rather drown the demand in blood." An unarmed population, according to Mitchel, weakened the Irish bargaining position. "Denied the privilege of bearing arms," he wrote, "forbidden education—prohibited to exercise trade or commerce in any corporate town—excluded from all profession, . . . it was no wonder they had become impoverished in spirit as well as in means."[42] Irish and British interests increasingly diverged.

O'Connell hoped to force policy changes with a series of monster meetings. At one meeting, O'Connell called out, "Ireland! Land of my fathers. Ireland! Birthplace of my children. Ireland! That shall hold my grave. Ireland! That I love with the fondest aspirations, your men are too brave, your women are too beautiful and good, you are too elevated among nations of the earth, too moral, too religious, to be slaves. I promise you that you shall be free!" Obviously, O'Connell referred to the political, economic, and social oppression suffered by Ireland at the hands of the British.

The authorities perceived the meetings as a precursor to rebellion. "In point of national *prestige*," Mitchel declared, "England could still less afford to repeal the Union, because all the world would know the concession had been wrung from her against her will." Before the next mass meeting, at historic Clontarf, on October 8, 1843, the authorities prohibited the assembly. Despite the meeting's cancellation, the British charged O'Connell with "conspiracy and other misdemeanors." The authorities made sure of a guilty verdict by packing the jury with "Orangemen, Englishmen, and tradesmen." The law lords eventually reversed the decision.[43]

The arrest of O'Connell revived his Repeal Association and insti-gated young nationalists. However, O'Connell's supporters questioned the broad religious base of the Young Ireland movement, which in-cluded Protestant dissenters such as Mitchel. The British authorities did notice the rift in the Irish national movement: "We have reason to belive [sic] that the younger part of the Irish agitators are a far more serious set of men than their fathers," the *Morning Post* re-ported. "They look forward to the slaughter of those they hate as the greatest enjoyment they could experience. . . . The young men of the movement are Jacobin Republicans." The young radicals employed a new language of violence against oppression. As the *Nation* took on a more belligerent tone, promoting household suffrage and the secret ballot, O'Connell distanced himself from the Young Ireland move-ment and its willingness to use force.[44] However, all Irish politicians worried about the suffering people whose main food crop was being decimated by the potato blight.

The entire agricultural population of Ireland, regardless of reli-gious affiliation, suffered under the destruction of the potato crop. The Protestant Cleburnes were no exception. With the death of his father in 1843 and the ever-tightening financial situation, Patrick Cle-burne had left school and entered an apprenticeship with a traveling doctor. His family struggled to maintain the Grange House estate, and Cleburne failed the entry exam at Apothecaries Hall in Dublin. Faced with what he perceived as a personal failure, Cleburne enlisted in the British Forty-First Regiment of Foot, which was supposed to go to Madras.[45] Domestic unrest required the unit to remain at home, however, forcing Cleburne to potentially fire on fellow Irishmen.

Belatedly joining the Repeal Association, Thomas Francis Mea-gher agreed with the need to repeal the Union. "A nation organized and disciplined, instructed and inspired," he argued, "under the guid-ance of wise spirits, and in the dawning light of a glorious future, makes head against a powerful supremacy." Even more important, "If the majority rule, let the minority be heard," he said. "Toleration of opinion will generate confidence amongst all classes and lay the sure basis of national independence. But, sir, whilst we thus endeavor wisely to conciliate, let us not, to the strongest foe, nor in the most tempting emergency, weakly capitulate."[46] Meagher used legal and constitutional arguments to make his case against the Act of Union and British oppression.

The unimaginable suffering destroyed all faith in a constitutional solution. In criticizing the Irish Poor Law of 1842, Mitchel argued that the poorhouses did not address poverty but increased starvation. In addition, laws undermining tenant rights had forced people from their land. With the famine, political agitation for autonomy or independence grew. "Both government and landlords had been thoroughly frightened by that vast parade of a nation," Mitchel observed, "and they knew they had only been saved by O'Connell and his Peace-principle." Mitchel was not alone in questioning British policy, but his belligerency drew the ire of the authorities. The government unsuccessfully charged the *Nation*'s chief editor, Charles Duffy, with sedition.[47]

On February 16, 1846, Meagher highlighted how Ireland was at the mercy of the English government. He told his audience, "The Russian sympathizes not with the Pole whom he has struck down; and if you expect it to be otherwise, you do not possess the sagacity of men, and are only qualified to be slaves." Meagher briefly embraced a language similar to O'Connell's to describe British oppression: "In the name of freedom, Circassia guards her mountain passes," Meagher told the crowd two weeks later, "Italy organizes—Poland strikes! Sir, we weep no more for Poland, for Poland is in arms! The spirit of Kosciusko sleeps no more in the Cathedral of Cracow! It walks the Carpathian heights, and is heard in the cry—there is hope for Poland, whilst in Poland there a life to lose!" Like Mazzini, Meagher assumed there was a possibility of assisting the Poles, either by direct intervention or with a distracting revolution in Ireland. He considered the three eastern monarchies intent on destroying the Polish nation. He used his international comparison to emphasize that only independence could protect against English policies: "We being Irish—this land being Ireland," Meagher shouted, "I demand an Irish viceroy for the Irish court."[48]

Meagher questioned the liberal spirit and compassion of the British government. "Even from the royal lips, with an expression of pity for our country," he said, "there came a cold, harsh threat of coercion." He challenged, "Legislation will never effect what nature has forbidden," especially unity between Ireland and Great Britain. Meagher hoped for a better future. "After years of social disorder, years of detestable recrimination between factions, and provinces, and creeds," he said, "we are on the march to freedom. A nation, organized and disciplined, instructed and inspired, under the guidance of wise spirits, and in the dawning light of a glorious future, makes head against a powerful supremacy." He vehemently opposed the recent coercion bill. He told the British, "Let them test it in the country of the Sikhs! There they have to civilize a most disordered people! There they have to deal, not with a defenceless, but an armed people!" Meagher accepted notions of white racial superiority, but he continued to call on all "friends of freedom" to stand up to the English and bring about Irish independence. Assuming "Ireland does not belong to the Irish," he insisted on repeal.[49]

However, internal divisions undermined the Irish nationalists. In the Kilkenny by-election, O'Connell urged voters to "return a Repealer, and I cannot possibly permit it to return either a Tory or Whig or an animal more mischievous than either of the others, called a Young Irelander." The schism in the Irish repeal movement had materialized on July 13, 1846, when O'Connell called for the passage of a resolution that pledged the Repeal Association to abstain from violence and physical force. Meagher spoke up against the peace resolution. The forceful argument in favor of violence gained Meagher the nom de guerre "Meagher of the Sword."[50]

Meagher started with a powerful explanation about why British oppression, which left Ireland unable to prosper, had to end. He hoped that once Ireland had its independence, the people could create a strong national identity. The Irish people should not confuse the "boons of a Whig government to that which would be the abiding blessing of an Irish parliament." In pointing once more to the example of oppressed Poland, Meagher called for an end of the Act of Union, which should be the only issue on the people's mind. He did caution that "no member of this Association suggested an appeal to arms. No member of this Association advised it." Meagher was not in favor of violent revolution because "an excitement to arms would be senseless—and wicked, because irrational." Nevertheless, he disagreed with the peace resolution. He could not pledge "the unqualified repudiation of physical force in all countries, at all times, and under every circumstance." He reasoned that violence as a last resort was sometimes necessary:

> There are times when arms will alone suffice, and when political amelioration call for a drop of blood, and many thousand drops of blood. . . .
> Abhor the sword—stigmatize the sword? No, my Lord, for, in the passes of Tyrol, it cut to pieces the banner of the Bavarian, and, through those cragged passes, struck a path to fame for the peasant insurrectionist of Inspruck.
> Abhor the sword—stigmatize the sword? No, my Lord, for, at its blow, a giant nation started from the waters of the Atlantic, and by its redeeming magic, and it the quivering of its crimson light, the crippled Colony sprang into the attitude of a proud Republic. . . .
> Abhor the sword—stigmatize the sword? No, my Lord, for it swept the Dutch marauders out of the fine old towns of Belgium.[51]

Irish freedom might be the result of political agitation, but physical violence had to remain a last resort.

Members of Young Ireland perceived that the peace resolution was an intentional maneuver to remove their vocal and belligerent attitudes from the organization. In the next meeting, on July 28, Meagher tried to continue his speech, but John O'Connell demanded that Meagher stop his promotion of violence. William Smith O'Brien rose in defense. "Mr. Meagher has distinctly stated that he joined this Association for the purpose of obtaining repeal by peaceful and moral means alone. . . . You are charged with being a people who will never give fair play to an adversary. You are charged with being willing slaves to any despot who may obtain the reins of power at a particular moment." Since O'Connell refused to allow Meagher to finish, O'Brien walked out, and Young Ireland followed.[52] Secession divided the Irish national movement.

Meanwhile, Irish peasants worried about their survival. O'Brien agitated for a variety of measures in what he called the "imperial Parliament." Parliament refused to change the poor laws or adopt measures to assist the famine victims. Irish landowners, even politicians in the nationalist organizations, remained involved in the grain and livestock trade with the neighboring island, taking food away from the starving masses. The botched relief effort gave Irish nationalists an opportunity to accuse the British of purposefully engaging in thinning out the Irish population. "If Yorkshire and Lancashire had sustained a like calamity," Mitchel argued, "there is no doubt such measures as these would have been taken, promptly and liberally."

He presented an even more sinister comparison. When Britain abolished slavery, the country had borrowed £20 million to give "to their slave-holding colonists for a mischievous whim." Much to Mitchel's indignation, no money was available to help Ireland. He explained "the object must be popular in England; it must subserve some purpose of British policy;—as in the case of the twenty millions borrowed to turn negroes wild (set them 'free' as it was called)—or the loans afterwards freely taken to crush the people of India, and preserve and extend the opium trade with China." This perception of second-class status added to the perception of English oppression and the need for Irish independence.[53]

On January 13, 1847, Young Ireland created the Irish Confederation. The organization's constitution demanded the restoration of "the inalienable right, of the Irish Nation; . . . That a society be now formed under the title of 'The Irish Confederation,' for the purpose of protecting our national interests, and obtaining the Legislative independence of Ireland." At its opening meeting, Meagher questioned English control of Ireland. Britain had repeatedly violated Irish rights and refused to address demands for self-government. "England, in her lust for empire," Meagher argued, "has deprived us of those large means, that social wealth, that manufacturing capital, which would have enabled our country to meet the necessities of this dark crisis." Even more, England deliberately held Ireland down and removed its food. He suggested, "Let it be our motto. Union with England for no purpose—union with England for no price—union with England on no terms!" After more elaboration, Meagher concluded, "The spirit of Nationality, rooted in our hearts, is as immoveable as the alter of the Druid, pillared in our soil."[54]

The Confederation's leadership debated whether constitutional agitation or more violent means were the right approach to gaining Irish independence. "No nation," Meagher emphasized, "has won its independence by an accident." When the question of violence arose, Meagher challenged, "I will . . . ask you—is an insurrection practicable? Prove to me that it is, and I, for one, will vote for it this very night." He remained a voice of caution. The leaders did not want to rashly enter into a rebellion, especially if the people and country were not ready. While he sympathized with Mitchel, Meagher noted that the clergy, aristocracy, and middle class stood opposed to the idea of insurrection. At the same time, Meagher worried about giving in to democracy or social revolution. "The Polish peasants cut the throats of the Polish nobles," he observed, "and before the Vistula had washed away the blood, the free city of Cracow was proclaimed a dungeon." He was likely referring to the events of 1846. Meagher explained, "I am not for a democratic, I am for a national movement—not for a movement like that of Paris in 1793, but for a movement like that of Brussels in 1830—like that of Palermo in 1848."[55] As in many other parts of Europe, democracy was too radical and national independence based on separation remained the foremost desire.

Meagher argued, as early as April 1847, "The famine has been [England's] best swordsman—it has cut down thousands of her peasant foes." However, he hoped that the English vulture would not destroy the "generous and heroic" peasants. He called on the national spirit: "The Irish crown must no longer be a cipher. The Irish scepter and the Irish flag must cease to be mere figures of speech—they must become empowered and recognized realities." While Meagher wanted his fellow countrymen to take action and bring about independence, he did not desire a radical uprising. "I am one of the people, but I am no democrat. I am for an equality of civil rights—but I am no republican. I am for vesting the responsibilities and the duties of government in three estates." In order to help the Irish peasantry, Meagher suggested legal measures against foreign competition.[56]

John Mitchel, undeterred, called for violent rebellion. He was a liability for the Irish Confederation. In his editorials, he instructed the Irish people to stand up for their nationality and to arm themselves with rudimentary weapons. His appeals created tensions in the

Nation's offices. In early December 1847, Duffy suggested constitutional means to accomplish repeal; Mitchel resigned. After his retirement, however, Mitchel did not settle down. On February 12, his new newspaper, the *United Irishman*, appeared. "Mitchel was certainly the most hardline and confrontational of the Young Ireland group," wrote one of his biographers. "Mitchel was the sole advocate of armed revolution, something the other members believed the country was completely unprepared for." Mitchel and his editors believed "Ireland was our country. The Irish race was our flesh and blood. The alternative was, either to see a foreign enemy scourge our people from the face of their own land, by famine and pestilence, 'law,' political economy, and red tape, or to set our backs to the wall and fight to the death." At every turn, Mitchel insulted the British authorities. He called Clarendon a "butcher" and "high commissioner of spies," and he ended one editorial with "Your lordship's mortal enemy." Mitchel later elaborated: "We have all heard much of the espionage of France or Austria. Neither of them is furnished with a police so omnipresent, so inevitable,—above all so treacherous,—as Ireland." Ready for a violent rebellion, Mitchel made practical suggestions on how to construct barricades and fight with rudimentary weapons. Some Irish nationalists worried that Mitchel was another Robespierre, a "bloodthirsty villain."[57]

On March 15, 1848, the Irish Confederation met and agreed that only after they had exhausted all political options should the organization call for violence. Meagher called on Irish nationalists to demand the repeal of the union and, if "refused, let the Irish deputies pack up their court dresses—as Benjamin Franklin did, when repulsed from the court of George III—and let them, then and there, make solemn oath, that when next they demand admission to the throne room of St. James's, it shall be through the accredited ambassador of the Irish Republic." He asked the people to follow the example of the French and fight along barricades if the Irish government remained one "of dragoons and bombadiers, of detectives and light infantry." He hoped to not only mimic the French; even more, he asked for French assistance.[58] Ireland's radicals invoked both the United States and European revolutions. They hoped to enlist international support.

On March 28, O'Brien and Meagher arrived in Paris, but the cautious French foreign minister, Alphonse de Lamartine, explained that domestic uncertainty precluded any support for the Irish. Meagher tried to change opinions with an appeal to the French revolutionary spirit. "France proclaimed herself the protectress of weak nations" Meagher explained, "and is not the sword of the Republic pledged to the oppressed nationalities which, in Europe, and elsewhere, desire to reconstruct themselves?" Drawing comparisons, he observed, "The storm which dashed the crown of Orleans against the column of July, has rocked the foundations of the Castle. They have no longer a safe bedding in the Irish soil." He called out, "The world is in arms . . . prepared to grasp your freedom with an armed hand." Finally, he argued, "Taught by the examples of Italy, of France, of Sicily, the citizens of Ireland shall, at last, unite." The Irish had nothing to lose. "Should we succeed . . . the glory of this old Irish nation . . . will grow young and strong again. Should we fail—the country will not be worse than it is now—the sword of famine is less sparing than the bayonet of the soldier."[59] Meagher continued to hope for European assistance.

Meagher felt good about his visit to Paris. When he returned to Ireland, he told his audience, "I went to France animated with a love of freedom, and glorying in its service. I have returned from France with this love deepened in my soul." In presenting the people of Ireland with the Irish tricolor, he told them, "From Paris, the city of the tricolor and the barricade, this flag has been proudly borne. . . . The white in the centre signifies a lasting truce between the 'orange' and the 'green'—and I trust that beneath its folds, the hands of the Irish Protestant and the Irish Catholic may be clasped in generous and heroic brotherhood."[60] Meagher appealed to the nationalism of the Irish people with a symbol of identity and unity. The flag represented the Irish Confederation and its efforts to bridge the sectarian divide.

On April 7, O'Brien returned to Parliament to agitate for Irish independence. He explained, "Unlike all the other governments of Europe, the liberal government of England, instead of attempting to pacify the country which they are most closely connected by timely concessions, meet the demands of the people by prosecutions and by coercive laws." He pointed to the Italian state of the Two Sicilies, and to how the Naples government oppressed the Sicilians, to illustrate Ireland's suffering. O'Brien was confident that Irish independence could only be the result of Irish efforts, saying, "Irish freedom must be won by Irish courage and Irish firmness." He drew parallels with other independence struggles, such as the one in Poland. He warned, "I do, under these circumstances implore you, before it is too late, to consider the portentous warnings which have been presented by what had occurred in other countries." However, Parliament did not listen, and it further limited Irish freedoms. The Crown and Government Security Act, better known as the Treason Felony Act, provided the government with a broader interpretation of treason to include speaking in encouragement of rebellion. The penalty for this kind of treason was transportation.[61]

Undeterred, Mitchel continued his rabble-rousing campaign with calls for a democratic revolution and Irish independence. He cited Wolfe Tone, who had said, "Our independence must be won at all hazards. If the men of property will not support us, they must fall," in his attacks on the British government. "Mitchel's open defiance of British authority, coupled with his fire-spitting rhetoric, could only be interpreted as incitement and would not be tolerated for long by Dublin Castle," wrote one of his later biographers. On May 13, the authorities arrested Mitchel, charged him with violating the Treason Felony Act, and packed the jury with Protestant Irishmen. Found guilty, Mitchel summarized the problems of his trial in his "Speech from the Dock." "I have to say that I have been tried by a packed jury," he said, "by the jury of a partisan sheriff—by a jury not empanelled according to the law of England. I have been found guilty by packed jury, obtained by a juggle—a jury not empanelled by a sheriff but by a juggler. That is the reason why I object to the sentence being passed upon me." Mitchel explained that he had challenged Lord Clarendon to this standoff to embarrass the Lord Lieutenant, to force him to pack a jury and to convict an innocent person. Mitchel claimed victory, since he had "shown that Her Majesty's government sustains itself in Ireland by packed juries, by partisan judges, by perjured sheriffs." Even such an accusatory statement changed nothing. With great excitement in the streets and the courtroom, the authorities quickly removed Mitchel from the dock and from Ireland.[62]

The Irish Confederation did not call for violence after Mitchel's conviction. Meagher told a Dublin audience, "We are no longer masters of our lives. They belong to our country—to liberty—to vengeance. Upon the walls of Newgate a fettered hand has inscribed this destiny. We shall be the martyrs or the rulers of a revolution." He once more emphasized that a rescue attempt was unwise. He defended his personal perspective: "Call me coward—call me renegade. I will accept these titles as the penalties which a fidelity to my convictions has imposed." He asked for a reversal of the trial to allow "the triumphant felon [to set] his foot once more upon his native soil." Nevertheless, the Irish Confederation prepared for conflict by establishing clubs across the country.[63] While the Young Ireland movement prepared for an uprising, the British government prepared to crack down on any rebellious activities.

On July 21, the British cabinet, with parliamentary approval, suspended the writ of habeas corpus in Ireland. Realizing that their arrests were imminent and that they would face rigged juries, the leaders of the Irish Confederation determined to make County Kilkenny the center of the uprising. When they arrived in the region, they discovered that support for the uprising was minimal. In Killenaule, O'Brien urged the people to rebel but to avoid social revolution or destruction of property. Meagher called on the people. "Men of Tipperary," he said, "you have heard a true son of Irish soil, whose rugged virtues partake of the character of the country. . . . I am here not only to repent of nothing, but to dare them to do something worse." He urged the people to resist British oppression. Support for the uprising was limited, as many volunteers deserted the Irish revolutionary army within their hometown.[64]

The uprising started on July 28, when the revolutionaries encountered a detachment of Eighth Royal Irish Hussars. After verbal opposition, the soldiers marched through Killenaule without incident. The next day, a police force of forty-six, under Thomas Trant, approached Ballingarry, where the local population had erected barricades to prevent the arrest of the rebels. The police force retreated to Margaret McCormack's house. Sadly for the uprising, the children of the widow were inside the house with the police, who refused to surrender. The revolutionaries tried to negotiate, appealing to the nationalism of those inside.[65] The incident ended in defeat. The uprising had failed after only six days.

On August 3, Clarendon informed London that the country was at peace. In September and October, the leaders were put on trial. Their juries, much as in Mitchel's case, were carefully selected to secure guilty verdicts. During his trial, Meagher voiced his opposition to the rigged jury. He addressed the court's inadequacies: "My lords, previous to the jury being sworn," Meagher asked, "I respectfully beg leave to say a few words. I desire to protest against the construction of the panel from which the jury by which I am to be tried has been selected. . . . I feel that my cause, my honor, my liberty, my life are as safe in the hands of a jury composed exclusively of Protestants, as they would be with a jury composed exclusively of Roman Catholics." He protested that the sheriff was unable to locate a Catholic jury in a Catholic country. "No, I do not despair of my poor old country, her peace, her liberty, her glory," he explained. "For that country I can do no more than bid her hope. To lift this island up—to make her a benefactor to humanity, instead of being the meanest beggar in the world . . . this has been my ambition, and this ambition has been my crime. Judged by the law of England, I know this crime entails the penalty of death; but the history of Ireland explains this crime, and justifies it. . . . I deserve no punishment—we deserve no punishment."[66] His protest had no impact, and he was soon on his way to Van Diemen's Land (today's Tasmania).

According to Mitchel, the British had finally accomplished the conquest of Ireland. "What I wish to be fully understood," he wrote later, "is that this Act [the Incumbered Estates Act] was not intended to relieve, and did not relieve, anybody in Ireland; but that, under pretence of facilitating legal proceeding, it contemplated a sweeping confiscation and new 'Plantation' of the Island." Besides his invocation of a plantation, which had a long history in the northern parts of the island, he also drew parallels to continental European history. "No sack of Magdeburg, or ravage of the Palatinate," Michel continued, "ever approached in horror and desolation to the slaughter done in Ireland by mere official red tape and stationery, and the principles of Political Economy."[67] The Irish separatist uprising had failed.

The Irish Confederation had not overcome British oppression. In dramatic contrast to their predecessors, Young Ireland had infused a new language into the struggle to end the Act of Union and restore at least parliamentary autonomy. British oppression had to end, and if that required religious unity, then the Irish Confederation willingly embraced union between Catholics and Protestants. Furthermore, the Young Ireland movement committed to constitutional justifications and did not perceive of the Irish people as enslaved, as O'Connell did. The Irish reformers disagreed about when the use of violence was justified and when they had exhausted political means for change. Ireland had failed, in part, because the country's political leadership was fragmented and because Ireland was unable to gain any foreign support.

The United States suffered nonviolent challenge to the established order in 1848. Political crisis stemmed from long-standing sectional disagreements. Southerners had limited the embarrassment of ab-olitionist petitions with the congressional gag rule. Nevertheless, antislavery sentiment in the country grew. Political realignments altered the conversation from one about the humanity, morality, or economics of human bondage to one about the benefits of free and slave labor systems in the western territories.

The political crisis started when the United States provoked Mexico into war over the southern border of Texas. This was seen by some as an unjustified war of aggression on behalf of the southern slave states. Representative David Wilmot attached a proviso to a funding bill, which stated, "There shall be neither slavery, nor involuntary servitude in any territory on the continent of America which shall hereafter be acquired by or annexed to the United States by virtue of this appropriation, or in any other matter whatever, except for crime whereof the party shall have been duly convicted."[68] This caused a debate that highlighted the sectional differences in the United States and increased southern perceptions that their section was under at-tack. Southerners and their political allies defeated the Wilmot Pro-viso, but nobody could ignore the territorial slave question anymore.

In the ensuing debates, southerners demanded that the territorial slavery question be left alone and that the southern states would fight any attack on their rights. On February 14, 1849, South Carolina representative Daniel Wallace asserted, "Power uncheck and uncontrolled is incompatible with the existence of human liberty; it goes on from one step of misrule to another, until the liberties of the people are swallowed up in the vortex of despotism." Wallace feared that passage of any bill limiting the extension of slavery equaled an increase of the power of the central government and tyranny, which only a revolution could end. He feared a tyrannical majority forcing its will on the people. Foreshadowing secession, the South Carolinian argued, "The hour is rapidly approaching when the minority of sovereign parties to the compact of Union must act . . . to arrest the progress of aggressions."[69] He outlined a common perception among southern politicians that the Union was a compact of sovereign states and not one nation.

In the North, supporters of civil disobedience called on the people to resist the war. Disgruntled Whigs and Democrats prepared to challenge the established order with the Free Soil Party. Liberty men and dissenting Barnburners in New York joined with disgruntled members of the established parties. The Free Soil Party embraced a conditional antislavery platform with their main agenda, stating, "We have assembled in convention as a union of free men, for the sake of freedom, forgetting all past political differences, in a common resolve to maintain the rights of free labor against the aggression of the slave power, and to secure free soil to a free people." The party did not wish to destroy slavery where the institution already existed. The party simply opposed any farther expansion of slave territory. The key slogan of the party was "Free Soil, Free Speech, Free Labor, Free Men."[70]

In the southern states, fire-eaters fought against the free soilers. The "Platform of the South," suggested by John C. Calhoun, called for the protection of slavery. In the Senate, on February 15, 1847, Calhoun introduced a series of resolutions against these attacks on southern rights. "What if the decision of this body shall deny us this high constitutional right?" he asked.

If the decision should be adverse, I trust and do believe that they will take under solemn consideration what they ought to do. . . . There is my family and connections; there I drew my first breath; there are all my hopes. I am a planter—a cotton-planter. I am a Southern man and a slaveholder—a kind and a merciful one, I trust—and none the worse for being a slaveholder. . . . I would rather meet any extremity upon earth than give up one inch of our equality—one inch of what belongs to us as members of this great republic! What! Acknowledge inferiority!"[71]

However, Calhoun's brand of proslavery agitation was on the defensive. A new, younger, sectional version of nationalism, supported by William L. Yancey, had taken hold.[72] Extremism gained supporters in the South to defend a national identity centered on their peculiar form of republican democracy.

Having concluded the peace treaty of Guadalupe Hidalgo, the United States faced a presidential election. The Democratic convention in Baltimore encountered a schism. Selecting a candidate and agreeing on a party platform proved difficult. The party compromised on popular sovereignty and Lewis Cass. Offended, the New York Barnburners walked out. In a separate convention at Utica, they nominated Martin Van Buren for the Free Soil Party. Also present in Utica were "a small number of antislavery New York Whigs and about twenty antislavery Democratic representatives from Massachusetts, Connecticut, Ohio, Illinois, and Wisconsin." The Whig party picked, in Zachary Taylor, a popular general. The lack of a party platform allowed northern and southern Whigs to run mutually exclusive and contradictory campaigns. This Free Soil rebellion within the Democratic Party was not the only political challenge. At Seneca Falls, a meeting demanded rights for women, abolition, and legal reforms.[73]

Just as the United States agreed to peace terms, settlers discovered gold near Sutter's Mill in Sacramento Valley. With thousands of people making the long trek across the continent to the goldfields, the population of California exploded, which allowed California to seek entry into the Union as a free state. The request increased the tensions between free soilers and fire-eaters. Congress tried to resolve the outstanding questions, including the organization of the Mexican Cession, the slave trade in the District of Columbia, and the effectiveness of the Fugitive Slave Law.

Henry Clay bundled all the provisions into one large bill, in 1849, but despite his previous successes, the so-called omnibus bill failed to win the necessary majority. Stephen Douglas took up the scepter of compromise and broke up the compromise bill into individual pieces. There were northern majorities to admit California as a free state, to abolish the slave trade in the District of Columbia, and to adjust the border of Texas. A majority consisting of southern congressmen and northern Democratic supporters passed a second set of measures that strengthened the Fugitive Slave Law and allowed for popular sovereignty in New Mexico and the Utah Territory.[74] The old political leadership faced an uncompromising, young, nationalistic elite filled with sectional ambitions. Extremists from both sections made their voices heard.

Southerners prepared for the eventuality of failure. In June 1850, fire-eaters from nine southern slave states held a convention in Nashville. The convention was to determine what the southern states should do if the federal government prevented the expansion of slavery into the western territories. In October 1849, fire-eaters had already called for a meeting in Jackson, Mississippi, to prevent the federal government from infringing on what southerners perceived as their right to expand westward. However, even in the southern states, opposition existed. The delegation from Louisiana was unable to attend because moderates in the state legislature prohibited their attendance. Secession was on the table, but the Compromise of 1850 and moderate desires to prevent fire-eater extremism prevented a break in the Union.[75]

Southern fire-eaters perceived that their section's political independence, sovereignty, and future were under attack by northern abolitionists. Even though the main issue was the expansion of slavery into the newly acquired western territories, and not the end of the institution itself, southerners often conflated the two. Any indication that a northern politician or political group was against slavery caused defensiveness among southerners and fostered the argument that southern identity and autonomy were under attack.

The events of 1848 caused major international upheaval. Uprisings throughout Europe and the Americas demanded changes to political and state structures. Some groups demanded radical reforms to establish republican or democratic governments. Others wanted the unification of culturally cohesive people into nation-states. Yet these requests did not encompass all the rebellions of 1848. Radical nationalists, who felt oppressed, insisted on separation. A growing perception of oppression often went hand in hand with calls for constitutional governments, separate from the former state entity.

Separatists shared many arguments against oppressors. In Hungary, Ireland, Poland, Schleswig-Holstein, and the southern U.S. states, separatists used legal arguments against attacks on their constitutional rights. Separatists felt the need to defend their rights or to seek independence. Initially, the struggle to regain their rights focused on the political process. When these demands fell on deaf ears or were ignored, separatists demanded outright independence. In the United States, separatists did not embrace the final stage, but in Hungary, Ireland, Poland, and Schleswig-Holstein, radical separatists did.

Despite the many similarities, however, there were differences. Abandoning the unity between Schleswig and Holstein, Olshausen and his Neuholsteiners focused on legal arguments against Danish oppression. These radicals willingly used force rather than peaceful constitutional means to protect the rights of the duchies. The Irish Confederation's leaders also favored legal means over violence, but, here too, radicals had no such qualms. Neither group perceived of its status as enslavement. The Hungarians and Poles frequently invoked enslavement to justify their rebellion against their oppressive Austrian and Russian overlords, and European separatists carried these arguments against oppression with them after the failure of their rebellions.

Separatist fire-eaters in the United States had long felt oppressed by the northern states and the increasingly vocal abolitionist movement. The question over the expansion of slavery drove the sections apart. Nonetheless, despite vocal proponents of separation, the majority of southerners were not ready to challenge the United States outright. Political divisions within the separatist community grew, which undermined the ability of the separatists to win. Disunity prevented separatist movements from gaining independence, resulting in their failure.

3

EUROPEAN SECESSIONIST MIGRATION

After the rebellions of 1830 and 1848, facing charges of treason, long prison sentences, and likely execution, many separatists migrated. Some stayed in Great Britain, France, or Switzerland, hoping for a second chance to bring political changes to their homelands. Others went to the United States. All of them carried their political views, separatist language, and revolutionary ideals with them to their new homes. Eventually, the Civil War allowed individuals from all four European uprisings an opportunity to alter the political and national identities of their new homes. This chapter will look at the movement of key members of the Irish, Hungarian, Polish, and Schleswig-Holstein uprisings to the United States. During this transition, many found themselves in an unfamiliar environment where the respect and deference they were used to did not exist anymore.

Between 1848 and 1853, 1.64 million economic and social migrants arrived in the United States. In addition, there were hundreds of political refugees. To individuals who had suffered under overpopulation, health issues, detrimental industrial working conditions, and land shortages, the United States, with its booming economy, growing infrastructure network, and an abundance of open land, looked like a paradise. However, travel across the Atlantic remained a hazardous journey that could take anywhere from twenty-five to one hundred days, and the often poor sanitation on board caused serious illness and death. Even though, by the 1850s, steamships allowed for faster and more reliable travel, the vast majority of migrants continued to use older sailing vessels.

Once migrants arrived in the country, many moved farther inland along the extensive canal, railroad, and river system. Cities, as centers of transportation and industry, attracted many migrants, who formed communities.[1] However, each person had his or her own personal experiences. Similarly, political refugees came to the United States in various ways and either embraced and integrated into their new home country or remained reluctant.

Suffering defeat first, Irish rebels came last to the United States. John Mitchel, sentenced to fourteen years of transportation, left Ireland for Bermuda on June 1, 1848, where the unprepared authorities initially quartered him in what he described as a "dog house." Even as his accommodations improved, his health deteriorated, as he was suffering from asthma. By December, Mitchel requested relocation or, he said, he would die. After a successful appeal to the authorities, Mitchel left for the Cape Colony, in South Africa. The ship arrived in Simon's Bay on September 19, 1849, where the local residents refused to allow the ship to land its human cargo. Five months of waiting followed before the ship finally received permission to leave for Van Diemen's Land (modern Tasmania). Here, Mitchel joined Thomas Francis Meagher, William Smith O'Brien, John Martin, and Kevin O'Doherty. Mitchel illegally made contact with many of his fellow convicts.[2] He did not remain docile for long.

Some Irish rebels had no desire to stay, and Meagher was the first successful escapee. On January 3, 1852, he handed back his "ticket of leave," revoking his promise to not make an escape attempt. When the police arrived at Meagher's cottage to arrest him, he had already left for the coast, where a boat with a sympathetic captain waited. By way of Pernambuco, Brazil, Meagher reached New York, arriving to a hero's welcome. People across the country expressed their sympathy. In Cleveland, an Irish American meeting articulated its "highest gratification" that Meagher had escaped from British custody. In Savannah, a newspaper reported, "Meagher is a man of unquestionable talent. . . . He comes now to the United States to seek a refuge and a home . . . Meagher, it is said, is a man of spirit—an admirer of personal as well as political independence."[3] Meagher was a hero in both the North and the South.

"Save Lafayette alone, no foreign-born visitor to this Republic was ever accorded such a generous, hearty, and spontaneous welcome, as that given to Thomas Francis Meagher," exaggerated a later biographer. Awaiting Meagher in New York were Richard O'Gorman, John Dillon, Thomas Reilly, Michael Doheny, and other compatriots of the 1848 uprising. Once in New York, Meagher went on lecture tours. He told a New York audience, "The feelings and conviction which influences my career in Ireland, have undergone no change. Still, as ever, I perceive within my country the faculties that fit her for a useful and honorable position, and believing that they require only to be set in motion to prove successful, I still would prompt her to put them forth. . . . Hopes may have darkened, but the destiny, to which I would see my country lifted, is before me still." On July 27, 1852, New York's Irish militia units paraded at Castle Garden to celebrate Meagher.[4]

On June 9, 1853, Mitchel rode into Bothwell, walked into the police station, and likewise returned his ticket of leave. He was down the road before the police officers could arrest him. However, the escapee's ship had left without him. Mitchel decided to alter his looks and hide in plain sight. On July 18, he boarded the *Emma* to Sydney, Australia. When the ship put into Sydney, Mitchel got off before the authorities conducted a proper search. Leaving Sydney, Mitchel's family traveled on board the *Julia Ann* and Mitchel traveled on board the U.S.-flagged *Orkney Lass*. In Tahiti, the *Orkney Lass* and the *Julia Ann* rendezvoused and Mitchel joined his family. By early October, he was in California. In a short speech, he explained that he had "not come here to whine about my own suffering." "I was not liberated by their Queen's pardon," he said, "but by the disloyal aid of some of her Majesty's subjects in Australia." He promised to be "a true and thorough American." However, California offered few opportunities, and on November 1 he embarked on a trans-Isthmian crossing. At the end of the month, he arrived to an extraordinary welcome in New York.[5]

For every political leader arriving with fanfare and celebration, there were thousands of unnamed migrants. Among them was Patrick Cleburne, who came to the United States for economic reasons after buying his way out of the British army. With three of his siblings, Cleburne left on the *Bridgetown* for New Orleans, where they arrived on December 25, 1849. After a brief stay in Cincinnati, Cleburne relocated to Helena, Arkansas, in June 1850, where he worked in a drugstore.[6] Their arrival in the United States forced Irish migrants to adjust to their new environment.

After the fighting in Hungary stopped, some prominent Hungarians and about five thousand soldiers fled into the Ottoman Empire. While most of the soldiers soon returned home, the leadership faced treason charges and an Austrian firing squad. Russia and Austria pressured the Ottomans to hand over the refugees. The Russians demanded any Poles who had served the Hungarian cause. Austria demanded the return of "bandits and rebels," per treaty requirement. At the same time, Great Britain and France supported the Ottoman refusal. The belligerent British minister in Constantinople, Stratford Canning, called on the Mediterranean fleet to make a show of force. However, a naval force could not prevent the kidnapping or murder of Lajos Kossuth and other ranking Hungarian leaders.[7] The Hungarian refugees were not safe.

From his prison in Kütahya, Turkey,[8] Kossuth wrote a lengthy address to the people of the United States. He once more explained the Hungarian demands. First, "the inalienable rights sanctioned by a thousand years, and by the constitution of my father-land, should be guaranteed by a national and responsible administration," he demanded. Second, the monarchy had violated the liberty of the people, their freedom to speak their own language and exercise their religion. Kossuth concluded, "No nation ever manifested more faithfulness to their rulers. And though we poor Hungarians made endless sacrifices, often at the expense of our national welfare . . . they deceived us a thousand times, and made our conditions worse." He also claimed that the Hungarians had "not asked liberty for ourselves alone: we would not boast of privileges that others did not enjoy, but desire to be free in fellowship with free nations around us."

The United States was a chosen country for Kossuth. "Free citizens of America! From your history, as from the star of hope in midnight gloom," he wrote, "we drew our confidence and resolution in the doubtful days of severe trial." He wanted the Hungarians to imitate the United States. He connected the two countries, since "among the nations of the world, there are two which demand our gratitude and affection. England, no less powerful than she is free and glorious, supported us by her sympathy, . . . And that chosen land of freedom beyond the ocean—the all-powerful people of the United States." He was glad for the support of the United States.

Kossuth cautiously explained to his U.S. audience, "No, no! Hungary is not lost! By her faith, bravery, and by her foresight, which teaches her to abide her time, she will be yet among the foremost in the war of universal liberty!" In a dangerous statement that mimicked much of what he had said during the uprising, Kossuth claimed that his people had suffered enslavement: "This people [Austrians], who for centuries had endured slavery, fought against their own freedom! God forgive them." Such an appeal was a double-edged sword in the United States. Kossuth closed with a universal hope: "May your great example, noble Americans, be to other nations the source of social virtue; your power be the terror of all tyrants . . . and your free country ever continue to be the asylum for the oppressed of all nations."[9] The Hungarian rebels carried with them perceptions of enslavement.

In February 1851, the U.S. government offered Kossuth asylum, inviting him as the "nation's guest," which he accepted. On September 10, 1851, about fifty Hungarian refugees, among them Alexander Asbóth, departed the Ottoman Empire. They arrived in New York on November 10. Kossuth briefly visited Great Britain before continuing to the United States. When Kossuth arrived, on December 4, 1851, 200,000 people supposedly lined New York harbor. "No foreigner had ever seen such a reception as he did," a later historian exaggerated, "save for the French champion of freedom Marquis de La Fayette." Kossuth's visit created euphoria as he called for assistance from the United States and a renewal of the fight for Hungarian independence. His speaking tour brought out many people and substantial contributions to the Hungarian cause. However, Kossuth did not find the political environment in the United States favorable, and he soon departed for Great Britain.[10] Many Hungarians stayed, but with their only professional experience being fighting and politics, they had a hard time finding employment.

Hungarians migrated in small numbers. The Kossuth euphoria in the United States opened doors for individuals to shed their European identity and assume a more popular Hungarian identity. Many Hungarian refugees left Europe either in 1848, through German ports such as Hamburg and Bremen, or in 1849, through British ports such as Liverpool, Southampton, Glasgow, or London. Initially, Hungarians could sustain themselves by giving public lectures. Over time, they dispersed. Some remained in New York and other eastern port cities. Many left for the Midwest, in states like Wisconsin and Iowa, to embrace farming. A few settled in Missouri and Texas. Skills and opportunities determined where Hungarians settled.[11]

The Hungarian migrant population remained too small for a vibrant community to emerge. Hungarian newspapers lasted only short periods, lacking readership. Hungarians made the best of their situation. Ferenc Varga wrote, "I became separated from my adored homeland, but the Almighty blessed me with a family in which I found compensation." Asbóth belonged to the group of Hungarians who were slightly better off, because he had useful skills that were needed in the modernizing United States. As an engineer, he found work on railroad projects such as the Syracuse–New York and the Binghamton–New York. He also assisted Frederick Law Olmsted in the surveying of Central Park.

In contrast, Charles Zagonyi belonged to the second wave of Hungarian migrants. He had fought for the duration of the war in Hungary and then fled to the Ottoman Empire. Zagonyi arrived in the United States on July 21, 1851, and stayed in New York. Lacking a skill, he struggled as a member of the short-lived Hungarian vocalist society, which was booed off the stage in New York, and as an equestrian instructor in Boston. Around Davenport, Iowa, Ladislaus Újházy and a contingent of forty Hungarians created the short-lived New Buda.[12] Coming along with the Hungarians were many Polish revolutionaries who had taken refuge in Hungary and had fought with them in 1848.

The Austrians had allowed Polish revolutionaries into their territory after the 1830–1831 uprising. However, Austrian hospitality did not last, and in November 1833 the authorities in Trieste put 234 Poles on the *Hebe* and the *Guerriere* for passage to the United States. More than eight hundred Poles of the 1830 separatist uprising came to the United States.

Among the Novembrists, Adam Gurowski was unique. He did not arrive until almost two decades later, in 1849. Immediately after the uprising, Gurowski, like many Poles, went into exile in Paris, where he served on the Polish Revolutionary Committee and helped draft a democratic constitution. In the course of his exile, he rethought his political opinions and started to argue that Poland would never be an independent and prosperous country without strong leadership. Within five years, he embraced Pan-Slavism and reconciliation with the tsar, accepting a position within the tsarist government in Saint Petersburg, Russia, and supporting the Russian-ization of Poland. Having offended the tsar by supporting the idea of peasant communes, Gurowski left Russia in 1844 and lectured on political economy in Bern, Switzerland, where he encountered Giuseppe Mazzini's republican and nationalist views. Gurowski left for the United States in November 1849.[13]

Little is known about many of the other former Polish rebels. After the uprising, Kacper Tochman, like Gurowski, Joachim Lelewel, Adam Jerzy Czartoryski, and Józef Zachariasz Bem, went to Paris to agitate for Polish independence. Tochman tried to mediate between the Lelewel and the Czartoryski-Bem factions. Unsuccessful, Tochman migrated to the United States in 1837, where he practiced law.[14]

When Ignatius Szymański left Europe is unknown, but he was in Boston shortly after the uprising to publish Harring's memoir. Szymański eventually moved to New Orleans, where he started with cotton pressing before acquiring thirty slaves and a sugar plantation. He was a Louisiana aristocrat with a manor, similar to his status in Poland.[15]

Among the small group of Polish Forty-Eighters, the leader of the provisional government of Cracow, Jan Józef Tyssowski, who left Europe in 1847, is the most prominent. In the United States, he worked for the German-language paper *Deutsche Schnellpost*. Włodzimierz Krzyżanowski reached the United States by way of Hamburg and worked as an engineer. Joseph Kargé arrived in the United States in 1851 and taught modern languages.[16] Sadly, like the Hungarians, the Poles are an understudied group and little is known about their transition.

The Schleswig-Holstein Germans were the last to arrive. In April 1852, the Danes announced the names of twenty-two men not included in the armistice. The list was a who's who of the Schleswig-Holstein uprising. First were Fürst Christian Carl Frederik August von Schleswig-Holstein-Sonderburg-Augustenburg and Prinz Friedrich Emil August von Schleswig-Holstein-Sonderburg-Augustenburg. Next came all the prominent members of the Schleswig-Holstein government, including Wilhelm Hartwig Beseler, Friedrich Graf von Reventlow-Preetz, M. Andreas Paul Adolph von Harbou, Georg Friedrich von Krogh, Karl Philipp Francke, Freiherr Friedrich Nicolaus, and Adam Ludwig von Liliencron. Lesser political figures on the list included Theodor Olshausen, Rudolph Schleiden, and Hans Reimer Claussen.[17]

Having previously been in exile, Theodor Olshausen was much better prepared for the difficult transition. On July 14, 1851, he secretly boarded a ship in Hamburg, bound for New York. He then moved to Saint Louis, Missouri. Olshausen had read about the United States, and he found many of the reports accurate. However, German American immigrants and native residents were at odds. He mused about the informal separation between Germans and the native population. A side effect of the large German population in Saint Louis was that Olshausen could communicate in his native tongue, not improving his English. Professionally, Olshausen decided to write a series of books about the geography, economics, and culture of the United States for the German immigrant market.[18]

Hans R. Claussen also settled in Saint Louis. From the start, Claussen worked hard to learn the language. He also studied the legal and constitutional system of the United States. In contrast to Olshausen, who accepted Saint Louis as a permanent residence, Claussen intended to stay only briefly. He visited Illinois and other neighboring states before deciding to settle in Iowa. Building on his background in law, Claussen took up residence in Davenport, first as a farmer and then later, and more successfully, as a notary public. Since Davenport was the destination of many immigrants from Holstein, Claussen likely found many familiar faces—or at least people who knew his name and so brought their business to him. However, in 1855, Claussen, for unknown reasons, left Davenport for Lyon, Iowa, where he became involved in a corn mill business.[19] His agricultural roots had returned.

Having arrived in the United States at the time of the 1852 presidential election, Claussen witnessed the American political system, which he so admired, firsthand. He saw various speakers in person. Most impressive to him was the civilized manner of political debates. Audiences even granted the opposition speaker the benefit of the doubt. Initially, Claussen was drawn to the Democratic Party, which presented itself to immigrants as the party of progress and stigmatized the Whigs as conservative, even reactionary. Claussen appreciated the possibilities for personal success offered by a constitutional and democratic system. He wrote of Stephen Douglas, "In Europe, he would have made it only to a good master craftsman, but here he has the bright future of one day being an equal of a crowned head; he might even be able to crush them to dust. Here you see the power of a constitution, which fosters the development of strength and does not hinder it."[20]

Among all the immigrants, Rudolph Schleiden was an exception. He had previous personal contact with the Atlantic World—his father and his brother Emil had worked in Mexico. On June 8, 1852, he visited Bremen and made contact with the governing oligarchy, two of whom, Arnold Duckwitz and Johann Smidt, he knew from his days in Frankfurt. As he lobbied for a diplomatic post, Schleiden read about Bremen's trade, politics, and international relations and devoured issues of the *Economist*. Because of Bremen's growing trade interests and a desire for better communications, the city contemplated sending a representative of its own to Washington, DC. By March 1853, Bremen's senate agreed to the creation of a new mission and unanimously confirmed Schleiden.

Having departed from Liverpool, Schleiden reached New York on June 21, 1853, where he looked into the creation of a steamship line. On June 30, 1853, Schleiden arrived in Washington.[21] Like many Forty-Eighters, Schleiden had transitioned from a stateless former revolutionary diplomat into a respectable diplomat. The Schleswig-Holstein revolutionaries joined a large German immigrant community. They were the last to arrive in the United States. They quickly assumed community leadership roles and adjusted to the situation in the United States.

Like the migrants themselves, the story of how the Novembrists from Poland and the Forty-Eighters from Hungary, Ireland, Poland, and Schleswig-Holstein arrived in the United States is diverse. Some fled under cover to avoid detection; others hid in plain sight. They looked to the United States as the example of democratic and republican government. Felons from Ireland, traitors from Hungary, revolutionaries from Schleswig-Holstein, and Polish turncoats all got a second chance in the United States.

4

ANTEBELLUM SEPARATIST INTERACTION

"Disunion must be the work of time. It is only through a long process, and successively, that the cords can be snapped until the whole fabric falls asunder. Already the agitation of the slavery question has snapped some of the most important, and has greatly weakened all the others."[1]

When John C. Calhoun spoke these words, in 1850, the ties holding North and South together had loosened. Nevertheless, the country remained a beacon of democracy and republicanism. The revolutionary upheavals of the previous two years and arrival of proponents of dramatic change, such as Novembrists and Forty-Eighters, helped to escalate tensions. Calhoun had called for revolutionary changes as early as 1832 and had influenced many young fire-eaters to protect southern rights against an increasingly oppressive union, dominated by northern special interests. European revolutionaries, and especially separatists, who arrived in the United States after 1848, entered a country on the verge of its own separatist revolution. The clash of European and U.S. separatist ideologies forced difficult decisions on everybody.

As the sectional tensions between the northern and southern states increased, European separatists infused their revolutionary language into the struggle in North America. They could sympathize with the arguments of both northern and southern politicians. After all, many had used the same arguments against their own oppressors in Europe. Even though European separatists and southerners had much in common, the vast majority of European separatists sided with the Union. To them, the question was whether to support an oppressed minority and help southerners defend their constitutional and democratic rights or to fight against an oppressive minority/aristocracy and uphold the principles of republican and democratic government.

European separatism cast a long shadow over the United States during the 1850s. The visit of Lajos Kossuth was a reminder that the United States represented democracy and republicanism, but Kossuth was the emissary of independence and secession. Thousands welcomed him in New York, and he unsuccessfully called on the people to support the Hungarian independence movement. He frequently referenced the Hungarian status of enslavement in his speeches. In Baltimore, on December 27, 1851, he asserted, "Without the restoration of Hungary, Europe cannot be free from Russian thralldom, under which nationalities are erased, no freedom is possible, all religions are subjected to like slavery." At another speaking engagement, on February 7, Kossuth reminded listeners about Hungary's role in stopping the onslaught of eastern barbarians. However, "all which Hungary has ever suffered is far less than it has to suffer now from the tyrant of Austria, himself in his turn nothing but the slave of ambitious Russia."[2] In his many appeals for assistance, Kossuth used the words "slavery" and "oppression" interchangeably.

The principles Kossuth stood for did not receive universal support in the United States. His separatism was not welcome in the South. On April 3, he told an audience in Mobile, Alabama, of the hostile reception from Alabama Senator Jeremiah Clemens. However, to his surprise, the crowd in Mobile welcomed him warmly, convincing him that the people of Alabama were friends of Hungary. In his speech, Kossuth invoked George Washington and established the Hungarian right to national sovereignty. After all, Washington had said, "Every nation has a right to establish that form of government under which it conceives it may live most happy."[3] Widespread support for the "principle of self-government" existed in both Hungary and the United States, according to Kossuth. Europe faced a struggle between tyranny and freedom, but Kossuth's main interest in the United States was in financial assistance to bring about Hungarian independence.

Like the Hungarians, Irish migrants continued their agitation for independence. In July 1852, Michael Doheny welcomed Thomas Francis Meagher with the Irish New York militia. "You see here many of

your countrymen in arms," Doheny told Meagher. "The flag of freedom, the integrity, the glory of the mightiest of nations, have been
committed to their valor and loyalty. In a grateful and proudly confident spirit, they rally round. . . . Those who accept the arms of liberty
assume the responsibility of defending her; they become her sentinels
and her guardians. . . . Armed men do not rail; they do not beg; nor
do they idly menace. These are the tricks of slaves." Even though
many Irish had not thought of their oppression as enslavement, in the
United States, former members of the Irish Confederation observed
political slavery. "The example of Kosciusco requires no apology or
panegyric. The world is the temple of his fame," Meagher told his
Irish audience, "the sun his coronet of glory. Leaving his native land
in the days of his fresh and radient [*sic*] youth, he plunged himself
into the red sea, that lay between America and her liberties."[4] Meagher called on the United States to continue to promote liberty.

As their exile turned permanent, migrants engaged in politics. The
Irish people were torn between supporting the Democratic Party or
the newly emerging third parties. When he reentered politics, Meagher supported the Democratic Party. "In the controversy between
the North and the South [Meagher's] sympathies were entirely with
the latter," a later biographer explained, "up to the moment when, by
an overt act of treason, the integrity of the Union was menaced and
the mask of constitutionality cast aside." John Mitchel worried about
the escalating territorial slavery question and nativist reformism.

Not all Irish supported the Democrats. Likely because of his father's political reform views in Ireland, Patrick Cleburne found a
home within the Whig party in Arkansas, but he eventually supported
the fire-eater Democrat Thomas C. Hindman. Schleswig-Holstein
Forty-Eighters similarly distrusted the Know-Nothings, but they
quickly turned to the new Republican Party. In 1855, Theodor Olshausen observed that the Know-Nothings had "lost all of their power" as
the Republican Party gained in strength. Olshausen's animosity toward nativism caused him to see the process of party realignment in
favor of the Republicans proceeding more rapidly than it did.[5] Identities in their new homeland remained malleable.

The Kansas–Nebraska Act, passed in 1853, organized the Louisiana Purchase, opened the way for a transcontinental railroad line,

and abolished the Missouri Compromise. As Congress debated the act, politicians frequently employed terms like "freedom," "sectional peace," "oppression," and "constitutional rights" to voice support or opposition. Ohio's representative Andrew J. Harlan worried about the implications of the repeal of the Missouri Compromise. "Yes, sir," he said, "freedom is about to break loose and overrun this vast empire, and it must now be arrested and driven back, or the power of slavery within its borders is broken forever." William Barksdale questioned the compromise: "It is not true that any such compact was made between the North and the South. The southern Representatives had no right, and did not, in fact, undertake to make such a compact for the South, and the action of no southern State can be found, pledging the people forever to the Missouri restriction." The southern states accepted but did not support the compromise.[6] The opening of Kansas and Nebraska to slavery increased sectional tensions.

The territorial slave question spelled the demise of the Know-Nothings, opening the door to the Republican Party. In the western states, especially, Germans such as Friedrich Hecker and Carl Schurz attracted ethnic voters to the new party's ideology of "free soil, free labor, free men." Besides Illinois and Wisconsin, Iowa was crucial for the young party. Between 1854 and 1856, as the Republicans won many state offices, immigrant voters and their leaders were instrumental. As a result, Hans Reimer Claussen and Olshausen once more assumed community leadership roles.[7] These early political engagements coincided with one more hope for a renewed European revolution.

The Crimean War between Russia on one side and Great Britain, France, and the Ottoman Empire on the other raised hopes among European separatist migrants. Irish migrants yearned for another rebellion. In violent anti-British language, Mitchel called on the people to change their sympathies and support the Russians. Demanding independence, he suggested that Irish migrants should start an uprising or attack the British in Canada. Both Mitchel and Emmet Monument Association members John O'Mahoney, Doheny, and Michael Corcoran contacted the Russian minister in Washington to inquire whether Russia would support a renewed Irish uprising.[8] They were unsuccessful but continued to give public speeches against Great Britain.

In contrast, Hungarians and Poles hated Russia and desired the tsar's defeat. Polish exile Adam Gurowski worked to turn public opinion against Russia with his articles in Horace Greeley's New York *Tribune*. Gurowski published *Russia as It Is,* later also reprinted as *Russia and Its People*. He argued that the Slavs were an agricultural people, but not a backward people. He asserted, "Liberty and the commune were anterior to monarchical power, that is to autocracy, to political or social enslavement. . . . Czarism levies war against every genuine impulse and idea," he concluded. "Panslavism . . . has reminded and reminds the nation that the bigotry of Czarism is comparatively modern, and that communal equality was the cradle and nursery of the Slavi for uncounted centuries."

Gurowski subjected the Russian army and peasants to detailed analysis to illustrate their enslavement. Despite lacking equality, Gurowski assumed, "The Russian officers would willingly wish to become the means, even the promoters, of a political—nay, even of a social internal emancipation. . . . For soldiers, the long years of service are but a daily, nay hourly, iron servitude," he wrote. The soldier "remains always the serf's brother, and both, however in a different way, bear on their necks the heavy pressure of caste and despotism." Like the soldiers, serfs were in a state of slavery.[9] While he was cautious in his use of the word "slavery," Gurowski implicitly indicated that the Russian people were enslaved, longing for emancipation.

Gurowski framed his desire for revolution in terms of both emancipation and the overthrow of oppressive institutions. He feared that "any liberties, political or social franchises, conceded by compact or granted as a favour, are no liberties at all." Since serfdom was detrimental to Russia, Gurowski felt that emancipation of the serfs was long overdue. "At present, despotism binds Russia awfully in its anaconda folds. Strict restrictions, called laws," he wrote, "twist harshly around all the various members of the political whole—the nation." The Polish exile believed in the higher principle of emancipation. He said, "The emancipation of Russia is an absolute condition of the emancipation of Europe, and thus of the future harmonious and progressive activity of the European or Christian World." As much as Gurowski desired change, he criticized the planter elite, which continued to rely on slave labor. Prophetically, Gurowski wondered, "Whatever may be the ambitious purpose of the Czars, and their hostility to the triumph of the principles of liberty and democracy, the enterprise set on foot against the world's welfare will turn against them. Emancipation and the destruction of autocracy will rise from the dreaded conflagration."[10] The state of oppression and slavery could not last forever in Russia or, for that matter, the United States.

Regardless of the existence of slavery in the United States, Gurowski considered the country a beacon of democracy. "America represents the concrete of the human family," he wrote, "Russia only one of its members; and thus what Russia represent in history is inferior to what is revealed by America. . . . America is the light and Russia the darkness; the one is life, the other inertia." Even recent event did not detract from the high standing of the United States: "How much soever one might wish to have seen American history purified from this obsolete and barbarous stigma—still the war of Mexico served to illustrate the vitality of the American constructive principle." Gurowski felt that Russia could learn from the United States. Nevertheless, he wondered how a member of Congress from New Orleans could call the Ottoman Empire a symbol of liberty and civilization, especially since slavery in the Ottoman Empire had "not even the excuse of being a necessity for the cultivation of the soil."[11] Gurowski drew connections between oppressive systems of labor and sociopolitical control in an effort to paint Russia as the enemy.

The Crimean War offered the United States opportunities for its own Caribbean expansion. On his way from California to New York, Mitchel had visited the Caribbean Basin. Going through Nicaragua, he had a few racist words for the Mosquito Protectorate: "The British have never, it seems, formally given up their protectorate of the Mosquito 'kingdom' and its Sambo sovereign." On the steamer to Cuba, an unknown individual had told Mitchel about the oppressed status of the Cuban people. The individual was angry about the treatment the Spanish authorities had given to the recent filibusters. The assumption that "Cuba is bound to come in" was widespread. Mitchel wondered whether the United States had a right to Cuba and was immediately correct that "the Cubans have a right to Cuba." Knowing Mitchel's strong Irish nationalism, his conversation partner asserted, "The Irish have a right to Ireland; and Spain holds it against the right owners with a monstrous garrison, as England holds Ireland against you. Would a filibuster expedition of Americans to Ireland, to aid you and your friends in driving out the British, appear to you an act of piracy and robbery?" Mitchel could not deny that such support was welcome.[12] If Cubans could receive their freedom by way of a filibuster, so could the Irish.

Filibusters offered those with military experience an opportunity to put their skills to work. Meagher perceived filibuster activities in Central America as positive for the United States, and he supported William Walker. Meagher even traveled to Central America himself. "I visit Central America—Costa Rica especially," he wrote later, "for the purpose of ascertaining the true conditions of affairs there, and becoming familiar with a noble region." There were plans for Irish migration to the region to escape oppression.[13]

In contrast to Meagher's peaceful migration, militarily experienced Hungarians were all too ready to support filibusters as soldiers of fortune. Joseph Csermelyi, Augustus Kováts, John Prágav, Emeric Radnich, and Louis A. Schlesinger joined Narciso López's failed filibuster to free Cuba in August 1851. Schlesinger explained that they had joined an army of liberation to bring freedom to the Cubans, something reminiscent of their own uprising only two years earlier.[14] Apparently, they willingly overlooked the slavery aspect of the filibusters. Expansion southward decreased in importance as public opinion shifted.

To influence public opinion, separatist leaders embraced the prospering newspaper business in the United States, where most towns had a paper. Ethnic or special interest groups offered reliable readership. German-language newspapers appeared in the major cities. Similarly, there were papers for the Irish, for abolitionists, for nativists. Shortly after his arrival, Mitchel started to write for Meagher's *Citizen,* which provided news to the growing Irish community of New York. In mid-April 1856, Olshausen relocated to Davenport, Iowa, where he took over *Der Demokrat,* a local German newspaper.[15] As editors and contributors to daily publications, these migrants became involved in the local and national political discourse, assuming leading roles within their communities. They used their positions to translate their European experiences to the United States. Irish migrants frequently sympathized with the political arguments voiced by southerners against oppression by a northern imperialist majority; Schleswig-Holstein Germans did not. Schleswig-Holstein Germans perceived of proponents of chattel slavery in the United States as the oppressors.

Among the separatists, only Mitchel defended the institution of human bondage. He argued that founders like George Washington had owned slaves without moral or conscience issues. He told abolitionists, "You will have it that those who differ from you, and agree with the wisest of mankind, are fools or villains." There were both historical and religious arguments justifying slavery. Slaveholding, according to Mitchel, was no crime. He used the ideas of Thomas Jefferson and Thomas Carlyle to connect liberty and slavery. At the same time, Mitchel defended his people. "My principle was simply," he wrote, "that *Irishmen* were fitted for a higher destiny and sphere, and they all ought to feel British dominion as intolerable as I did."

Mitchel did not restrict his defense of racial slavery to historical arguments. "He would be a bad Irishman," Mitchel claimed, "who voted for principles which jeopardized the present freedom of a nation of white men, for the vague hope of elevating blacks to a level which it is at least problematic whether God and Nature intended them." Mitchel believed that Africans were inherently made for slavery. "African Negro was born and bred to slavery," he wrote, "and therefore to set him free was impossible." Even more, he denied "that it is a crime, or a wrong, or even a peccadillo, to hold slaves, to buy slaves, to keep slaves to their work by flogging or other needful coercion." He agreed with the harsh system of punishment. More troubling, the Irish exile wished "we had a good plantation, well-stocked with healthy negroes, in Alabama." Ironically, he accepted the degradation of slavery in southern society, which some Irish compared to their own treatment at the hands of the British.[16] Mitchel approached slavery as a social status and not one of political oppression, which allowed him to sympathize with the southern states' rights arguments against political oppression.

Few migrants had the money to purchase a plantation. Irish migrants, in particular, lacked the wealth, and those who had the wealth perceived investment in slavery as not necessarily profitable. In Arkansas, Patrick Cleburne worked hard to make his drugstore venture profitable. While his employers and future partners invested their income in plantations, Cleburne initially refused to do so. Eventually, after changing to law, Cleburne owned real estate worth $20,000. There is no indication whether Cleburne owned slaves or, if so, how many.[17]

In contrast, Polish separatists in the South embraced slavery. Ignatius Szymański owned a large plantation on Bayou Terre-aux-Boeufs in Louisiana, with thirty slaves producing sugar and wealth for the Polish offspring of a noble family.[18] Szymański translated his family's serf-worked estate into a rich slave-based sugar plantation. For these two adopted southerners, political liberty mattered more than the human liberty of their enslaved workers.

Considering how little contact some individuals, especially Mitchel, had with slavery, Mitchel had embraced an extraordinary opinion. One has to wonder whether Mitchel still relied on his brief contact with slavery in Brazil during his voyage to Van Diemen's Land. In *Jail Journal*, he wrote, "These slaves in Brazil are fat and merry, obviously not overworked nor underfed, and it is a pleasure to see the lazy rogues lolling in their boats, sucking a piece of green sugar-cane, and grinning and jabbering together, not knowing that there is such an atrocity as a *Palladium* in the whole world. . . . Slaves in Brazil are expected to work moderately, but are not treated with contumely. They are often admitted to the society of the families they serve, and lead in some measure the life of human beings."[19] Mitchel's view of Africans had not changed since this encounter, and his proslavery attitude only hardened after his arrival in the United States.

His views on slavery created many enemies. Friends and acquaintances unsuccessfully urged Mitchel to soften the tone of his proslavery articles. Undeterred, Mitchel pointed to the hypocrisy of abolitionists. They only focused on the plight of African Americans and ignored the conditions of workers in northern factories. The moral tone and millenarianism of abolitionists offended Mitchel. Even more, he wondered whether every individual was equal and had the right to "life, liberty, and happiness."[20] Mitchel embraced a view of liberty that excluded some and protected others.

Mitchel's views produced sectional popularity and anger. "Is this the friend of oppressed Ireland, the man who has made the earth echo with the story of her wrongs, her oppressions?" the *Ohio Observer* asked. The paper could not understand Mitchel's support for racial slavery. If he was proslavery, he should have "staid [*sic*] in New South Wales." The Ohio paper wondered, "Is it the outcome of a slavish nature, or of a nature soured by oppression; or is it one of the ordinary inconsistencies of fallen humanity, which allows a love of freedom and a hatred of oppression in the heart of the oppressor?" While eloquently explaining the symbiotic relationship between slavery and liberty, the paper went a step further. "None make louder claims of a love of freedom than the slave-holders of the South," the paper said. "And at the North we have seen the fiercest intolerance of free speech in those making the boldest boast of freedom." To abolitionists, Mitchel was already, in Ireland, "a tyrant, a despot, a slaveholder."[21] Where Europeans had used the word "slavery" to describe political, social, economic, and cultural oppression, in the United States "slavery" had a much more sinister meaning.

In the *Liberator,* Henry C. Wright argued that Mitchel was "the slave-breeder, slave-trader, and slave-driver." Wright was aware that Mitchel's invocation of religion to justify slavery was a common theme in churches throughout the country. However, Wright turned the situation against Mitchel and the Irish. "*Irish* patriotism and *Irish* religion," he wrote, "are just as hostile to mankind, as *American* patriotism and *American* religion." Mitchel's call to the Irish to become slaveholders was offensive and only made him look like the "European tyrants." There was an inherent contradiction in Mitchel's arguments. "*Liberty* and *slavery* are his watchwords," Wright wrote. "Liberty for the Irish, Slavery for Americans; Liberty for the laborers of Ireland, Slavery for the laborers of the United States." As a result, Mitchel was a modern-day "Irish Benedict Arnold." Wright suggested that, "as a traitor to liberty," Mitchel should go the route of Judas and hang himself.[22] What seemed like a paradox to contemporaries in the United States made sense to Mitchel; he and the Irish suffered from a different oppression than that of slaves in the United States.

In June 1854, Mitchel spoke at the University of Virginia at Chancellorsville, where his audience appreciated his proslavery tirades.[23] Aware of Irish suffering, the *Richmond Dispatch* described Mitchel as "a worthy representative of his gallant and generous race" and representative of the South. "If we have been called to select a champion to advocate Southern rights in the North," the paper wrote, "we could not have found a man in the United States more to our liking than John Mitchel." Feeling welcome, Mitchel resettled his family on a 140-acre farm in Tucaleechee Cove, about thirty-five miles from Knoxville. As Mitchel quickly learned, however, he was not cut out for farming, and the lack of good conversation partners depressed him. He did appreciate the egalitarianism and self-reliance of the people. For Mitchel, Eastern Tennessee was an agrarian paradise. Judging by the values southerners espoused, Mitchel perceived the South as the closest any place in the world would come to classical republicanism. Furthermore, the planter aristocracy espoused European manners.

Once he had relocated to Knoxville, and in cooperation with William Swan, Mitchel published the *Southern Citizen*. In the paper, he defended slavery and suggested the reopening of the international slave trade. Already, in New York, Mitchel had suggested that, because most people in Africa were "ignorant and brutal negroes," they should be brought to the United States to improve their situation. He firmly believed that "the cause of negro slavery is the cause of true philanthropy, so far as that race is concerned."[24]

Northern anger against Mitchel's proslavery and pro–slave trade arguments continued unabated. The New York *Tribune* told Mitchel to remain silent on the issue of reopening the slave trade. The paper knew of the racism underlying Mitchel's support. "But the Africans are black, and the Irishmen are white, when they are not very dirty. . . . Color has not therefore saved the Irish people from the most terrible oppression, as, we think, J. M. will admit," the paper posited. There were many other comparisons between the Irish and the Africans, such as their "shiftless and degraded" state. The paper posed an important question to Mitchel: "When an Irish patriot, as Mitchel professes to have been, argues that the black man is not fit for freedom because he is not free, it is perfectly proper for us to ask this Irishman why the rule is not applicable to the condition of his own countrymen?" Mitchel countered with his own comparison: "The North is England; the South is Ireland."[25]

Mitchel argued against a northern-imposed industrial system. Industry would eradicate the agricultural way of life. "The South, like

Ireland, was fighting for the right to govern itself," Mitchel insisted.
He drew parallels between the British legal oppression of Ireland
and northern oppression of the southern states. In the South, Mitchel's rhetoric to defend slavery and reopen the slave trade appealed;
his anti-British attitudes did not. Great Britain was the single most
important consumer of southern cotton and an essential provider
of industrial commodities. To obtain a broader audience, Mitchel
relocated to Washington, DC, but he closed the paper down in July
1859. Soon after, Mitchel was on his way to Paris to assist the newly
created Irish Republican Brotherhood.[26] At heart, Mitchel was always
an Irish patriot.

In dramatic contrast to Mitchel, Schleswig-Holstein's separatists
hated slavery. The slavery-related conflict in the Kansas Territory, in
particular, drew the ire of German separatists. Always the pacifist,
Rudolph Schleiden sympathized with the Free Soil movement. He
was glad when the House of Representatives voted down the bill to
incorporate Kansas under the proslavery Lecompton Constitution.
He appreciated New York senator William H. Seward's aggressive
April 30, 1858, speech supporting the antislavery elements in Kansas.

In Iowa, Schleiden's revolutionary colleagues provided the back-
bone of the Republican Party coalition, though the party had to
reconcile its western immigrant constituency with its nativist supporters. Their congressional candidate in Iowa, William Vandever,
needed to garner the vote of the state's large foreign-born population without offending the nativist constituency. Claussen questioned
Vandever's position on immigration, asking how he would deal with
proposed laws to make immigration more difficult and to make the
right to vote harder for immigrants to obtain. Vandever indicated
that he was disinclined to support any changes to naturalization or
voting rights.[27]

The slavery question drove a constitutional and sectional wedge
between North and South. Many migrants failed to understand the
political dilemmas associated with slavery. Olshausen had no appre-
ciation for the intricate nature of the slavery question. In *Mississippi
Thales*, a book for Germans planning to immigrate, Olshausen called
slavery a "shocking institution" that should have long since been
eradicated. There was, he incorrectly claimed, no widespread sup-

port for slavery, even in the South. Olshausen noted that slaveholders hypocritically prohibited the education of slaves while, at the same time, insisting that educating slaves was impossible. Slaveholders, he said, feared that education would instill a desire for freedom and thus undermine the institution.

He further dismissed claims that slaves were treated well, pointing to their lack of education. Slaves and free people of color had limited legal rights. Olshausen did not go so far as to say that slavery was holding back the South, but his book implied as much, which was reminiscent of his opinion of Denmark and Schleswig in the lead-up to 1848. His views were controversial. German-language New York papers reviewed the work and praised his critical opinion of slavery. No translation ever appeared, for lack of marketability.

Despite knowing about the racial and economic fears of whites and concerns about vagrancy, Olshausen, as a democratic radical, opposed any further compromise, such as the Compromise of 1850, which only protected an inhumane and unjust institution. No party could call itself "Democratic" and yet support slavery.[28] As in Europe, he continued to stand against any form of oppression and supported the spread of democracy.

Also as in Europe, a disillusioned and radical-minded Olshausen became increasingly pessimistic. He perceived that the U.S. system of government was drifting backwards, with civil war the inevitable result. The slavery question was bound to present the next Congress with major difficulties. "It is very likely," he said, "that in the near future an attempt will be made to separate the free and slave states. It will likely remain only an attempt, because I do not think that the slave states will maintain themselves alone, because a war over slavery would occur." Olshausen believed that a civil war was already being fought in Kansas and that it was only a question of time until the rest of the country would be drawn into war as well. He knew that abolitionists were a minority, and he cautioned that a foreign war or the question of emancipation could easily slow down western expansion. The core issue was slavery. In Olshausen's opinion, democrats and slaveholders were institutionally at odds and could no longer form a united country. Like William Lloyd Garrison, he insisted that "the question is of separation or of emancipation."[29]

Ironically, Olshausen probably never realized how close his own arguments in Schleswig-Holstein were to those of southerners. In 1848, he had fought against Danish oppression, for a democratic, separate nation; in the United States, he stood opposed to a secession movement that argued against northern oppression and democracy. To Olshausen, southerners were representative of oppressive aristocrats and only the northern states embraced democracy and republicanism.

The slavery question divided the Polish immigrant community. Despite the occasional Polish slaveholder, many Poles opposed southern slavery. Gurowski was vocal in his opposition to the Compromise of 1850, saying "What do I care for Mr. Webster? I can read the Constitution as well as Mr. Webster." Continuing to point out that the Fugitive Slave Law was unconstitutional, Gurowski attacked: "Mr. Webster should be hung for advocating it. He is a humbug or an ass. An ass if he believes such an infamous law to be constitutional; and if he does not believe it, he is a humbug and a scoundrel for advocating it."

In 1860, he published *Slavery in History*. His comparative work illustrated how slavery caused the end of "freedom, free labor, and the free yeomanry." "Already some of the violent proslavery militants in the slave section," Gurowski claimed, "express their purpose to invoke the aid of France in their schemes of secession and conquest, and propose that their cities be occupied by French garrisons." Aware of the use of Biblical slavery, Gurowski dismissed invocations of the Bible to justify slavery as "modern sophistry attempts to give a divine and moral sanction to chattel slavery, and [to base] its justice on the absolute and predestined inferiority of the *black race*." Although scientific racism was still in its infancy, Gurowski lashed out against the idea and questioned the abuse of science to justify slavery. "Science emancipates the mind from prejudices, falsehoods, and superstitions, and from the tyranny exercised over man by the elements and forces of nature, as well as from the far more malignant forces of social oppression." At the same time, religion could serve both sides of the sectional divide. Gurowski noted, "It is a significant feature that in the American Union almost every religious denomination has its proslavery and its antislavery factions."[30]

Ancient history offered many comparisons that were unfavorable to the South. Gurowski wondered whether southerners would ever put weapons into the hands of the slaves, as some states in Greece had done. Similarities between slaveholders of Sparta and the South indicated that both societies eventually declined. "The sword was the soul of Spartan institution," Gurowski wrote. "The pure and elevated conception of an American social structure rests not on physical but on intellectual and moral force; but its deterioration is visible in the new conception of slavery inaugurated and sustained by the militant oligarchs." Furthermore, slavery did not guarantee agricultural prosperity. Gurowski wrote, "What a wide difference between the agriculture of the free and slave sections of the United States! And that, too, though the region of slave culture enjoys advantages both in climate and soil." If the southern states formed an independent country, the Union support against servile insurrection would disappear. Gurowski perceived that southern society was on the same road to self-destruction that had brought down Spartan and Roman society.[31]

In conclusion, Gurowski explained, historical lessons of slavery allowed for only one outcome. "These analogies prove beyond doubt," he asserted, "that slavery always corrupts the slaveholder and the whole community." He wondered how the Irish could support slavery. "Such are the Irish, en masse," he wrote, "and some others who escape oppression in Europe only to support slavery in America." By 1860, the United States faced a historic dilemma. "Slavery is as fatal to society as are the Southern and tropical swamps to human life," he claimed. After calling John Brown a martyr, Gurowski connected the institution of slavery to the oppressive political system in the United States. "The oligarchic despotism in the Slave States runs rapidly through all the stages," the Polish exile wrote, "with which individual despotism has filled the dark records of history." The lesson of slavery was clear: "Slavery generates bloody struggles. Many of these have resulted in the slaves violently regaining their liberty, while others have destroyed the whole state."[32] Having participated in the Polish uprising against Russian enslavement and oppression, Gurowski voiced opposition not just to the institution of slavery but also to the oppressive political system within the southern states, where a minority controlled politics.

Even as southerners made arguments against what they perceived as northern political oppression, they knew how much foreigners despised slavery. Southern social theorist George Fitzhugh published an analysis in *DeBow's Review*, in April 1861, in which he blamed a small group of agitators in the northern states for the sectional tensions. He wrote derogatorily, "We see a small squad, among them [William H.] Seward and [Horace] Greeley, . . . and very many half-starved, half-naked Frenchmen, and Infidel Germans, flanked by a crowd of unsexed women, and free negroes."[33] Despite the support provided by individuals like John Mitchel, southerners continued to distrust European intellectuals and rabble-rousing, radical Forty-Eighters, who associated with abolitionism.

Nevertheless, some fire-eaters looked to European rebels as their own revolutionary plans took shape. They drew parallels between their own struggle against political oppression and the revolutions of 1848. "Washington was a rebel! Lafayette was a rebel" wrote Alabamian William Yancey, "and so was Tell and so is Kossuth—rebels against abuse of power; and welcome to us be the appellation received in defense of our right and liberties." South Carolina fire-eater Robert Barnwell Rhett agreed. "Even now the heart of the Pole yearns for the tempestuous and capacious despotism of his nobles in olden times, rather than the steady and more advantageous rule of Russian domination. Are the people of Ireland, to this day, content with her identification with England? The people of England and Ireland, Russia and Poland, Austria and Italy, are not more distinct and antagonistic in their characters, pursuits, and institutions, their sympathies and views, than the people of our Northern and Southern states."

South Carolinian Lewis M. Ayer claimed that Hungary, Ireland, and Poland lacked independence and self-government; therefore, their separatism was justified. Ayer implicitly sought the same right of separation and self-government for the southern states. Comparisons of this nature were common among southerners. Fire-eaters perceived that they were engaged in a struggle for independence from oppression, just like their Hungarian, Irish, or Polish counterparts in 1848. The political, economic, and sectional challenges of the 1850s created not only tensions within the country but also southern perceptions of being an oppressed minority. South Carolina's D. H. Hamilton explained, "The South is almost entirely hemmed in and nothing is left to us but desperate fighting."[34] This sentiment had been shared by separatist movements across the North Atlantic for the previous fifty years.

However, southerners and their separatist counterparts also shared concerns about democracy. Nathaniel B. Tucker worried about democracy disintegrating into mob rule. In his opinion, slavery was a mechanism to prevent the excesses of democracy. Similar, Mississippian John A. Quitman fretted about the involvement of too many people in political decision-making; nevertheless, he was always in favor of universal male suffrage. According to Louis T. Wigfall, secession had separated the southern states from the political corruption of the North and restored a purer form of republicanism to the South. European separatists such as Mitchel agreed with the southern perception of a purer form of democracy. He looked to the United States for a place supportive of freedom, democracy, and paternalism.[35] To some separatists, slavery helped maintain democracy.

As sectional tensions increased, southerners worried about the possibility of their political and social enslavement at the hands of the North. Contributing to *DeBow's Review*, A. Roane asserted that southern rights and the section's place within the country had eroded in the previous decade. He argued for self-defense. Roane claimed, "Whoever holds his liberty, his property, or any right whatever, at the mercy of another, however wise or benevolent he may be, is to that extent a slave. This is equally applicable to individuals, to States, to sections, and to entire nations." He worried about majority oppression, especially a majority interpreting constitutional rights for its own benefit.[36] Southerners feared political, social, and economic oppression and enslavement, just as European separatists had.

When separatists of the Polish uprising of 1830 and the Hungarian, Irish, Polish, and Schleswig-Holstein uprisings of 1848 arrived in the United States, their initial goal was to continue the struggle for the freedom of their homelands. As their stay became protracted and no new revolutions materialized, however, they reconciled with the permanency of their exile. Once separatist migrants became politically involved, they faced a difficult decision. Was their sympathy with the northern states, against a perceived slave-power conspiracy, which saw the southern minority dictate terms, and with an enslaved population working southern fields? Or were they to remain loyal to their separatist identity and sympathize with the perceived politically oppressed southerners, who had to defend their social system against northern aggression?

European experiences informed separatist migrants' decisions in the United States. However, economic, political, or social enslavement and actual human enslavement were quite different. Europeans had to reconcile their various constitutional and legal arguments to fit the situation in the United States. Polish and Hungarian separatists associated their uprising with the plight of African American slaves in the southern states, but even more, they saw in southern society a political system of oppression against the entire country. Others saw the southern social and political system as oppressive. European separatists who had described their oppression in political terms, like the Irish, were likely to side with the constitutional arguments of the southern states again northern imperial oppression. However, the 1850s had not required European separatist to pick sides; the election of 1860 did.

5

SECESSION AND A SEPARATIST'S DILEMMA

> On the 4th day of March, 1861, the Federal Government will pass
> into the hands of the Abolitionists. It will then cease to have the
> slightest claim either upon your confidence or your loyalty.
>
> —HOWELL COBB, "Letter . . . to the People of Georgia"

When South Carolina seceded from the Union, on December 20, 1860,
everybody in the country had a difficult decision to make. Secession
and the eventual outbreak of the Civil War were the culmination of
decades of sectional strife. Novembrists and Forty-Eighters watched
closely as the events unfolded. Many European separatists actively
precipitated the break between the two sections. The politically active German Americans, in particular, had an impact on the policies of the new Republican Party. Their activism raised fears in the
South that the Republicans intended to destroy the southern way of
life. Many Forty-Eighters sympathized with the northern position,
though there were exceptions, who identified with the South. Thus,
Novembrists and Forty-Eighters faced a difficult decision. They had
supported separatist causes in Europe and therefore were familiar
with the arguments used by the southern states. Nevertheless, few
joined the southern states.

With the presidential elections looming large, the year started om-
inously. Rudolph Schleiden forebodingly ended his traditional New
Year's Eve diary entry for 1859 with a wish "to see this quietness as a
sign that the new year would maintain and foster the just recreated
peace in the nation." Schleiden doubted that either section would
be so foolish as to allow an election to cause conflict. He hoped that
moderates would force the extremists to back down.[1]

In a skewed view of reality, Theodor Olshausen believed that the election of Stephen A. Douglas, or of a southern presidential candidate, could cause war but that conflict was less likely if a northern radical such as William H. Seward were elected. Olshausen's personal choice for the Republican nomination was John C. Frémont.[2] Apparently, the Schleswig-Holstein radical did not understand that the election of a Republican northern sectional candidate could prompt southern secession.

The Democratic convention met on April 23 in Charleston, South Carolina. The party's platform committee failed to come to an agreement on the slavery question. As southern delegations departed in protest and the convention disintegrated, the party failed to nominate a presidential candidate. They decided to reconvene six weeks later, in Baltimore. In the intervening weeks, supporters of the Democratic front-runner, Stephen A. Douglas, replaced the seceded southern delegations, but southern Democrats continued to demand a plank to protect slavery.

In Baltimore, the second convention witnessed its own controversy when southern delegates who had walked out of the Charleston convention were denied participation. They continued their secession. Mississippi delegate Powhattan Ellis Sr. argued that northern Democrats had refused "to join us on fair and equal terms." The Mississippian announced, "If the flag of our country cannot protect me and my property wherever it can be rightfully raised," then the South needed to find protections of its own.

Sympathizers from other state delegations joined southern separatists in an independent convention. Northern Democrats nominated Stephen Douglas; southern Democrats selected John C. Breckenridge, on a proslavery platform. The only national party had broken apart along sectional lines.[3]

On May 16, the Republican Party opened its convention in Chicago. Preceding the convention, German Americans held their own meeting to present the general convention with a German platform. In Iowa, the leaders of the immigrant community, including the two Schleswig-Holstein radicals Olshausen and Hans Reimer Claussen, had their own ideas about who the party's candidate should be. They opposed any further expansion of slavery, which was the party's main plank for the upcoming election. When it came to the nomination of a presidential candidate, they opposed Missourian Edward Bates. They criticized him for staying in the race in 1856 and for supporting the Know-Nothing Millard Fillmore in order to hurt the Frémont ticket. His support for the enforcement of the Fugitive Slave Law further irritated the Schleswig-Holstein radicals. This debate among the German immigrant community, and its decisions, resulted in the Davenport resolutions, which other German groups in the northwestern states adopted.[4] The radicals had a significant impact on the emergence of a German American bloc within the Republican Party.

For German Americans, Seward, with his strong antislavery record, remained the preferred candidate. However, Olshausen apparently considered Abraham Lincoln the party's best choice. As long as the candidate had a strong antislavery record, the Holstein radicals were satisfied. Since the party wanted to improve on its 1856 success, the selection of such a candidate was unwise, and it opened the door for the moderate Lincoln. The party platform continued to oppose the expansion of slavery, but Republicans broadened their appeal by adding support for a homestead act, for internal improvements, for the construction of a transcontinental railroad, and for tariffs.[5] They hoped that those proposals would win over moderate northerners with Whig leanings and disgruntled northern Democrats. Despite or because of their separatist origins and radical views, Schleswig-Holstein radicals embraced the sectional Republican Party and its perceived antislavery program.

Novembrists and Forty-Eighters were torn about Lincoln's nomination. In June 1860, John Mitchel was in Illinois, speaking against the Republican Party. He was glad that the Democratic Party, which "was kept alive four years longer than it had any right to live," had finally passed away. Irish voters, in particular, he said, should carefully consider whether a party supportive of protective tariffs and free western land was not a party worthy of their vote. Irish migrants should shed their concern for the southern states. "The South," Mitchel explained, "cannot be saved in the North, not by the North, and must either save herself or go unsaved." He was implicitly foreshadowing secession. Therefore, Mitchell agreed with both Seward's "irrepressible conflict" and William L. Yancey's "dissolution of the Confederacy."[6] Despite seeing benefits in the Republican program, Mitchel did not think the South had much to gain from the Union and that it should stand on its own. The sectional division of the parties increased the likelihood of a sectional break.

After Lincoln's election victory, southern fire-eaters determined that the time for secession had arrived. Southern state governments called conventions to decide their future within the Union. The democratic elections allowed the people to voice their opinion on the future of the country. In some states, like Mississippi, turnout significantly declined between the regular election, when almost 70,000 voters participated, and the secession vote, where only 29,000 votes were cast. In Louisiana, where the plurality of 50,510 had voted for John C. Breckenridge, 38,665 residents participated in the secession election, with the majority favoring secession. There also were undemocratic decisions leading to secession, such as the suppression of the apparently cooperationist victory in Georgia.[7] Other than the anomaly of Georgia, the southern states used the democratic process to leave the Union.

South Carolina announced its departure from the Union on December 20, 1861, with a well-reasoned declaration of independence. Like the thirteen colonies in 1776 and Hungary in 1848, South Carolina claimed that the federal government had regularly violated the state's constitutional rights. A Virginian explained that what the southern states were doing was "hard to comprehend . . . but we all know the meaning of *Revolution*!" The state "resumed her separate and equal place among nations, deems it due to herself, to the remaining United States of America, and to the nations of the world, that she should declare the immediate causes which had led to this act."[8]

As with all separatist movements, South Carolina claimed that the state was "free and independent," with all the privileges that came with independence. The Articles of Confederation had brought the states together as "free, sovereign and independent states." The United States consisted of a group of sovereign states and granted, according to South Carolina, "the right of a people to abolish a Government when it becomes destructive." The states had ratified the Constitution, which granted substantial powers to the states. South

Carolina asserted that the states remained associated with one another in a compact after ratification.

Since the Union was a compact, the states and the central power had mutual obligations to one another. If one party failed to follow those obligations, the other was released from its obligations. "Fourteen of the States have deliberately refused, for years past," South Carolina claimed, "to fulfill their constitutional obligations, and we refer to their own Statutes for the proof." In particular, northern resistance to returning runaway slaves irritated the southern states. The right of property owners, slaveholders, from the southern states was dramatically curtailed. South Carolina further explained, in detail, its constitutional argument. "Each State was recognized as an equal," South Carolina's declaration read, "and had separate control over its own institutions. The right of property in slaves was recognized by giving to free persons distinct political rights, by giving them the right to represent, and burthening them with direct taxes for three-fifths of their slaves; by authorizing the importation of slaves for twenty years; and by stipulating for the rendition of fugitives from labor." The state's fear of legal oppression, which had grown over the previous decades, culminated in the secession of the state.

The emergence of a northern party that undermined the constitutional rights of the individual states concerned South Carolina. With the election of a candidate who had stated publicly that a "government cannot endure permanently half slave, half free," the southern states felt the time for action had arrived. There was also what South Carolina called the exclusion of the South from the common territory in the western states. They assumed that the North waged a war on slavery. With the equality of the states and protection of the Constitution gone, South Carolina reasoned, "the slaveholding States will no longer have the power of self-government, or self-protection, and the Federal Government will have become their enemy." The declaration closed by saying, "We, therefore, the People of South Carolina, by our delegates in Convention assembled, appealing to the Supreme Judge of the world for the rectitude of our intentions, have solemnly declared that the Union heretofore existing between this State and the other States of North America, is dissolved, and that the State of

South Carolina has resumed her position among the nations of the world, as a separate and independent State."

The Hungarians had made a similar statement only twelve years earlier. Separatists shared a perception of being an oppressed minority without constitutional rights. However, in contrast to Hungary and Poland, and more like Ireland, the southern states focused on constitutional arguments, to avoid any moral or ethical questions about the institution of human slavery.

In contrast to South Carolina, Georgia focused on the economic divergence between the northern and southern states. Georgia claimed that the northern states had "endeavored to weaken our security, to disturb our domestic peace and tranquility, and persistently refused to comply with their express constitutional obligations to us in reference to that property."[9] After the Mexican War, the southern states felt they did not receive their fair share of the new western territory. The loss was especially offensive because the Constitution guaranteed equal access to the western land.

Misconceptions were everywhere. Georgia declared that the Republican Party stood for "the prohibition of slavery in the Territories, hostility to it everywhere, the equality of the black and white races, disregard of all constitutional guarantees in its favor." With the election, a majority of northerners had overruled the alliance of a northern minority and southern majority. Like South Carolina, Georgia outlined how the northern states had violated the constitutional requirements placed upon them with regard to the protection of property and the return of fugitives. The declaration concluded, "The people of Georgia have ever been willing to stand by this bargain, this contract; they have never sought to evade any of its obligations; they have never hitherto sought to establish any new government; they have struggled to maintain the ancient right of themselves and the human race through and by that Constitution. . . . To avoid these evils we resume the powers which our fathers delegated to the Government of the United States, and henceforth will seek new safeguards for our liberty, equality, security, and tranquility." Like other separatist movements, Georgia had to act to stop additional violations of its rights.

Mississippi's declaration of secession listed the reasons for separation. The declaration outlined the historical progression of antislavery policies in the United States, including the Northwest Ordinance and the Missouri Compromise. Grievances had increased with the prohibition of slavery from new territories and the refusal to admit new slave states. Mississippi incorrectly assumed that the Republican Party stood for "negro equality, socially and politically, and promote[d] insurrection and incendiarism in our midst." Especially concerning to the southern state was that North's desire to destroy slavery without providing a replacement. The Republican Party intended to destroy the social and economic system in the southern states. The party's victory, Mississippi argued, had "destroyed the last expectation of living together in friendship and brotherhood." Finally, the declaration argued against remaining in the Union: "Utter subjugation awaits us in the Union, if we should consent longer to remain in it," the declaration read. "We must either submit to degradation, and to the loss of property . . . or we must secede from the Union framed by our fathers . . . Our decision is made. . . . We embrace the alternative of separation; and for the reasons here stated, we resolve to maintain our rights with the full consciousness of the justice of our course, and the undoubting belief of our ability to maintain it."[10] These declarations are reminiscent of the arguments used by European separatist movements.

European separatists debated whether southern secession was legitimate or premature. As a former separatist, Schleiden criticized the undue haste of southerners. He saw no genuine political threats. Given how long he had waited before deciding to join the duchies' uprising, one can easily understand his response and the reasons why he would refuse to support this separatist nationalist revolution.

However, the Schleswig-Holstein uprising had started as a reaction to perceived threats. Schleiden had been critical, in 1848, of Friedrich Hecker and Gustav von Struve because they had not waited and had acted rashly. He had even accused them of not being good republicans. The same criticism applied to the South. While the Schleswig-Holstein rebel disagreed with southern secession, he had justified the 1848 uprising by saying, "Not opposition or indignation caused the proclamation of the provisional government but a desire for self-preservation." No southern fire-eater could have said it better. Even the Polish separatist Adam Gurowski agreed. He viewed the events in the South with suspicion and thought of secession as a conspiracy. "The people of the free states," Gurowski wrote, "their representatives in Congress, were to be played with like children." Despite, his hope for a Virginia-sponsored compromise solution, he called for preparation for war.[11]

In February, leaders of the rebellious states came together in Montgomery, Alabama, to form the Confederate States of America. Appointed to the highest office was the moderate former U.S. senator from Mississippi, Jefferson Davis.[12] The decision to appoint a moderate and not a fire-eater mirrored the decision of separatist governments during this period. Hungary, Poland, and Schleswig-Holstein all had appointed moderate leaders to their first provisional governments, and only as the conflict escalated did more radical individuals such as Lajos Kossuth take control. In many regards, Kossuth and Davis were remarkably similar in their micromanagement.

The spirit of revolution gripped the country. In Helena, Patrick Cleburne wrote to his brother, "I hardly know what to say to you about politicks [sic]. The fever of revolution is very contagious. . . . My own opinion is that the first blood shed on Southern soil in a collision between the Federal troops and the State authorities of any Southern state will be the signal for civil war." Cleburne felt the necessity to defend the constitutional rights of his home state and the other southern states, but he remained open to compromise. "I hope to see the Union preserved by granting to the South the full measure of her constitutional rights." He was an Arkansan and was ready to defend the rights of Arkansas. Cleburne, like many southerners, feared that the northern states aimed to oppress and enslave the southern states. "If the stars and stripes become the standard of a tirancial [sic] majority," he wrote in January 1861, "the ensign of a violated league, it will no longer command our love or respect but will command our best efforts to drive it from the state." Slavery did not figure into Cleburne's decision; only constitutional rights mattered. However, the southern army "is for protection, Lincoln's to subjugate and enslave the whole Southern people and divide their property among his vulgar unprincipled mob."[13] Common southern fears of northern oppression and enslavement explained Cleburne's decision to fight northern "invaders."

Polish residents in the South agreed with Cleburne's assessment. In Europe, Kacper Tochman had perceived of Poland's rebellion as an assault against "utter centralized and despotic authority." Similarly, southerners feared oppression by a "despotic North." Tochman believed that the southern states were about to mimic the Polish cause and shed tyranny. He agreed with the southern arguments that the United States was a collection of sovereign states and that the states rather than the people had ratified the Constitution. Even more, slavery was a beneficial institution and only a form of labor.[14] In his view, slavery did not matter, but oppression by a northern majority did.

The Hungarian separatists in Iowa immediately reemployed their battle-tested language against oppression and enslavement to justify their opposition to southern secession. In Davenport, Miklós Perczel opposed secession. "We pointed out that the Union is a constitutional law of the land, the cornerstone of the entire organization of the nation," he explained, "the disturbance of which is politically unsound and should not go unpunished, because it would result not only in the dissolution of the country, but also threaten the very existence of the republican form of government since the aristocratically inclined citizens of the pro-secession states would soon seek to establish a monarchy to ensure the security of their institutions and the fruition of their grandiose plans." Perczel was not the only Hungarian to support the Union. According to one historian, Hungarians fought against "the tyrant of slavery" and for "the Grand Cause of the emancipation of slaves." They wanted to defend the country's democratic principles against aristocracy and oppression. This war was not about the institution of slavery but about political oppression, which was synonymous with enslavement.[15]

On March 4, 1861, Abraham Lincoln's inaugural address extended a conciliatory hand to the seceded states, indicating Lincoln's constitutional perception that he had no authority to interfere with slavery where it already existed. He did indicate that he would not tolerate secession and that he hoped for the restoration of the Union. The speech lacked moral arguments, only advanced legal justifications, and even those were not as aggressive as Lincoln had initially intended.

Many, including Gurowski, considered the inaugural address insufficient. Gurowski claimed, "The insurrection of the slave-drivers will not end in smoke." He felt more forceful measures were necessary. "It may turn out more interesting than anything since that great renovation of humanity by the great French Revolution," he wrote. Gurowski had little confidence in Lincoln's cabinet, and Secretary of State William H. Seward, especially, struck him as incompetent and ill-suited for such an important position. "For the present complications," Gurowski wrote, "diplomatic relations ought to be conducted with firmness, with dignity, but not with an arrogant, offensive assumption, not in the spirit of spread-eagleism; no brass, but reason and decision."[16] Gurowski had set himself up as a constant critic of the Lincoln administration.

Once in office, the Lincoln administration faced the difficult decision of what to do about the two remaining federal installations in the Confederacy, Fort Sumter in Charleston, South Carolina, and Fort Pickens in Pensacola Bay, Florida. Should the government retain them or passively relinquish the last two U.S. flags flying in the seceded states?

The Confederates wanted a peaceful resolution of the issue and sent Andre B. Roman, Martin J. Crawford, and John Forsyth as envoys to Washington. The presence of a Confederate peace mission was an open secret, similar to what Schleswig-Holstein Germans, Poles, and Hungarians had done in the past. Gurowski referred to them as "rebels, slave-drivers, slave-breeders" and was upset that Seward communicated with the delegation. Union at any price was unacceptable, and compromise would negate Lincoln's election victory, according to Gurowski.[17] The uncompromising separatist radicals had never supported concessions. In any event, the Confederate emissaries were as unsuccessful as their Polish, Irish, Hungarian, or Schleswig-Holstein counterparts.

After the March 16 cabinet meeting, Lincoln was unsure whether he should surrender either fort or prepare for conflict. Being unaware of the president's plans, Seward gave the erroneous impression that the forts' evacuation was imminent. Until the very end, Seward continued to support evacuation, hoping for a Unionist resurgence in the southern states. Gurowski thought this was to make the people in the North accept the inevitability of separation.

Meanwhile, secessionists made inroads in the upper South. Neither Seward nor Gurowski considered Lincoln up to the challenges of the presidency. Southerners were unable to get a hearing in Washington, much like the experience of their Schleswig-Holstein predecessors in Copenhagen or the Hungarians in Vienna. By early April, with no news from the Fort Pickens's relief mission, Lincoln determined that he could not surrender Fort Sumter.[18] The president informed South Carolina's Governor Charles Pickens about the intention to resupply Fort Sumter. The governor asked the Confederate government in Montgomery, Alabama, for advice. President Davis ordered the capture of Fort Sumter, and with the first shot on April 12, 1861, the Civil War commenced.

The start of war forced Lincoln to adopt new policies. On April 15, the president called for 75,000 ninety-day volunteers to serve in the Union army. The population of the free states flocked to the colors in overwhelming numbers. The enthusiasm that swept through the country drew in Novembrists and Forty-Eighters. The Polish Novembrist Gasper Tochman, residing in Charleston, commented, "The church bells began to peal, and the cheers and shouts, and the bombastic boasting and speechifying of men in a condition of mind more like that of lunatics than reasonable beings, produced a most disagreeable impression upon me." Despite the early enthusiasm, Tochman was not a committed Confederate.[19]

On April 19, the Sixth Massachusetts passed through Baltimore on its way to Washington. The sympathetic southern population of the city pelted the soldiers with rocks. A fight ensued. Four soldiers and twelve residents of the city died. The incident of mob action raised fears about the security of Washington, which was defended by only 3,500 soldiers.

Schleiden approved of the right to revolution, but he believed that southerners had acted preemptively. No violation of southern rights had occurred. Faced with bloodshed and the carnage of war, Schleiden's humanitarianism took over, and he desired to prevent unnecessary slaughter. Despite thinking compromises impossible, Schleiden thought about proposing a three-month cease-fire so that Congress could meet in extraordinary session on July 4 and determine a policy.

On the morning of April 24, 1861, Schleiden heard that the vice president of the Confederacy, Alexander Stephens, was in Richmond.

Knowing Stephens from the Georgian's time in Congress, when the two had resided in the same house, Schleiden saw an opportunity to communicate with one of the highest officials in the Confederacy. He talked with Salmon P. Chase and Seward. Schleiden knew that Seward was unlikely to comment until he had consulted with the president. Seward cautioned that the president and the government could not publicly acknowledge such negotiations or give Schleiden specific terms, but he suggested that Schleiden should present his ideas to Lincoln.[20]

In the afternoon, Seward and Schleiden visited Lincoln. The president thanked Schleiden for his willingness to help prevent bloodshed. He expressed regret that Schleiden had not gone to Richmond on his own, without consulting Lincoln or Seward. Schleiden countered that it would have exposed him and his government to accusations of conspiring with the enemy against the lawful U.S. government. Lincoln accepted that explanation. Obviously, Schleiden was painfully aware of the reason why he was in the United States. His participation in a separatist insurgency had made him an outcast once; there was no need to reprise that role for a cause in which he did not believe.

Lincoln continued that his peaceful intentions, which he had expressed more than once, had all too often been misinterpreted. He insisted, therefore, that this conversation be kept completely confidential. He stressed that military preparations were not aggressive in nature. The president believed that he could not give any authority "to enter into negotiations or to invite propositions," but he promised to consider "with equal respect and care" all propositions he received from Schleiden. Schleiden gained the impression that Seward and Lincoln wished that he would unofficially consult with Stephens to reach an agreement to prevent bloodshed.[21]

Schleiden had accomplished less than he had hoped, but he remained undeterred. That evening, he went to Alexandria, Virginia, to take the morning train to Richmond. One has to wonder whether, as Schleiden crossed the bridge over the Potomac, his mind wandered back to his departure from Copenhagen thirteen years earlier. In contrast to Kiel in 1848, however, Schleiden found Richmond to be more of an army camp. The railroad stations were full of young volunteers, eager to fight. The newspapers had a belligerent tone. In the lobby of the Spotswood Hotel, Schleiden found Senator Robert M. T. Hunter and other prominent southerners, who were anxious to find out what had brought Schleiden to Richmond and to give their opinions about recent events.[22]

Upon his arrival in Richmond, Schleiden contacted Stephens, and the two had a three-hour conversation. Stephens wanted to help foster peace, but he saw little prospect for success. Reminding Schleiden of the treatment the southern commissioners had received in Washington, Stephens argued that the Confederacy would not renew steps toward peace. Even Judge John Archibald Campbell, who had been an intermediary between Seward and the southern commissioners, had sent an outraged letter to Jefferson Davis to protest the Lincoln government's intentions. Stephens believed that the attack on Fort Sumter had been unnecessary. He thought Lincoln had used the rumors that the Confederate Army was about to attack Washington to draw troops to the capital, even though the governments of neither the Confederacy nor Virginia had shown any inclination to attack. The recent events in Baltimore, according to Stephens, placed Maryland in the secessionist camp. The Confederacy was honor-bound to come to the state's assistance. Thus, one aspect of the cease-fire had to be either Maryland's inclusion in the Confederacy or the end of troop movements through the state. In addition, the high spirits of the population would not allow for a cease-fire. The final and gravest problem was that Stephens had no authority to negotiate. At the end of the conversation, he requested time to think about the offer.[23]

Schleiden requested a formal written statement of the terms. He discovered that Stephens's terms were almost word for word what Davis had told the Confederate Congress on March 29. The vice president regretted the "threatening prospect of a general war," and he stressed that it was not the intention of the Confederacy to provoke a war with the Union. However, peace without independence was not acceptable. The bombardment of Fort Sumter had occurred only after all possibilities for peace had been exhausted. The main point, which would never be acceptable to Seward or Lincoln, was, he wrote, "From all evidence and manifestations of their design which have reached me, it seems to be their policy to wage a war for the recapture of former possessions, looking to the ultimate coercion and subjugation of the people of the Confederate States to their former dominion. With such an object on their part persevered in, no power on earth can arrest or prevent a most bloody conflict." Stephens then left it up to Lincoln to offer terms.

With this letter as a basis, Stephens and Schleiden debated for another two hours. Schleiden pressed Stephens on the need to modify some passages. Most significantly, he told Stephens, "a significant amount of mistrust shined through the letter, coupled with, in his opinion, a substantial amount of misplaced honor, which threatened the impact of the letter because in Washington the letter would meet a similar mistrust and false, misplaced honor that shied away from making the first step." In the end, both men agreed to keep their talks confidential. Schleiden did not record in his diary the second conversation with Stephens, perhaps because he had lost hope for an agreement. Schleiden returned to Washington on April 27, and the Lincoln government saw no reason to further pursue negotiations.[24]

One has to wonder whether Schleiden ever noticed how the roles had changed. In 1848, he was the secessionist, much like Stephens. Schleiden himself, as the go-between, had stepped into the shoes of Great Britain and Sweden. One has to wonder whether he realized which role he had assumed during his trip to Richmond. After all, Stephens's statements could just as well have come from a Schleswig-Holstein German in 1848.

Having failed to gain the Union's acceptance of their independence, the southern states searched for legitimacy through foreign recognition. In his first diplomatic instructions, the Confederate secretary of state argued, "Reasons no less grave and valid than those which actuated the people of Sicily and Naples to cast off a government not of their choice and detrimental to their interests have impelled the people of the Confederate States to dissolve the compact with the United States." In a similar vein, the *Richmond Examiner* emphasized the southern right to self-government by pointing out, "They were all agog at the notion of freedom for Ireland. They exulted at the movement for Hungarian liberty, and rushed forward to flatter and fawn upon Kossuth."[25] Confederate independence, however, was unacceptable. Even European separatist denied the Confederacy the right to self-government.

Missouri, with its large European separatist population and divided loyalties, faced difficult decisions. In Saint Louis, the radical Olshausen illustrated how a separatist nationalist could fight a secession movement with the same ferocity that had characterized his fight for a separatist uprising. In Saint Louis, at the start of the war, Olshausen observed the turbulence between the various immigrant communities. His radical ideals led him to believe that slavery was a major cause of the war and that everyone's freedom was at stake. A Republican newspaper summarized, "The throne of the despot is to be raised up in the ruins of citizen self-government. Henceforth the citizens of Saint Louis are to be subject to the will of a dictator. . . . Soon we shall lose the freedom of the press. Austria and South Carolina will be at home in Missouri."[26] The arguments advanced in the paper were similar to those made by Hungary, Ireland, Schleswig-Holstein, or Poland, but also the U.S. South over the previous fifty years.

Olshausen was well aware of Missouri's divided loyalties. He claimed that most of the early Unionists in the state were Germans. He associated the "freedom fighters" of 1848 with the defense of the Union. Based on his experiences, support for separatism would have made equal sense. Olshausen had harsh words for people who did not support the Union. For the South, Olshausen had even harsher words. He called secessionists a band of guerrillas and believed that all people in the South were barbarians, worse than their Native American allies. He must have forgotten that he himself was a barbarian at one time.[27]

In Washington, Gurowski's hatred for the Confederacy increased. He wrote, "I throw in a cesspool my document of naturalization, and shall return to Europe, even if working my passage," if secessionists were to win the war. "Not self-government is on trial, and not the genuine principle of democracy," Gurowski reasoned. "It is not the genuine, virtual democracy which conspired against the republic, and which rebels, but an unprincipled, infamous oligarchy, risen in arms to destroy democracy." Compromise was unacceptable, and the Union had to "first kill the secesh, destroy the rebel power, that is, the army, and then look for the Union men in the South."[28] Gurowski opposed any compromise with a separatist movement, as did many others.

On May 3, 1861, Alexander Asbóth published in the *New York Times* an appeal to his fellow Hungarians to join the Union army. In his effort, Asbóth connected U.S. and Hungarian history and insisted that the Hungarians should show their support to the Union as the United States had supported Hungarian independence in 1848.[29] Asbóth observed that Hungary's failure allowed those who had worked against Hungarian independence to claim the mantle of liberty. But the Hungarians were not defeated. There was hope for "a renewed gigantic united outburst in behalf and in vindication of our ancient constitution and independence."[30] As a Hungarian separatist, Asbóth was deeply troubled by the dissolution of the United States. Like many others, he worried that the success of secession "would be a triumph for all despots and the doom of self-government." Hungary and all other people who fought oppression would suffer if the Confederacy succeeded. The Hungarian separatists had no sympathy for southern separatism.

Asbóth did not stop there. He asked Hungarians "to remember that we belong to that nation which struggled gallantly, but unsuccessfully, for that same liberty, which crowned the efforts of Washington." They had lost in 1849 against Austrian and Russian armies, which forced Hungarian leaders, including Kossuth, into exile. At that time, the United States had stepped in and safely removed them, under the protection of the "glorious flag of Stars and Stripes." The Hungarians were honor-bound to support the United States. "The sympathy and assistance thus bestowed upon down-trodden Hungary and its scattered exiled sons imbued me with a feeling of everlasting gratitude," Asbóth wrote. This support required him to defend the country.

Furthermore, Asbóth explained to his fellow Hungarians, "I have already offered my military services to the Government. Many of you have done the same, and I feel confident that you all share my sense of indebtedness to the United States." Having fought in a revolutionary uprising before, and bringing European military experience with them, Asbóth and his fellow Hungarians were sought after in the United States. Asbóth closed his appeal by noting how important the United States was as a symbol for the rest of the world. "You all know the value of the Union as it was, and will stand by it faithful and true, and defend it at all hazards, with that same firmness and gallantry displayed so emphatically in the defence of your own native land, the rights and Constitution of Hungary." Asbóth, like many fellow

Hungarians, thought that an oppressive minority in the southern states had taken the United States hostage and that only victory in the coming war could end southern enslavement.

European separatist migrants had little sympathy for southern secessionists, despite their shared experiences. Separatists had a difficult decision to make. Based on their European experiences, many connected slavery, planter oppression, and aristocratic oppression, justifying their support for the Union. Others saw constitutional oppression and sided with the new southern union. Their reaction depended on those European experiences. As secession broke the United States apart, separatists built on their perceptions of the two sections to decide which section better represented their ideology. In some cases, that meant fighting against an oppressive slaveholding minority that held the United States hostage and undermined the democratic process. In other cases, that meant fighting against an oppressive northern majority imperialistically forcing its way on the southern people.

6

NORTH AMERICA'S SEPARATIST REVOLUTION

> An appalling list of foreigners in the Yankee army. These newspapers tell of the Hungarians, Russians, Prussians—French dukes de Chartres and Joinville. We have Polignac as a setoff.
> —MARY CHESNUT, *Mary Chesnut's Civil War*

Many separatist migrants had military and political experience that they could put to good use in the course of the war. Radical separatists tended to uphold democratic principles against government infringements at all times. The followers of Lajos Kossuth and Theodor Olshausen had challenged moderate governments during their European rebellions, when those governments rescinded civil liberties, and they continued to do so. In addition, the war required European separatist to pick a side. Migrants with military experience, such as the Hungarians, provided essential services to the understaffed U.S. Army. Mary Chesnut commented on the "appalling list of foreigners" fighting in the Union army, but she forgot that some former separatists fought for the Confederacy.

Across the country, migrant communities came together to form military units with ethnic cohesion. Since few Hungarians resided in the United States, there were not enough for an entire regiment. Hungarians usually served as officers. On December 1, 1861, László Újházy, who had fought in the Hungarian war for independence, explained Hungarian separatists support for the Union:

> The miserable Hungarian exiles became dispersed on the entire globe and still: we have come together here in such great numbers! One might ask: "How come?" The main reason is that wherever the

bugle-call of freedom blares, Hungarians leave all of their proper-
ties behind no matter how cherished they had been to them, and
they rush to the battle field where honor and valor can triumph
against villainy and tyranny. You have gathered in defense of the
sacred cause of freedom, helping to defend the government of this
republic, which was attacked by an evil and pretentious aristocracy—such an aristocracy that not only forces other human beings
to serve them, but degrades them to the level of animals. . . . As long
as we don't get the chance to fight for our constitutional existence
against blood-sucking Austrians, let us fight here, for our adopted
country. And once the day of triumph comes, and not only the old
glory of the Republic will be restored, but it will become an even
shinier example for other nations to follow, we will be able to stand
out with our arms toughened in fight to the battlefield where we
have to take revenge for our many martyred fellow countrymen.[1]

Újházy connected the Hungarian struggle for independence with the
war in the United States. Implicitly, he compared southern slaveholders to oppressive European aristocrats. Újházy saw the Civil War as
part of a larger struggle against oppression.

Especially difficult was the decision for Irish Americans who had
participated in the Irish Confederation's uprising and who sympathized with the political arguments of the southern states. Meagher
frequently expressed his support for the South. However, when the
war started, Meagher explained his action: "Duty and patriotism alike
prompt me to it. The Republic, that gave us an asylum and an honorable career,—that is the mainstay of human freedom, the world
over—is threatened with disruption. . . . Above all is it the duty of us
Irish citizens, who aspire to establish a similar form of government in
our native land. It is not only our duty to America, but also to Ireland.
We could not hope to succeed in our effort to make Ireland a Republic
without the moral and material aid of the liberty-loving citizens of
these United States." The writers of *Harper's Weekly* similarly perceived that some Irish compared "southern aristocracy" with "British
aristocracy."[2] For Meagher and many Irish residents, the Civil War
was a continuation of their struggle for Irish independence. He felt
honor-bound to help the country that supported Ireland.

After Abraham Lincoln's call for volunteers, ethnic groups in New York sprang into action, forming regiments. The substantial Irish population of New York City produced a number of regiments. Thomas Francis Meagher joined the Sixty-Ninth New York Volunteer Regiment under the command of Michael Corcoran. After its formation, they quickly reached Washington by way of Annapolis, Maryland. Irish Americans embraced the Union cause with great enthusiasm. Meanwhile, Stephen Kovács, a Hungarians exile in New York, tried to recruit a Hungarian regiment. The result was the multiethnic, Garibaldi Guard, though only one-tenth of the soldiers were from Hungary.

Alexander Asbóth and Frederick George D'Utassy assisted in the recruitment of the Garibaldi Guard. Asbóth explained to D'Utassy, "Both Hungarians, and having fought for the laws and constitutional rights of our native country, we are now ready to take the field for the maintenance of the Union." Such a statement raises questions about why Asbóth did not join the Confederacy, which also fought for its constitutional rights. Apparently, Asbóth felt that the southern states were not showing any "patriotic virtue" and that they had in fact violated the Constitution. To encourage enlistment, Asbóth asked his fellow Hungarians to be mindful of their past and how their experiences in 1848 compared to the United States becoming an independent country. Both Hungary and the United States struggled for liberty. He wrote, "You all know the value of the Union as it was, and will stand by it, faithful and true, and defend it at all hazards with the same firmness and gallantry displayed so emphatically in the defence of your native land, the rights and constitution of Hungary."[3] Therefore, the struggle to defend the Union was just like the struggle for Hungarian independence.

Experienced leadership was badly needed, as the first military engagements showed. Confederate troops broke the Union lines and sent troops running back to Washington, DC—Corcoran, Meagher, and the Sixty-Ninth among them. Some blamed Corcoran and William T. Sherman for the disintegration of the regiment. Apparently, Sherman had told soldiers to flee, making it impossible for Corcoran to maintain a square formation. Despite its performance, many soldiers of the Sixty-Ninth reenlisted. The regiment became the cornerstone of the Irish Brigade, recruited from among the Irish community of New England.

As one of the most prominent Irish migrants in the United States, Meagher actively recruited, making speeches among New England's Irish residents. The Irish were fighters and had fought in many different wars over the years. Meagher argued, "The South had been the ruling party. . . . The Southerner had become so accustomed to rule that he could not be reconciled to the will of the majority, constitutionally expressed, when that will took the reins of power from his hands."[4] For Meagher, the war was not about slavery but about constitutional principles, just like the Irish struggle.

Officers within the Irish Brigade successfully lobbied the government to place Meagher in command of the brigade. In their effort, they overcame much of the latent nativism in the country. Lauding the Irish fighting ability, Meagher told his soldiers,

> The reputation of the Irish soldier, achieved in the wars of France, of Austria, and of Spain, in days long gone by—transmitted to the New World, and there renewed and replenished in the struggles that gave birth to the Republics which disenthralled the Andes from the yoke of Spain, and which at a still later day, proved itself fresh as ever, and bright as ever in the full blaze of that sun which blazed, fiercely as the death-dealing arrows of Apollo, upon the plains of Cerro Gordo,—the reputation of the Irish soldiers thus made good and thus transmitted is now to be maintained and still further to be perpetuated by the Irish Brigade.[5]

The Irish saw their struggle as part of a larger international conflict to restore the Union. Meagher did not mention Ireland, but he had Ireland in mind when he thought about the larger implications of the war.

The early military disasters brought out many wannabe generals, such as Adam Gurowski. Harshly criticizing Winfield Scott's leadership, Gurowski initially praised George B. McClellan. However, the disillusioned Pole eventually called McClellan "McNapoleon" when the general did not respond to the Pole's suggestions. Gurowski felt that too many politicians were involved in military decision-making.

He even questioned Lincoln's leadership and suggested the German Forty-Eighter Franz Sigel as chief of staff. The failure of the Union left Gurowski saddened with "a more rending pain now than I felt thirty years ago when Poland was entombed."[6] Remembering the events in Poland, Gurowski worried that the United States might suffer a similar fate. Others made comparisons to their own European experiences.

In Missouri, revolutionaries from the various migrant groups played an essential role on both sides. At the start of the war, Missouri's governor, Claiborne F. Jackson, favored secession, and the commander of the U.S. arsenal at Saint Louis, Captain Nathaniel Lyons wanted to protect Union interests. He was in charge of the largest arsenal in the slave South, which contained sixty thousand muskets and other war matériel. Jackson and his pro-southern friends moved quickly, in the aftermath of Fort Sumter, to secure Missouri for the Confederacy. He called out the southern-favorable militia and seized a small arsenal near Kansas City, Missouri. On May 8, 1861, additional weapons arrived from the South. Lyons prepared to attack the secessionists at Camp Jackson, and thanks to the German and Hungarian community, he had loyal troops at his disposal.[7]

However, European migrants fought on both sides in Missouri. Some Irish immigrants fought for the Confederacy, and at least one soldier compared the struggle of the southern states to the desire for independence and self-government in Ireland. Their decision found the support of Catholic archbishop Peter R. Kenrick in Saint Louis. One Irish Catholic wrote sympathetically, "The South has the right to self-government as clearly as the Belgians, Italians, Poles, or the Irish." German Americans argued instead that there was a secessionist conspiracy in Missouri. The *Anzeiger des Westens* wrote, "The leading conspirators are slave owners and as such form an oligarchy which is a conscious enemy of all free institutions."[8] The two positions represent a microcosm of the larger problem faced by the European separatist community: they fought either for self-government against northern oppression or against a minority oppressing a majority.

On May 10, Lyons took his troops to Camp Jackson, surrounded the encampment, and captured the secessionists. Upon the party's return to Saint Louis, the southern-sympathetic population attacked the troops. A melee ensued, which left twenty-eight civilians and two soldiers dead. Violence continued into the next days. The state deteriorated into chaos. Jackson called on Sterling Price to lead the pro-southern forces. On June 11, the leaders of the two sides met for a conference in which Jackson offered to turn Missouri into a neutral state like Kentucky. Lyons refused to let the governor dictate terms to the federal government. Instead, he decided to accept the challenge. When the government appointed John C. Frémont to head the Western Department, including Missouri, the Union general became a love child of the radical separatist.[9]

Frémont assembled an ethnically diverse staff. Alexander Asbóth joined Frémont's staff and helped organize the raw recruits into effective regiments. Two more Hungarians were on Frémont's staff. Charles Zagonyi commanded Frémont's bodyguard. To address accusations that he had joined the army as a mercenary, Zagonyi explained, "I took service in the United States army only for the reason that I wanted to see this great country united again, and put down the rebellion, and not to divide it more and more." The pompous uniforms of his 150 mounted soldiers, which worked as a police force in Saint Louis, gave rise to the feeling that the unit was unfit for a republic.

On August 15, 1861, Frémont offered to make Meagher an aide-de-camp. The Irish exile refused: "I cannot find it in my heart to part from my tried and honored comrades." Asbóth did not remain in his position for long, either. When Frémont's troops marched into southern Missouri, the Hungarian was in command of a division, but while Asbóth did not make much of an impact in the campaign, Zagonyi supposedly led a valiant charge, on October 25, in skirmishes around Springfield, Missouri. Some contemporaries, however, compared Zagonyi's charge to the light brigade's disastrous attack during the Crimean War.[10] The Hungarians continued their fight against enslavement and oppression, just as they had fought the Austrians.

To deal with the complicated political and military situation in Missouri, Frémont imposed martial law and, on August 30, issued an emancipation proclamation for slaves of disloyal masters. Concerned about the impact of the proclamation, Lincoln countermanded the decree and removed Frémont from command. Olshausen was outraged and sympathized with the disgraced general. Having already established slavery as a major factor causing the war, Olshausen favored Frémont's emancipation proclamation. For the Schleswig-Holstein radical, the proclamation was one of the most important gestures of the war. It was regrettable, Olshausen thought, that the general's effort had put him in such rough waters, for only the total end of slavery would restore peace and harmony to the United States.[11] Olshausen had returned to a familiar posture: opposition to government policies during wartime.

In Iowa, Hans Reimer Claussen disapproved of the Lincoln administration's decision to stress unification over the issue of slavery. Like Olshausen, Claussen abhorred slavery and wanted nothing less than its complete abolition. As during the election campaign of 1860, Claussen said, no Republican was worthy of support who did not subscribe to abolition. Slavery needed to take center stage in the war. In a newspaper article, reacting to the dismissal of Frémont and the end of his emancipation edict, Claussen made an exaggerated claim that the vast majority of northerners wanted the end of slavery.[12] Claussen's radicalism and narrow-mindedness, which had seen the radicals demand the continuation of the first Schleswig-Holstein war against all of Europe, had resurfaced.

Sacking Frémont had another effect. Asbóth, Zagonyi, and the other foreign officers suddenly found themselves under fire when the government discovered irregularities with their appointments. Zagonyi faced a court of inquiry because his report of the engagement at Springfield contained inaccuracies. Zagonyi refused to accept the findings of the commission but was temporarily without command. Asbóth had to wait until March 21, 1862, to receive his commission as brigadier general, instead of the original appointment on September 7, 1861. Despite these issues, Asbóth remained in Missouri and continued to fight for the Union. In early 1862, Asbóth occupied northwestern Arkansas. Wounded at the Battle of Pea Ridge, he temporarily withdrew from service.[13]

The majority of Hungarians fought for the Union, but both sides frequently invoked the Hungarian struggle of 1848 to justify and explain their own actions. Union soldier Alfred L. Castleman wrote, "Hungary, with its population of only 3,000,000, and without revenue, withstood the whole power of Austria, till the hordes of Russia had to be called in to aid in their subjugation." Many southern news-papers made similar statements and comparisons. The Richmond, Virginia, *Enquirer* used the Hungarian struggle for its own purposes. Historian Andre Fleche wrote, "The paper charged that northerners 'were all agog at the notion of freedom for Ireland' and that 'they ex-ulted at the movement for Hungarian liberty.'. . . [and] 'hooted at the idea of union between Ireland and Great Britain or between Austria and her dependencies.' Yet, the author lamented, 'they deny, in effect, the claim of thirteen sovereign States to be free.'"[14] The European separatist rebellions provided both sides with arguments.

Nevertheless, some separatists embraced the Confederacy. At the outbreak of the Civil War, Mitchel watched with great interest as the sectional tensions escalated and two of his sons enlisted in the Confederate Army. Mitchel remained loyal to the southern states. Wanting to support his adopted section, Mitchel arrived in New York in September 1862 and secretly made his way through Union lines. Northern newspapers criticized Mitchel's decision to join the Con-federacy. At the same time, Mitchel maintained his defiance toward government oppression. According to the New York *Herald*, Mitchel's "tone is more violent than it ever was in Ireland." Mitchel seemed to work hard to prevent reconciliation between the two sections and thus to create a permanent separation. Therefore, the *Herald* won-dered how much Mitchel actually helped the South. "He is just the man to create a revolution with a revolution," commented the paper. "For some time symptoms of revolt against the despot at Richmond have been manifesting themselves."[15] Radicals in all European upris-ings had given their revolutionary governments a hard time. Mitchel's radical ideas had resulted in his dismissal from *The Nation* in Ireland. Mitchel had changed little.

In Richmond, Mitchel initially worked for the *Enquirer,* which supported the Jefferson Davis government. Since Mitchel disagreed with the Davis government's indecisive attitude and unwillingness to pursue the war with all ruthlessness, he quit his job and joined the *Richmond Examiner,* in December 1863. Mitchel's call for ruthless conduct of the war mirrored his call to the Irish people to arm them-selves with farm tools to fight English oppression. Despite a series of family tragedies, including the death of one of his sons at Gettysburg, the death of his daughter in Paris in 1863, and the death of another son in the defense of Fort Sumter the following year, Mitchel continued his support for the Confederacy. As the war turned south, Mitchel became disillusioned.[16]

The Polish Novembrist Kacper Tochman had military experience that he unsuccessfully offered to the South. He went to Montgomery on May 11, 1861, and received permission to recruit a Polish brigade, consisting of two regiments. The regiments eventually had 1,700 soldiers between them, but they consist largely of Irish, German, and French immigrants. The soldiers were a rowdy bunch. Tochman purposefully appealed to the "Fellow-Countrymen of the Old World" in his recruitment. He did not receive permission to accompany his little brigade into battle. This is in dramatic contrast to Ignatius Szymański, who helped with the defense of New Orleans against David G. Farragut in 1862. The Confederate government insisted that Tochman's authority was to raise regiments in the North, not in the South. The government dismissed Tochman's contention that he had received verbal promises. Tochman appealed to the Confederate Congress's Committee on Claims, which eventually granted compensation, but the Confederacy collapsed before payment was made.[17]

For many Poles, both in the United States and in Europe, Tochman's support for the Confederacy did not align with their country's past. In December 1863, the Polish democratic societies in Europe questioned how Tochman could be in such gross violation of their constitutional principles and support the Confederacy. Tochman claimed that, as a citizen of Virginia, he had not violated any laws. He embraced the states' rights identity so dear to many southerners. He rejected any notion that he had violated the principles of the Polish national cause, a constitutional oppression on the part of Russia. However, Tochman's actions in the South brought northern action. Northern authorities arrested his wife, searched their house, and confiscated their private correspondence.[18]

In contrast to the Poles, Patrick Cleburne got his chance to serve his country and quickly advanced to brigade command, but he stagnated at division commander for most of the war. He served with distinction at Shiloh, Perryville, and Murfreesboro. After the defeat of Braxton Bragg's army, Cleburne became involved in the political, military, and personal squabbles within the Army of Tennessee. However, Cleburne's ability to fight did not save Bragg's incompetently placed army at the Battle of Chattanooga or John B. Hood's depleted army in Atlanta. Eventually, Hood's wrath against the Irish general for a missed opportunity resulted in Cleburne's fatal charge at the Battle of Franklin, in November 1864.[19]

As the war progressed, criticism of both governments' conduct of the war increased. Novembrists and Forty-Eighters in the North questioned the Lincoln government's conduct. The decision to emphasize union over slavery was a political necessity for Lincoln, but many separatists disagreed. The president had to placate slaveholders in the loyal slave states, but he also had to maintain a broader political *Burgfrieden*, or fortress truce, a state in which a society within a particular jurisdiction avoids political infighting. Democrats, who opposed emancipation, would support a war effort to end disunion but would not support emancipation. Despite the relatively cooperative spirit in the North, opposition existed, and the government wasted little time in arresting opposition leaders, closing newspapers, and suspending the writ of habeas corpus.[20]

Across the country, but especially in Missouri, the anti-Lincoln press faced stringent limitations. Olshausen had printed articles containing anti-Lincoln opinions. Frémont's successor, Henry W. Halleck, notified Olshausen at the *Westliche Post* that unless the tone of the paper changed, he would suspend the paper. Later in the war, Olshausen complained to Lincoln directly about the censorship and policies undermining freedom of speech. He had done the same in Schleswig-Holstein. He was still the radical who challenged the government for undermining civil liberties. Gurowski agreed that the protection of liberty and democracy was immensely important: "Democracy, the true, the noble, that which constitutes the signification of America in the progress of our race," Gurowski claimed, "democracy will not be destroyed. . . . Democracy will emerge more pure, more powerful, more rational; destroyed will be the most infamous oligarchy ever known in history."[21] These separatists had not changed their liberal outlook on politics and continued to demand the protection of democratic principles.

In the fall of 1862, Lincoln issued the preliminary Emancipation

Proclamation, giving the war a new meaning. The proclamation sig-
naled not only the demise of slavery but also an end of the *Burgfrieden* in the United States. Northern Democrats, who had supported
a war for union, opposed abolition. The same people who had seen
slavery as a divisive factor withheld their support for the "Great
Emancipator." Most concerning was Lincoln's conduct of the war and
the limits on civil liberties. Olshausen called Lincoln's government a
"pitiful administration, the country overrun by corruption and fraud,
and a miserable war effort." He had equally harsh words for the Confederates, whom he called "barbarous rebels."[22] This came from a
separatist nationalist who himself had been a "barbarous rebel" only
fifteen years earlier.

Olshausen was not the only one to voice such a negative opinion of
the government. "I am sure that a great drama will be played, equal
to any one known in history and that the insurrection of the slave-
drivers will not end in smoke," Gurowski wrote in his diary. "This
insurrection may turn very complicated; if so, it must generate more
than one revolutionary manifestation." He did support emancipation.
As early as 1861, Gurowski had called for the use of slavery as a moral
weapon in the war. The Polish exile perceived that "slavery has become a traitor, is arrogant, blood-thirsty, worse than a jackal and a
hyena." He disagreed with the assumption that runaway slaves would
come to the northern states once slavery ended. Instead, Gurowski
believed, "the colored population from the free States, incited and
stirred up by natural attractions, will leave the North for the South."
Even more, he assumed that African Americans, once freed, would
embrace agriculture and increase southern productivity and prosperity, with planters hiring freedmen.[23]

Even more, Gurowski frequently commented about the necessity
of enlisting African Americans in the war effort. He was glad that
the Emancipation Proclamation opened the door to the arming of
African Americans. "The military organization of Africo-Americans
is a powerful social and military engine by which slavery, secession,
rebellion, and all other dark and criminal Northern and Southern
excrescences can be crushed and pulverized to atoms," Gurowski
claimed. Assuming that Lincoln intended to rescue slavery from its
eventual demise, he complained, "The *conditional* is the last desper-

ate effort made by Mr. Lincoln and by Mr. [William] Seward to save slavery. Poor Mr. Lincoln was obliged to strike such a blow at his *mammy!*" He wondered about the tone, which he called "written in the meanest and the most dry routine style."[24] There was much to criticize, and Gurowski was a vocal critic.

While European separatists found reasons to question Lincoln's Emancipation Proclamation, the arming of African Americans had a positive impact on the Union's manpower requirements. Confederates felt the pressure. Perceiving that slavery was not a reason for his enlistment and therefore was not important in the war, Cleburne made a bold and radical proposal. In January 1864, Cleburne outlined that the Union had a superior army, which relied on the greater manpower of the northern states, on African Americans, and on Europeans who opposed the institution of slavery. Therefore, the southern protection of slavery provided foreign soldiers and runaway slaves to the Union army. Unless something happened, the southern states would be crushed and "subjugated" by the Union. If that occurred, slaves, "personal property, lands, homesteads, liberty, justice, safety, pride, manhood," would all be lost, and all the "gallant dead [seen] as traitors." Therefore, Cleburne concluded, "slavery is comparatively valueless to us for labor, but of great and increasing worth to the enemy."[25]

Cleburne believed that the Confederate government had to address its manpower shortage. Therefore, he proposed that "we immediately commence training a large reserve of the most courageous of our slaves, and further that we guarantee freedom within a reasonable time to every slave in the South who shall remain true to the Confederacy in this war." He then explained why arming slaves would save the Confederacy. "Between the loss of independence and the loss of slavery," Cleburne explained, "we assume that every patriot will freely give up the latter—give up the negro slave rather than be a slave himself." Again, Cleburne established the difference between chattel slavery, which he cared little about, and the more important enslavement of people by an oppressive government.

The arming of slaves would dramatically undercut the manpower of the Union and ultimately would turn the support of European powers in favor of the Confederacy. Cleburne understood that if the slavery issue were eliminated, the Union's reasoning for the war would no longer hold up. Without the moral high ground, the Union would simply be engaged in a "bloody ambition for more territory." With freed slaves serving in the Confederate Army, Cleburne argued, the country would "instantly remove all the vulnerability, embarrassment, and inherent weakness" of its cause. Cleburne knew that states' right theories stood in the way of outright emancipation, but emancipation, including acceptance of "marriage and parental relations," was necessary if the Confederacy was to survive.

In answering southern fears about slaves fighting for the Confederacy, Cleburne pointed to historic precedents in which Spartans used slaves in battle. Most controversial, considering how southerners had used the precedent of the Saint-Domingue uprising, Cleburne claimed that "negro slaves of Saint Domingo, fighting for freedom, defeated their white masters and the French troops sent against them."[26] If his fellow officers read this far, they likely were outraged by the comparison, which linked the most devastating slave uprising with the arming of slaves to fight for the Confederacy. Although Cleburne probably never read Gurowski's book on slavery, he knew enough about the history of slave societies to make comparisons and to know what fate awaited the Confederacy.

Finally, Cleburne dismissed common and long-held assumptions. For example, he rejected the idea that slavery and republicanism were connected. Having a government of the South's choice was still better than having a government "forced upon us by a conqueror." At the same time, Cleburne did not accept the notion that white people would not be able to work in the southern environment. If the war had shown anything, it was that white southerners were capable of doing hard manual labor. Cleburne concluded, "It is said slavery is all we are fighting for, and if we give it up we give up all. Even if this were true, which we deny, slavery is not all our enemies are fighting for. It is merely the pretense to establish sectional superiority and a more centralized form of government, and to deprive us of our rights and liberties. . . . It may be imperfect, but in all human probability it would give us our independence." Cleburne assumed that a Union victory would cause southern enslavement; he was too radical for the Confederacy.

In the North, Meagher sympathized with the idea of arming slaves. Likely because he saw the carnage among the Irish troops, he embraced a position close to that of Cleburne. In a speech, Meagher asserted that African Americans who had fought in the Union army should receive political rights, including the right to vote. "The black heroes of the Union army have not only entitled themselves to liberty," he claimed, "but to citizenship." Meagher continued to view the Civil War in terms of a political struggle. "It is full time for them to emancipate themselves from the control of the politicians who have held them in ignoble captivity for many years," he said, "and to whose vulgar dictations they surrender the intelligence and high spirit which should be as precious as their citizenship."[27] Meagher had gained respect for African American soldiers, but he still viewed the war in constitutional terms. In any event, African American soldiers did not immediately turn the tide in the war.

As battlefield successes continued to elude the Union in the east, the Irish Brigade required replenishing. After the devastation of Fredericksburg, the brigade received new Irish green flags. However, they entered the 1863 campaign season without replacement soldiers. After the defeat at Chancellorsville, Meagher decided that he could no longer justify staying in command. In his resignation, he complained about the "exhausted condition" of his unit and how the regiments were not permitted to "renew" themselves. A later biographer wrote, "The battle of Chancellorsville was the last engagement in which General Meagher participated . . . He could not in self-respect—or in justice to his command—submit any longer to the treatment to which both were subjected by the official dictators of the War Department—[Edwin] Stanton and Halleck."[28] The Irish general left the war behind.

Nevertheless, Meagher remained loyal to the cause and continued to speak in support of Union victory. In a ceremony honoring his service, Meagher questioned the claim that the southern Confederacy had inherited the legacy of the American Revolution: "The authority of a government founded on the free will and votes of the people, disputed at the outset before even that government had an opportunity to vindicate or compromise itself; the national property fraudulently surrendered or seized; merchant ships waylaid by buccaneers and strewn in ashes on the seas." The Irish exile opposed any compromising peace, but at the same time, as for all Irish migrants, the war was for him a constitutional dispute.[29]

Other separatist radicals increased their pressure on the government. The new commander of the Army of the Potomac, Joseph Hooker, drew Gurowski's ire after the Battle of Chancellorsville. Gurowski pointed out that when the Russian army attacked Warsaw, "Prince Paschkewitsch . . . was disabled or stunned, and his chief of staff, Count Toll, directed the storm for two days." After the Battle of Gettysburg, on the other hand, [George] Meade allowed [Robert E.] Lee to slip across the Potomac into Virginia. Gurowski wrote, disgusted, "If only Meade had imitated [Joseph] *Radetzky*. In 1849 after the denunciation of the Armistice of Milan, *Radetzky* called a council of war to decide whether the Po was to be crossed and Piedmont invaded. All the best Austrian generals . . . voted against the proposition. Radetzky quietly listened, then rose and give orders to cross immediately." The action resulted in the Battle of Novara, a victory for Austrian arms.[30]

The criticisms against the Lincoln government culminated in 1864. The election year offered radicals an abundance of opportunities to work against Lincoln. Gurowski confided to his diary:

> The next presidential election is ominous not only for the American Union, but its influence will powerfully affect the destinies of Central and South America, and therefore also influence Europe. . . . If the American people show a decided and stern purpose, the *Decembriseur*'s liberticide schemes will be checked; Maximilian may not come; and if he comes, he will pack his trunks and return to his Bourg as soon as the American people emphatically declare that his Hapsburg rags must no more pollute this continent. Spain will come to her senses, and give up her appetite for Peru and for San Domingo. . . . Spain ought to absorb, or to unite with, Portugal.[31]

Gurowski's statement was remarkable in how he connected many different parts of the world to the election in North America. In particular, his invocation of the Decembriseur, a group of revolutionaries in Russia in 1825, indicated that he continued to associate the struggle in the United States with the one in Poland and Russia.

European radical separatists in the North and the South agreed on few things, but they shared a dislike of Lincoln. As a southern sympathizer, Mitchel had a low opinion of Lincoln. He described the president as an "ignoramus and a boor; not an apostle at all; no grand reformer; not so much an abolitionist, except by accident—a man of very small account in every way." Gurowski wrote, in regard to Lincoln's reelection, "Re-election! re-election! it is sickening to mind and body. Why has not Congress the pluck to assert its power; crush the politicians; take Lincoln, Seward, and [Francis] Blair by the collar; shake their scheming, sham souls from them, and throw them into the deepest dungeons of Fort LaFayette, all the tribe of Weeds."[32]

The Schleswig-Holstein radicals agreed. In Saint Louis, Olshausen wanted the Republican Party to adopt a radical program. If the party refused such a program, he favored running a third presidential candidate. To promote his views, Olshausen attended the Louisville Freedom Convention of the Slave States, in late February 1864. Over the following months, he sought a radical candidate to challenge Lincoln. The choice was easy; the radicals had found their hero in 1861: John C. Frémont. Olshausen lauded Frémont as a "noble, educated, and reasonable man," while casting Lincoln as a "narrow-minded, finance-political rural Illinois lawyer."[33] In early May, the call went out for a radical convention, separate from the general party convention. As during the first Schleswig-Holstein war, Olshausen challenged the government during a time of grave crisis.

The radical separatists in Iowa welcomed the call. Like Olshausen, Claussen was critical of Lincoln's policies. After their disagreement in 1861, Claussen and the editor of *Der Demokrat* jointly opposed Lincoln's nomination. At a public meeting, which voiced the German opposition to Lincoln's reelection, Claussen criticized the president's policies toward Missouri, which he did not explain further, and the nonacceptance of African American recruits in Kentucky. Claussen supported Frémont and criticized the Lincoln administration's patronage, foreign policy, and military strategy. Like Olshausen, he detested the president. He characterized Lincoln as a brakeman who had prevented liberty from coming to terms.[34] United in their opposition to Lincoln, the delegates went to the radical convention in Cleveland intending to nominate another candidate with a radical program.

State conventions, often constituted as the Radical Democracy movement, assembled to nominated delegates for Cleveland. The radicals in Missouri nominated Olshausen to represent them. The party name, Radical Democracy, was ill advised, because many moderate politicians in the United States already viewed the radical Forty-Eighters with suspicion. Olshausen was one of many Forty-Eighters present; however, this party was far from a German opposition group. Resentment of the Lincoln administration was widespread, even among native-born citizens.

The Cleveland Convention agreed to a diverse program that included the restoration of the Union, the suppression of secession, and the end of slavery, ensured by a constitutional amendment. The delegates criticized Lincoln's attack on civil liberties, demanding a guarantee of freedom of speech and of the press. They wanted to amend the Constitution to limit the presidency to a single term. In response to the French-supported monarchical experiment in Mexico, Radical Democracy supported a vigorous enforcement of the Monroe Doctrine against unrepublican governments. Looking toward the end of the war, the radicals opposed Lincoln's "Ten Percent Plan" for the reconstruction of the southern states.[35] Having written its platform, the convention nominated Frémont as their presidential candidate.

Since it was not advisable to split the party in the face of George B. McClellan's strong Democratic challenge, Frémont reevaluated his position. The Frémont candidacy lasted only until September. Olshausen remained an active supporter, giving speeches in support of Radical Democracy. Frémont's decision to drop out angered many radicals. One letter to the editor denigrated the radicals in Missouri as the "Olshausen clique." Claussen quickly abandoned Radical Democracy. He blamed the convention for nominating Frémont instead of working toward a broader opposition to Lincoln. Apparently, he, like many others, believed that the strong presence of Germans in Cleveland undermined the movement's success. *Der Demokrat* even pointed to the hypocrisy of those German immigrants who had opposed the nomination of Lincoln but then supported him in the election, and it ridiculed the radical elements of the party.[36] The radicals and their unwelcome challenges were just as despised in the United States as they had been in Europe in 1848.

The election campaign between Lincoln, who by early September could rely on the fall of Atlanta and on Philip H. Sheridan's successes in the Shenandoah Valley to bolster his campaign, and his Democratic opponent, George B. McClellan, was hard fought. Lincoln carried the nation with a comfortable margin in the popular vote and an even stronger majority in the Electoral College. With the reelection of Lincoln, Olshausen decided there was nothing left for him in the United States. Like many radicals, Olshausen loved the concept of democracy, but when democracy did not work in his favor, he ran or fought the results. Gurowski agreed with Olshausen's disillusionment. "I wish myself far off in Europe," he wrote, "but when I consider this great people outside of the governmental spheres, then I am proud to be one of the people, and shall stay and fall with them." After the election victory, Gurowski erratically wrote, "Poor Lincoln accused of tyranny! He has not nerve enough, not mind enough to be a tyrant. . . . Lincoln has not put one man in prison who has not richly deserved to be put there and kept to the end of the rebellion. . . . Freedom of the press put in danger by Lincoln! I wish Lincoln had the pluck to suppress the treasonable *Worlds, Intelligencers,* Boston *Couriers,* and all such prints which all over the country preach treason to right and to humanity, and poison the minds of the people."[37] While the older political radicals, especially those who had stood against the government during the election, were upset with Lincoln's reelection victory, the younger ones, who had supported the war and government, continued to support the military effort.

By the end of the war, many militarily experienced Novembrists and Forty-Eighters were still in positions of power. In the fall of 1864, Meagher returned to the war and assumed command in Tennessee, where Major General James B. Steedman had a difficult time defending the railroad line against guerrilla activities. Meagher enjoyed contributing to Union victory; fighting behind the line against guerillas required means not favored by the Irish radical. He did not remain in Tennessee long and was soon on the way to new opportunities in

Montana. Meanwhile, in Florida, Asbóth commanded African American soldiers, but also a number of Hungarians. Historian Stephen Beszedits lists some:

> The [Ladislas and Emil] Zulavsky brothers were veterans of the Hungarian Legion in Italy and participated in Giuseppe Garibaldi's triumphant campaign against the Kingdom of Naples. [Joseph] Csermelyi, a soldier in the War of Liberation, was among the dozen Hungarians who accompanied Narciso Lopez in his tragic filibustering expedition against Cuba in August 1850. [Emeric] Meszaros served with Asbóth in the Pea Ridge campaign as commander of the Frémont Hussars with the rank of major, while [Alexander] Gaal was a recent arrival from Hungary expelled by the Hapsburg authorities for taking part in the abortive Polish uprising of 1863 against the Russians.[38]

In mid-September 1864, Asbóth suffered a wound that left him crippled and that eventually killed him, three years later. He retired from the army on August 25, 1865. The *New York Times* lauded his contributions:

> Gen. Asboth is one of the oldest and most meritorious of the foreign officers who entered our service when the rebellion broke out. He is a man of high character and of very marked ability. He bore a prominent and most honorable part in the active scenes of the Hungarian Revolution, being one of the few in that contest who brought practical military knowledge and experience to the aid of the cause. During his residence in this country he has won the respect and friendship of all who knew him by the sterling qualities of his character, and by the modest manliness of his demeanor. So far as we are aware, all the Hungarians in this country who are in the war at all, are enlisted on the Union side.[39]

The war offered many separatists a second chance to embrace their revolutionary ideology and support a cause against oppression and for democracy. European separatists continued to disagree about where oppression in the United States originated. To some former members of the Irish Confederation, oppression came from the northern states forcing an alien way of life on the southern people. For the vast majority of those who came from Poland and Hungary, who had opposed Russian and Austrian enslavement, oppression came from a southern aristocratic minority. Many Irish, Poles, and Hungarians contributed their military knowledge to the war, at times leading troops into battle.

Radicals who had opposed their governments in Europe continued their opposition to discriminatory policies. In Europe, men like Mitchel or Olshausen had questioned their government at times of crisis because the rights and freedoms of the people were curtailed or because the revolutionary movement had refused to embrace independence. Similarly, when Lincoln revoked the writ of habeas corpus and limited the freedom of the press, Olshausen and Gurowski spoke out. They were ready to challenge Lincoln, just as they had done in Europe. In Richmond, Davis's conduct of the war was too timid for Mitchel, who had called for the arming and the uprising of people in Ireland. The Irish exile worked hard writing anti-Davis articles. Not much had changed; European radical separatists experienced their second separatist revolution.

When European separatists arrived in the United States in the early 1850s, they carried with them a fully developed ideology that included their opposition to oppressive government. This legacy clouded their approach to the sectional conflict in their new country. The slavery question was everywhere—in relation to the expansion of slavery into Kansas, the institution itself, and the perception of the slave-power conspiracy. The arguments of the sections held sway, with both claiming oppression by the other. European separatists could pick from an abundance of opinions, many of which were reminiscent of their own. If European separatist had argued for their status in Europe as being one of oppression and enslavement, they were likely to side with the northern states, seeing the slave-based aristocracy in the southern states in the same light as they had their European oppressors. However, if their arguments in Europe focused on legal oppression and avoided the terminology of slavery, as in Ireland, the community divided.

Overall, however, the enthusiasm of European separatists for the Confederacy was small. Despite what seemed like a desertion of their separatist principles, they remained true to their political radicalism and their European identity. They always desired independence for their home country, regardless of which side they supported in the Civil War.

7

THE DEFEAT OF SECESSION IN
THE NORTH ATLANTIC

My theory is to hold fast to the Constitution . . . it is our sheet an-
chor. . . . By our system of government minorities are protected
from like oppression of majorities; do away with this and our government becomes anarchical.
  —J. ADOLPHUS ROZIER, *New Orleans Times*, April 9, 1867

The surrender of the Confederate armies in 1865 spelled the end
of secession in the United States. Another separatist movement
had fallen victim to internal division. The defeat of the separatist
Confederate States of America indicated the decline of separatism
during the nineteenth century. Since the success of Belgium, Greece,
and Texas, separatist movements had failed. Hungary, Ireland, Poland, Schleswig-Holstein, and the Confederacy were just a few of the
states that tried to win back their sovereignty. A fragmentation of
the international state system was as acceptable in an increasingly
conservative-democratic world as it was during the reactionary Congress of Vienna era. These five separatist rebellions challenged the
established world order and failed. However, the fiasco of separatism
in the United States did not spell the end of separatist rumblings. Separatists did not engage in another full-scale uprising; nevertheless,
they continued to challenge oppressive governments.

The end of secession in the United States rang in another period of
separatist aspirations. Hungary, Ireland, Poland, Schleswig-Holstein,
and the southern states made one final attempt to gain autonomy.
Their bids had mixed results. In Ireland, a terror campaign and efforts to provoke a war between the United States and Great Britain

failed to bring about Irish home rule or independence. Radical separatists tried to restore Polish independence during the early 1860s; however, Russian military power and the lack of foreign support precluded success. Similarly, Schleswig-Holstein was the cause of two more wars. Neither war brought independence to the duchies; instead, they were a diplomatic tool for Otto von Bismarck to accomplish German unification. The Hungarians enjoyed partial success when the defeat of Austria in the Austro-Prussian War of 1866 forced the Habsburgs to make concessions, which included home rule.

Overall, independence continued to elude separatist movements in Europe. Ultimately, however, the southern states did not accept defeat and remained resilient. With violence by white supremacist organizations and political challenges to racial equality, the southern states regained home rule by the end of the century. Ironically, during Reconstruction, southern politicians embraced the notion of enslavement to describe their oppression.

———

Irish desires for independence increased after 1848, when the Irish Republican Brotherhood, also known as the Fenians, emerged to continue the fight of the Irish Confederation. Exiles of the 1848 rebellion supported and sometimes joined the Irish Republican Brotherhood. Although Thomas Francis Meagher and John Mitchel refused to assume leadership positions, the Irish in New York named their club in honor of Meagher. As a transatlantic organization, the Fenians required leadership in North America and Europe. John O'Mahony and Michael Doheny guided the Fenians in North America, and even though Mitchel was not interested in leadership, he helped. He used the famine to question Britain as a champion of nationalism and liberalism. In *An Apology for the British Government in Ireland,* Mitchel intended "to prove that the British government encouraged and aggravated Famine in Ireland, to thin the population." Almost two decades after the famine, Mitchel still wondered how the British could pay £20 million to West Indian planters to free the slaves, "turning their negroes wild," but provide no help to the Irish. He questioned how the British government could pay only "£50,000 [to help Ireland, which] was precisely the sum which was voted that same year out of that same Treasury, to improve the British Museum."[1] Only Irish independence could end British oppression.

Mitchel's literary barrage came to a halt when the U.S. government temporarily incarcerated him for his pro-Confederate activities. In November 1865, Mitchel returned to Paris and worked as a financial agent for the Fenians. However, even his meticulous commitment could not solve years of financial mismanagement. He also was unsure whether James Stephens was the right person to bring about Irish independence. In October 1867, Mitchel relocated to New York, where he published the *Irish Citizen*. The Fenians continued to look to him for guidance, which he refused. Their terror and bombing campaign caused resentment but did not accomplish Irish independence. Finally, the Fenians in North America, who tried to bring about a war between Great Britain and the United States with border skirmishes, failed as well.

The British did placate the Irish by disestablishing the Church of Ireland, but this was a far cry from home rule. Mitchel saw through the ploy and dismissed it as a fraud. After twenty-six years in exile, Mitchel returned home, in the summer of 1874. The next year, he won Tipperary's seat in Parliament, but as a convicted and escaped felon, he was ineligible to assume the office.[2] Mitchel and the leaders of the Irish Confederation never achieved Irish independence. Nevertheless, Ireland and Great Britain took early steps toward home rule.

———

In early 1863, Poland rose up a second time. Polish grievances against Russia had increased after 1831. The Russian Imperial Army's manpower requirement forced many young Poles to fill its ranks. Poles resented conscription. After the Crimean War (1853–1856), protests against conscription increased. In 1861, Polish protesters and Russian troops clashed in Warsaw in what became known as the Warsaw Massacre. By October, the Russian government declared martial law. As a result, the authorities dramatically curtailed Polish freedoms. Resentment built against the Russian oppressors.[3]

In Paris and London, exiled Poles prepared for a full-scale uprising, but they faced many obstacles in obtaining arms and equipment. At home, thousands of young workingmen were hiding in the woods to avoid conscription, ready to pick up arms for Polish independence. As in 1830, the rebellious Poles were ill-equipped and unprepared. In January 1863, the uprising started. By April, Adam Gurowski complained, "England plays as false in Europe as she does [in the United States]. England makes a noise about Poland, and after a few speeches will give up Poland," the Pole wrote. "In 1831, Englishmen made speeches, the Russian fought and finally overpowered us. England hates Russia as it hates this country, and fears them both."[4] There was no help.

From Washington, DC, Gurowski complained that Poland did not receive the same treatment that the southern Confederacy had. "The sympathies shown in certain quarters to the Southern traitors," he stated, "are neither so general nor so intense as was, and even is, the deep interest Europe felt in the fate of Poland and of the Poles. Poland periodically shakes Europe, evokes lively sympathies, even half-armed demonstrations, but never a recognition." The lack of recognition was even more offensive to the Poles because of Poland's long history. "And Poland is not a newcomer, not an offspring of dastardly treason to God and man like the South. Poland had geographical frontiers well known in Europe. For more than ten centuries Poland has had a large page in the world's history." Like their Confederate counterparts, the Poles immediately seized the Russian arsenals and obtained numerous weapons. Even with those weapons, the untrained Poles were no match for the Russian soldiers. By early May, the cause was lost.[5]

In the aftermath of the uprising, the Russian authorities captured and executed a number of Polish generals. Poland suffered more than 25,000 soldiers dead in the 650 engagements fought. The Russians harshly punished all those involved. If and how many 1830 revolutionaries participated in 1863 is unclear, as is the number of exiles returned from the United States. Like many, Kacper Tochman thought about returning but never did. In light of their advanced ages, many remained where they were and restricted their activities to moral and financial support. The Russian authorities executed more than 390 people and resettled another 18,600 to Siberia, the Caucasus, and the Urals.[6] Poland did not gain its independence until 1918.

In 1848, Schleswig-Holstein had distracted German attention away from Polish independence desires; the same happened in November 1863, when the Schleswig-Holstein issue reemerged. The Protocol of London of 1852 did not solve the Schleswig-Holstein question, but throughout the 1850s, Denmark, Schleswig-Holstein, and the German Bund debated about how a new constitution would protect the right of the duchies. By mid-January 1861, the German Bund threatened to occupy Holstein under a federal execution, because Denmark had violated Holstein's rights. Denmark's president of the council of ministers and foreign minister Carl C. Hall refused any compromise that could be "a sort of tribunal of censure over the Danish Monarchy."[7] Misunderstandings continued to prevail in the contested Dano-German borderland.

In 1863, the appointment of Otto von Bismarck as minister president of Prussia dramatically changed the dynamics of the Schleswig-Holstein question. While Bismarck worked to placate everybody, he recruited Austria to avoid a repetition of the first Schleswig-Holstein war. On November 15, King Frederik VII of Denmark died. His successor, Christian IX, ascended to the throne through the female line of succession, which was illegal under Schleswig-Holstein's laws. Many Forty-Eighters continued to support what they saw as their legitimate prince, Friedrich Christian August von Schleswig-Holstein-Sonderburg-Augustenburg.

In late December 1863, German forces occupied Holstein under a federal execution. On January 1, 1864, the new Danish constitution took effect. Sixteen days later, Bismarck dispatched an ultimatum to Copenhagen. After Denmark's refusal, Austrian and Prussian troops invaded Denmark and won a decisive victory at Düppeln/Dybbøl, on April 18. The invasion temporarily halted when the British suggested peace talks.[8] The negotiations stalled and war resumed. The resumption of the Dano-German War was a disaster for Denmark. On October 30, 1864, both sides ratified the final peace, with Denmark ceding Schleswig, Holstein, and Lauenburg.

Some Schleswig-Holstein exiles returned to once more support their duke; among them was Rudolph Schleiden. In London, during the armistice talks, he promoted the Augustenburg candidacy. He visited with Bismarck and Albrecht Theodor Emil Graf von Roon at Gastein, where Bismarck and Schleiden engaged in a three-hour conversation to bring independence to the duchies. In contrast, Theodor Olshausen was reluctant to support a monarchical Schleswig-Holstein. "It was clear to me from the start," he wrote his brother, "that the thing would take the same path as the events in 1848 had, because the Schleswig-Holstein elite had once more clung to the Duke of Augustenburg and the German princes."[9] Despite their opposition to American-style separatism, Schleiden and Olshausen still supported Schleswig-Holstein's separatism.

With the end of the Dano-German War, Schleswig-Holstein's search for independence continued. Austria and Prussia agreed, in the Convention of Gastein, to separately administer the duchies, thus violating the Treaty of Ribe and avoiding Schleswig-Holstein's independence. On June 1, 1866, Austria asked the Bund to settle the question. Offended, Bismarck claimed that Austria had violated the Convention of Gastein. When Prussian troops marched into Holstein, Austria asked for the mobilization of the armies of the Bund.

Prussia declared war on June 14, 1866. Only two years after fighting side by side in the Dano-German War, Austria and Prussia fought each other in the Austro-Prussian War. On July 3, 1866, the Prussians won the Battle of Königsgrätz/Sadowa, forcing Austria to relinquish leadership in the German states.

In many regards, the north–south division of the German states resembled the sectional division of the United States. Many Germans opposed a Prussianization of Germany, just as southerners had opposed an imposed northern nationalism. Schleswig-Holstein nationalists were similarly opposed to the integration of their homeland into Prussia. By the summer of 1862, the south German states were already voicing their opposition to north German—or, more precisely, Prussian—domination. "[Ludwig Karl Heinrich Freiherr] von der Pfordten frankly said to me that a determined majority in south Germany and especially in Bavaria was more likely to follow the example of the American slave states and let it come to a war with the north than to subject themselves to Prussian hegemony," Schleiden commented.

Schleiden sided with those who opposed an imposed national identity, just as he had in 1848. His dislike for Prussia was so strong that he resigned his diplomatic position in London in protest in 1866.[10]

Nevertheless, Bismarck had accomplished a partial unification of the German states, and unification was completed after the Franco-German War of 1870–1871. Schleswig-Holstein Forty-Eighters disagreed with Bismarck's means, and some disliked the new German state. Schleiden accommodated himself to the changed reality and was determined to find political means to protect his home state. He worked with a liberal nationalist party in Schleswig-Holstein and won the election to represent the port city of Altona.

Throughout his parliamentary career, Schleiden protected Schleswig-Holstein's interests. He fought to maintain Altona as a free port, pushed through a pension request from former Schleswig-Holstein officers, and cosponsored a naturalization treaty between Prussia and the United States. Schleiden did not take kindly to Karl Twesten's insinuation that the United States was unlikely to keep any promises made by the Confederate government to its citizens. Likewise, no government was under any obligation to maintain the promises made by the revolutionary government of Schleswig-Holstein. Schleiden dismissed any comparison between the dehumanizing slaveholding Confederate states and the internationally recognized government of Schleswig-Holstein.[11] Even long after the end of the Civil War and of the Schleswig-Holstein conflict, however, both questions lingered.

In the unified German Empire, national liberalism made way for new political ideologies. In 1873, Schleiden faced Social Democratic challenges and lost his reelection bid. In contrast to some fellow Schleswig-Holstein nationalists, he never reconciled to the Prussian occupation of the duchies.[12] The Schleswig-Holstein separatist nationalist cause was lost with the integration into Prussia. Schleswig-Holstein never gained its independence.

———

Where Poland suffered from the Schleswig-Holstein conflict, Hungary benefited and was successful in gaining autonomy. After 1848, the Hungarian question lost importance. However, Austria's diplomatic blunders during the Crimean War undermined the country's leadership within the German Bund and in Europe. Diplomatic isolation haunted the empire in 1859, when France and Piedmont-Sardinia forced Austrian territorial concession for the new unified Italian nation-state. In October 1860, Austria reinstituted the old constitution of Hungary. Furthermore, Austria restored electoral rights, the local parliament, and Magyar as the official language of the Hungarian bureaucracy and administration. Although the concessions were a step toward home rule, they were not independence.[13]

Magyar leaders wanted to reintroduce the laws of 1848. They asked for an amnesty for all participants in the uprising of 1848. In April 1861, Austria called for a new Hungarian parliament. The representatives wanted to reduce the influence of the Habsburgs by having the German royal family govern Austria and Hungary in personal union and restore autonomy to Hungary. Initially, the emperor did not respond well to these demands. After the discussions broke down, Austria once more embraced absolute rule and disbanded the Hungarian parliament. Nevertheless, the Austrians offered some concessions. Former revolutionaries and nationalists received an amnesty.

Government changes in Vienna restored a conservative, federal-minded government to power. In December 1865, the Hungarian parliament assembled again. At this point, the Austrians promised to restore the Hungarian crown and to accept, with revisions, the laws of 1848. The Austro-Prussian War, in 1866, temporarily delayed the reconciliation.[14]

At the end of the war, Ferenc Deák unequivocally demanded a compromise. Fearing the breakup of the empire into five different entities, the new Austrian minister-president, Friedrich Ferdinand von Beust, implemented a dual solution. In February 1867, Gyula Andrássy became the first Hungarian minister-president. The Hungarian Reichstag ratified the laws of 1848 with minor modifications. In mid-March, Emperor Franz Joseph I took the oath of office from the Andrássy government. Hungary gained full domestic political independence. Only finance, foreign affairs, and defense remained under imperial administration. With their own minister-president and cabinet, the two halves of the empire embraced different policies. The *Ausgleich* was accomplished.[15]

With the exception of Deák, the old radical separatists were not the driving force behind the Ausgleich. Of the hundreds of immigrants who had come to the United States in the aftermath of the failed uprising, only eleven returned. "Believe me, my friend, the Hungarian can never become American," John Xantus explained, "for his heart and soul can never become as hard as the metal from which the dollar is minted. There is only one place for us in this great world: 'Home,' which may not be great, magnificent or famous, and though poor, is still the most potent magnet for its wandering sons."[16]

Xantus returned to Hungary in 1861. Nicholas Perczel, Cornelius Fornet, and Ignátz Debreczeny obtained minor government jobs upon their return. Others returned as lawyers and physicians. The vast majority, however, remained in the United States, where their participation in the Civil War had raised their social status and gained them patronage positions.[17] The Hungarian nationalist had not achieved independence, but, more than other separatist movements, they had achieved autonomy.

———

The states of the former Confederacy achieved home rule in the aftermath of the Civil War. The end of the war had seen the disintegration of the Confederate government. In May 1865, President Andrew Johnson, who had replaced the slain Abraham Lincoln, issued a Proclamation of Amnesty and Reconstruction. He offered blanket pardons to all southerners who had served in the Confederacy, except those with $20,000 or more of property. He also turned the Reconstruction process into a civil affair, offering southerners a quick return to the Union with a lenient set of requirements, which included the acceptance of the Thirteenth Amendment and revocation of secession. However, when Congress reassembled at the end of 1865 and new southern Congressmen sought entrance without living up to even the lenient presidential demands, Congress balked. For the next few years, Congress and the president were at odds over Reconstruction policies. The Republican Party coalition of white northerners and southerners and African American freedmen used the opportunity to assume power throughout the southern states.[18]

Among many white southerners, a perception grew that northerners continued to impose their ways on the southern states, leaving the South defenseless against outside oppression. Southerners determined that they should wait until the national environment allowed them an opportunity to end northern oppression. The *Montgomery Advertiser* argued, "The threadbare cant of office-holding demagogues about treason, rebellion and confiscation will be hushed by the mighty hummings and heavings of that gigantic machinery which soon will be built up in the South if we go honestly to work about it. . . . Thus shall we deliver the South from oppression and the whole nation from the ruin of anarchy." Governor James W. Throckmorton perceived similarly: "When a great and gallant people are conquered and overcome, when they are oppressed and spurned, and their misfortune are heaped upon them as crimes, and every means are used to make them the instruments of their own torture and humiliation, it requires the loftiest courage to overcome the animosities and prejudices of the popular heart, and to combat the terrible surroundings of an outraged public sentiment."[19] Southerners felt oppressed, and having laws imposed upon them by the victorious northerners altered their descriptions of oppression.

The result of Congressional Reconstruction was an increase in violence across the southern states. White supremacy organizations like the Ku Klux Klan undermined the political process with a terror campaign against white outsiders and African Americans.[20] Their intimidation tactics were far more successful than those used by the Fenians in Great Britain. In addition, the Democratic Party's leadership worked hard within the political process to regain control of state governments. The South was in political, social, and economic turmoil.

Toward the end of the 1860s, Democratic governments reasserted control in many southern states, and by 1876, only South Carolina, Florida, and Louisiana had Republican governments remaining. Republicans maintained their power because they had U.S. troops to support them. There was also ballot box stuffing and voter intimidation on both sides. The election of 1876 caused a political dilemma. Both Rutherford B. Hays and Samuel J. Tilden were within reach of the presidency, with the votes in Louisiana, South Carolina, and Florida being claimed by both sides. Republicans and Democrats worked out a compromise solution, which eventually allowed Hays to become president but also ended Reconstruction and restored home rule to the southern states.[21]

The end of Reconstruction did not mean that all the accomplishments of racial equality disappeared immediately. Southerners understood that the racial control they had exercised during slavery was gone. Desiring to maintain a racial hierarchy, southern elites implemented segregation to avoid seeing rich African Americans. Segregation was the first step, followed by new laws to undermine the voting rights of African Americans. By the end of the nineteenth century, white segregationist southern elites were solidly in charge of the southern states and would remain so for half a century.[22] Southerners did not win their independence, and they temporarily lost the ability to determine their section's political future, but for most of the century following the Civil War southerners retained autonomy in racial and political matters.

———

Secession had lost. In the 1820s, separatists in Greece and Belgium had enjoyed some high-profile successes. Ireland, Poland, Hungary, Schleswig-Holstein, and the southern Confederacy were unsuccessful with their independence wars in 1830, 1848, or 1861. In the 1860s and 1870s, these five tried one last time to accomplish independence, with mixed results. The Irish, Polish, and Schleswig-Holstein Germans were unable to gain either independence or political autonomy. The Hungarians achieved autonomy within the Austro-Hungarian Empire. After losing the Civil War and being marginalized during Reconstruction, southerners soon regained power and embraced home rule. Secessionists had tried for forty years to gain political rights and to protect their national identities, without much success.

CONCLUSION

"I hear constantly used the terms Unionists and Separatists," said British prime minister William Ewart Gladstone. "But what I want to know is, who are the Unionists? I want to know who are the Separatists? I see this Bill described in newspapers of great circulation, and elsewhere, as a Separation Bill."[1] Gladstone posed these questions in 1886, when the House of Commons debated his proposal for an Irish Home Rule Bill. Gladstone's government suffered defeat, forcing the prime minister to step down after only a few months in office. Timothy Healy, who represented the Unionist district of South Londonderry, in Ulster, quipped, "I would ask the right hon. Gentleman the Prime Minister to remember the words of Frederick Douglas [sic], the Negro orator—'God and one make a majority.'"[2]

Whether Healy intended to draw any connection between Irish and Confederate separatists is unclear. Nevertheless, Gladstone raised important questions in his defense of the bill, questions that had troubled the Atlantic region for the previous fifty years. To contemporary and modern observers alike, the puzzling question was who was a Unionist and who a Separatist, with the answer often remaining shrouded in mystery based on circumstances. For European separatists who had struggled against oppression in 1830 or 1848, in particular, the question was all too real once they arrived in the United States.

When Gladstone stood before the assembled House of Commons in 1886 with his Home Rule Bill, separatism had failed in various independence struggles across the North Atlantic region. The hopes and dreams of an independent Ireland lay buried under the rubble of the Young Ireland and Fenian movements, the hope for an independent Schleswig-Holstein were crushed under a shiny Prussian military boot, and Polish independence desires had taken a frosty march to Russian gallows or Siberia. Nevertheless, hope remained for separatist independence aspirations. After all, failure was not universal, and some nations had gained independence in the course of the nineteenth century.

The autonomy-granting *Ausgleich* infused Hungarians with energy to use their new political freedom against other ethnic minorities in a rigorous Magyarization campaign within the boundaries of their realm, eventually turning the region into a "dungeon of nations." By this point, the United States Supreme Court had declared the civil rights acts passed during the Reconstruction era unconstitutional, which opened the door to discriminatory Jim Crow laws. Like Hungary, the states of the former Confederacy enjoyed home rule two decades after failing to gain independence. Autonomy was not the same as the independence enjoyed by Greece or Belgium, but it was a start.

Regardless of whether the separatists had lost their fight for independence, continued to suffer under oppressive overlords, or had gained home rule, nationalists in all regions, excluding Schleswig-Holstein, had gained a stronger sense of identity and connection with their homeland. Decades of struggle and suffering had allowed the elites to infuse the people with a sense of community. Lacking a coherent national identity, revolutionaries in 1830 and even 1848 struggled to convince the people of the necessity to rebel against oppressive governments. Even where a centuries-old identity existed, as in Poland or Ireland, political, religious, and social divisions often precluded a successful struggle for independence. Separatists not only had to confront their oppressors; they also had to convince the people that oppression of their nationality existed.

Despite growing efforts, creating a national identity was a slow effort. By the end of the nineteenth century, national identities had formed and strengthened to provide nationalists with popular support for their demands. At the same time, the emergence of nation-states allowed new identities to emerge; instead of a national community, people increasingly identified with social classification. An imagined community of suffering people with their shared views on politics, religion, culture, and heritage united people as they demanded freedom from oppression.

For most separatists, the enemy changed little in the course of the century. Still left without self-government or independence, Ireland's hatred for the oppressive British continued to grow. However, Wolfe Tone and Young Ireland's willingness to cooperate with Protestants was a thing of the past. Revolutionary upheaval needed the support and propagation of the Catholic clergy. Irish independence and Catholicism were intimately connected by the end of the century.

In the United States, slaves had always posed a threat to their masters, especially after the Nat Turner uprising rekindled white memories of the bloody Saint Dominigue slave rebellion. At the same time, the emergence of northern immediate abolitionists endangered the southern way of life. Agitators against the established order, regardless of race or gender, were never welcome in the southern states. These antebellum patterns continued in the New South. Free people of color were the "other" that white southern nationalists used to construct a unified white southern community. African Americans also served as scapegoats for problems in Southern society. The process of identity building was ongoing as defeated separatists had to reinforce their ties with the masses.

The need to overcome national oppression was closely associated with the desire for political progress. Ever since the American and French revolutions, people had demanded a say in politics and the right to vote. As much as political leaders in Europe in 1815 hoped to put the new ideas of republican and democratic government behind them, suppression of these political philosophies was impossible and states addressed them in a liberalization of the system. Since 1800, the United States had democratized, allowing virtually the entire white male population to vote. By the 1860s, Ireland and Schleswig-Holstein were part of increasingly democratic states, even if they remained underrepresented. The Russian and Austrian overlords of Poland and Hungary, respectively, retained restrictions with regard to the electoral franchise. Their reputation for autocratic government represented the lack of voice given to the people. One of the demands voiced by many revolutionaries, for a liberalization of the political system and expansion of the electoral franchise, increased in urgency during the nineteenth century.

Democracy, or more specifically representative government, did not mean the inclusion of everybody; property, race, and gender remained a common reason for exclusion. Even so, a democratic system of government offered voices to people, including those oppressed, and a means to bring change to their communities, however much being a minority undermined that ability. By the 1860s, Germany and Great Britain had moved quickly toward universal manhood suffrage. In the German Empire, all men voted in secret elections for their representatives to the Reichstag. The Reform Acts of 1867 and 1884 dramatically increased the number of Britons who could vote, while still falling short of universal manhood suffrage.

Meanwhile, the United States backtracked, limiting the electoral opportunities for African Americans in the southern states by imposing poll taxes, literacy tests, and other limitations. Southern elites were always suspicious of democracy and had embraced a limited republican-democratic system of government. Having temporarily lost their say in government during Reconstruction, white southerners now made efforts to exclude African Americans from the polls.

Even in democracies like Great Britain or Germany, the power of the people was limited. Irish voters sent representatives to Parliament, where Ireland lacked proportional equality with England. Schleswig-Holstein sent delegates to a Reichstag that had limited power in an emperor-chancellor-dominated system of government. Even with more representative governments, separatists still had not accomplished their goals of independence, and political engagement offered only limited opportunities for change.

Nevertheless, by the end of the nineteenth century, separatists had achieved some significant successes. Since the independence of the United States from the British Empire in 1783, all of Spanish America had gained its freedom. Texas had seceded from the Republic of Mexico in the 1830s, and other states of Spanish America faced similar challenges. In Europe, Greece and Belgium were separatist additions to the state system.

However, separatists were rarely successful thereafter. When Poland, Hungary, Ireland, and Schleswig-Holstein challenged their overlords, they threatened to undermine the established international order. Even secessionists in the U.S. South endangered the still youthful country with their demands for protections of human property. In their confrontations, separatists relied on a growing sense of national identity, based in part on ethnic distinctions but also on civic perceptions of a shared cultural, linguistic, political, and historical identity. This imagining of a unique national character was slow to form even in historically independent states like Poland or long-oppressed states like Ireland. As separatist confidence in their identity and their perception of oppression grew, separatist nationalists unsuccessfully used revolutionary upheavals as an outlet to challenge their overlords in 1830, 1848, and 1861.

Hungarian, Irish, Polish, and Schleswig-Holstein German revolutionary separatists had fought against outside oppression for ethnic, national, linguistic, economic, political, or constitutional reasons. They had voiced their feelings in a variety of forms, but many had described their status as a state of slavery—whether political, economic, or social—and demanded an end to their chained existence. Polish and Hungarian nationalists, in particular, perceived of their respective Russian and Austrian overlords not only as oppressors but as enslavers.

However, the younger generation of separatists, fighting in 1848, was more likely to see political oppression, not enslavement. Aristocratic overlords, majority oppression, or violations of constitutional rights were frequently used justifications for separatist uprisings. The use of violence to bring about independence was unsuccessful, due to a lack of planning or the overwhelming odds in favor of the oppressor state. The arguments used by European separatists were remarkably similar to those of southern secessionists; both sought independence from oppressors. Therefore, the U.S. South was not unique or exceptional in its demands to escape northern oppression, abolitionist rabble-rousers, detrimental economic policies, minority status, and violations of constitutional rights. Separatists universally used the same arguments against their oppressors.

When European separatist migrants of the failed 1830 and 1848 uprisings faced southern separatism, upon their arrival in the United States, they had to evaluate how their own experiences and arguments aligned with the two contending sections in the United States.

Many initially assumed they would return to Europe soon for another revolution. As their stay became protracted, separatist exiles returned to politics, searching for new political roles. They faced the country's questions over the expansion of slavery into the western territories, political party realignment, and abolitionism. Radical thinkers of the separatist uprisings from Europe added to the sectional escalation when they infused their language and community organization.

When the election of Abraham Lincoln finally triggered southern secessionism, European separatists faced a difficult choice: Could they remain true to their separatist identity and side with a slave-holding Confederacy whose constitutional rights faced violation by an oppressive, even imperial northern majority? Or would they side with a freedom-embracing North against a slaveholding southern aristocracy, which from its minority status tried to influence U.S. politics in an oppressive fashion? The translation of European experiences and perceptions about oppression meant that most European separatists abhorred the southern cause and fought against separatism. Some, however, perceived that the southern states had just as much right to independence and self-determination as Hungary, Ireland, or Poland had. Experiences and their translation into the sectional conflict in North America determined how European separatists reacted to the secession crisis.

NOTES

INTRODUCTION

1. Stephen Beszedits, *The Libby Prison Diary of Colonel Emeric Szabad*, 75.

2. Joachim Reppmann, program for "Legacy of 1848: German-American History Conference," 1.

3. Robert F. Durden, *The Self-Inflicted Wound*, 6; Ari Helo and Peter S. Onuf, "Jefferson, Morality, and the Problem of Slavery," 583–584; Edmond S. Morgan, *American Slavery, American Freedom*, chapter 18; Gordon S. Wood, *Empire of Liberty*, 514–515.

4. See the argument about political language in the Early Republic advanced in Lance Banning, *The Jeffersonian Persuasion*; and Lee Ward, *The Politics of Liberty in England and Revolutionary America*.

5. William III, "*The Declaration*, October 1688," in Steven C. A. Pincus, ed., *England's Glorious Revolution, 1688–1689*, 43; Colley Cibber, "*Memoir of the Revolution*, 1740," in Pincus, 49.

6. For works showing the evolving nature of politics after 1815, see Hartwig Brandt, *Europe, 1815–1850*; Jacques Droz, *Europe Between Revolutions, 1815–1848*; Dieter Langewiesche, *Europa zwischen Restauration und Revolution, 1815–1849*. The idea of nationalism being the creation of an imagined community is argued in Benedict Anderson, *Imagined Communities*.

7. Johann Gottlieb Fichte, *Addresses to the German Nation*, 136–138, 143–145. For a new study on the need to move beyond the dichotomy of ethnic and civic nationalism, see Timothy Baycroft and Mark Hewitson, eds., *What Is a Nation?*

8. Klemens von Metternich, *Memoirs of Prince Metternich, 1815–1829*, 3:456–463, 469–471, 473–476.

9. Giuseppe Mazzini, "*Manifesto of Young Italy* (1831)," in Stefano Recchia and Nadia Urbinati, eds., *A Cosmopolitanism of Nations*, 35; Mazzini, "*On the Duties of Man* (1841–60)," in Recchia and Urbinati, 96.

10. Giuseppe Mazzini, "General Instructions for the Members of Young Italy," in Nagendranath Gangulee, ed., *Selected Writings*, 129–131.

11. Two of the best works on world history during the nineteenth century are Christopher A. Bayly, *The Birth of the Modern World, 1780–1914*; and Jürgen Osterhammel,

Die Verwandlung der Welt. Neither author is interested in separatism and consider regions like Ireland, Hungary, and Poland to be of small importance.

12. Wolfram Siemann, *Die Deutsche Revolution von 1848/49,* 128. For works on German Forty-Eighters, see Charlotte L. Brancaforte, ed., *The German Forty-Eighters in the United States*; Sabine Freitag, *Friedrich Hecker*; Mischa Honeck, *We Are the Revolutionists*; Bruce Levine, *The Spirit of 1848*; Ernst-Erich Marhencke, *Hans Reimer Claussen*; Andrea Mehrländer, *The Germans of Charleston, Richmond and New Orleans During the Civil War Period, 1850–1870*; Daniel Nagel, *Von republikanischen Deutschen zu deutsch-amerikanischen Republikanern*; Jörg Nagler, *Fremont contra Lincoln*; Justine Davis Randers-Pehrson, *Adolf Douai, 1819–1888*; Joseph R. Reinhart, ed., *August Willich's Gallant Dutchmen*; Joachim Reppmann, *"Freedom, Education and Well-Being for All!"*; Hans L. Trefousse, *Carl Schurz*; Carl Wittke, *Refugees of Revolution*; Adolph E. Zucker, ed., *The Forty-Eighters.*

13. Shearer Davis Bowman, *Masters and Lords*; Enrico Dal Lago, *William Lloyd Garrison and Giuseppe Mazzini*; Don H. Doyle, *The Cause of All Nations*; Andre M. Fleche, *The Revolution of 1861*; Paul Quigley, *Shifting Grounds.*

14. Michael Kammen, "The Problem of American Exceptionalism," 1–43; Ian Tyrrell, "American Exceptionalism in an Age of International History," 1031–1055; Tyrrell, "What Is American Exceptionalism?"; Tyrrell, *Transnational Nation,* 84–93; James McPherson, "Antebellum Southern Exceptionalism," 230–244. Thomas Bender, *A Nation Among Nations,* chapter 3, makes a similar claim. His study of the Civil War era incorporates the uprising of 1848 and various aspects of national unification and military conflict. The contributors to L. Diane Barnes, Brian Schoen, and Frank Towers, eds., *The Old South's Modern Worlds* have argued similarly, but in contrast to McPherson, the authors argue that the southern states were part of the modernizing world. See Elisabeth Gläser and Hermann Wellenreuther, eds., *Bridging the Atlantic,* 2. For recent work placing the U.S. South in world history, see Cornelis Abraham Van Minnen and Manfred Berg, eds., *The U.S. South and Europe*; Jon Smith and Deborah N. Cohn, eds., *Look Away!*

15. Jean-Pierre Cabestan and Aleksandar Pavković, *Secessionism and Separatism in Europe and Asia,* 1–2. Richard Franklin Bensel indicates that the "northern oppression," or Union, interpretation appeared imperialistic from a southern perspective. Bensel, *Yankee Leviathan,* 62–63. Bridget L. Coggins asserts that the United States and the Confederate States were both secessionist creations. Coggins, "The History of Secession," in Aleksandar Pavković and Peter Radan, eds., *The Ashgate Research Companion to Secession,* 26.

16. Coggins, "History of Secession," 24, 32–35; James Mayall, "Secession and International Order," in Pavković and Radan, *Ashgate Research Companion,* 1–6, 14; Aleksandar Pavković and Peter Radan, "Introduction: What Is Secession?," in *Ashgate Research Companion*; Radan, "Secession in Constitutional Law," in Pavković and Radan, 333–334; Michel Seymour, "Internal Self-Determination and Secession," in Pavković and Radan, chapter 21.

17. Don H. Doyle, "Union and Secession in the Family of Nations," in Don H. Doyle, ed., *Secession as an International Phenomenon*, 1–5.

18. Michael Mann, *The Sources of Social Power*, 20. Also see Lloyd S. Kramer, *Nationalism in Europe and America*, 1. Interestingly enough for such an important work, Mann does not include Poland, Latin America, or the African continent in his analysis. Although Irish independence desires briefly appear, because of the impact of the American Revolution on British policy makers, Ireland, with its lack of industrialization, is otherwise of little importance to Mann. His treatment of Hungary is similar.

19. Michael Jeismann, "Nation, Identity, and Enmity: Towards a Theory of Political Identification," in Baycroft and Hewitson, *What Is a Nation?*, 27; Jörn Leonhard, "Nation-States and War: European and Transatlantic Perspectives," in Baycroft and Hewitson, 63–80; Maiken Umbach, "Nation and Region: Regionalism in Modern European Nation-States," in Baycroft and Hewitson, 231–254.

20. Novembrists are Poles who participated in the November 1830 uprising against Russia. The term *Dreissiger* has been used primarily for refugees from Germany who escaped the political repression following the Hambacher Fest in the early 1830s.

21. Doyle, *Secession as an International Phenomenon*. Many of the examples and evidence provided in Pavković and Radan, *Ashgate Research Companion* relate to the twentieth century. Similarly, Metta Spencer's compilation *Separatism: Democracy and Disintegration* starts in the late nineteenth century with the demise of the Austro-Hungarian Empire. Wayne J. Norman, *Negotiating Nationalism* acknowledges the American Civil War as a separatist and nation-building incident. He also indicates that the intellectual origins of later separatist movements trace back into the nineteenth century, but the century's events are of little concern for him.

22. See, for example, Honeck, *We Are the Revolutionists*.

CHAPTER ONE

1. Lucien Leopold Jottrand, *Louis de Potter*, 72–73. Original text reads, "Brave peuple belge, vous avez glorieusement vaincu. Sachez profiter de la victoire. Vos lâches ennemis sont dans la stupeur. . . . Liberté pour tous! Égalité de tous devant le pouvoir suprême: la nation; devant sa volonté: la loi. Vous avez écrasé le despotisme; par votre confiance dans le pouvoir que vous avez créé vous saurez vous tenir en garde contre l'anarchie et ses funestes suites. Les Belges ne doivent faire trembler que leurs ennemis."

2. Bridget L. Coggins, "The History of Secession: An Overview," in Aleksandar Pavković and Peter Radan, eds., *The Ashgate Research Companion to Secession*, chapter 2; Schmücker, "Remedial Theories of Secession," in Pavković and Radan, chapter 21; Seymour, "Internal Self-Determination and Secession," in Pavković and Radan, chapter 22; Mark Edelman Boren, *Student Resistance*, 28–34; William Carr, *The Origins of the Wars of German Unification*, 25–32; Walter Rüegg, *A History of the University in Europe*, 3:285–286.

3. For the literature on the Greek independence struggle, see David Brewer, *The Greek War of Independence*; Richard Clogg, ed., *The Movement for Greek Independence, 1770–1821*; Douglas Dakin, *The Greek Struggle for Independence, 1821–1833*.

4. For the literature on the French Revolution of 1830, see Bertrand Goujon, *Monarchies Postrévolutionnaires, 1814–1848*, chapter 4; J. Lucas-Dubreton, *The Restoration and the July Monarchy*.

5. J. A. Betley, *Belgium and Poland in International Relations, 1830–1831*; Robert Demoulin, *La Révolution de 1830*, chapters 1, 6–7.

6. R. F. Leslie, *Polish Politics and the Revolution of November 1830*, 9, 48, 98, 104–105, 109–113, 115.

7. Harro Harring, *Memoiren über Polen unter russischer Herrschaft*, 1:8, 2:224–225. The German original reads:

> Vergebens, ach umsonst sind die Gedanken
> An Rettung, den der Freiheit golden Licht
> Durchleuchtet nie des Despotismus Schranken,
> So lang' der Sklave nicht die Fesseln bricht.
> Das Reich der Willkür wird sobald nicht wanken,
> Denn das Gefühl der Freiheit lebt dort nicht
> Im Knechte, der den Herrn nur treuer liebt,
> Je öft'rer dieser ihm die Knute gibt.

8. Leslie, *Polish Politics*, 121–123, 126–127, 129.

9. Leslie, *Polish Politics*, 127, 138–140.

10. "Poland," *The Times* (London), February 12, 1831; Leslie, *Polish Politics*, 142–144, 152, 158–159.

11. "Tochman Kacper," in Rafał Gerber, *Studenci Uniwersytetu Warszawskiego 1808–1831*, 219; Mark F. Bielski, *Sons of the White Eagle in the American Civil War*, 65; Harro Harring, *Poland Under the Dominion of Russia*, 188. Since both Harring and Szymanski served in the same unit in the uprising, the two likely worked together to publish Harring's book in English. See also Leslie, *Polish Politics*, 163, 166–167; Lois Eugenia Rodgers, "Count Adam Gurowski," 1–2.

12. Leslie, *Polish Politics*, 171, 178, 194–195, 198–199, 212.

13. "Poland," *The Times* (London), June 15, 1831.

14. Leslie, *Polish Politics*, 234–235, 240–241, 243–244, 250–251, 252, 256–257.

15. "Polish Army," *The Times* (London), November 1, 1831; *Buffalo Journal and General Advertiser*, quoted in Florian Stasik, *Polish Political Emigrés in the United States of America, 1831–1864*, 16.

16. Joachim Lelewel, *Geschichte Polens*, 535.

17. For works on the English conquest of Ireland, see Nicholas P. Canny, *Making Ireland British, 1580–1650*; Steven G. Ellis, *Ireland in the Age of the Tudors, 1447–1603*; Pádraig Lenihan, *Consolidating Conquest*; John McGurk, *The Elizabethan Conquest of Ireland*. For works on the Rebellion of 1798 and Theobald Wolfe Tone, see Marianne

Elliott, *Wolfe Tone*; Jim Smyth, *The Men of No Property*; Kevin Whelan, *The Tree of Liberty*.

18. Theobald Wolfe Tone and William Theobald Wolfe Tone, *Memoirs of Theobald Wolfe Tone*, 1:xiv–xv, 263. Emphasis in original.

19. Daniel O'Connell and John O'Connell, *Life and Speeches of Daniel O'Connell, M.P.*, 51.

20. Angela F. Murphy, *American Slavery, Irish Freedom*, 30–31.

21. Aidan Hegarty, *John Mitchel*, 15, 17–18; James Quinn, *John Mitchel*, 4–5.

22. Michael Cavanagh, *Memoirs of General Thomas Francis Meagher*, 13, 19, 27–28; John M. Hearne and Rory T. Cornish, "An Introduction," in *Thomas Francis Meagher*, 1.

23. Howell Purdue and Elizabeth Purdue, *Pat Cleburne, Confederate General*, 5–8; Craig L. Symonds, *Stonewall of the West*, 11–15.

24. Oliver Auge and Burkhard Büsing, eds., *Der Vertrag von Ripen 1460 und die Anfänge der politischen Partizipation in Schleswig-Holstein, im Reich und in Nordeuropa*. Due to the contested nature of the region and the changes brought to Schleswig-Holstein in the twentieth century, the Schleswig-Holstein section will use both the Danish and German names for locations to illustrate the importance for both sides in this national conflict.

25. Gerd Steinwascher, *Die Oldenburger*.

26. "Waterloo Rede," in Anton Springer, *Friedrich Christoph Dahlmann*, 1:463–472. Dahlmann used the German term "*Knechtschaft*" in his speech. A *Knecht* is a slave or servant. The German word for "slave" as applicable to chattel slavery is *Sklave*. However, both the Sklave and the Knecht have limited legal rights, Sklaven more so than Knechte. It seems appropriate to translate *Knecht* here as "slave," since Dahlmann means individuals lacking political, social, or economic rights. Ulrich Lange, ed., *Geschichte Schleswig-Holsteins*, 285–286.

27. Jens U. Lornsen, *Die Unions-Verfassung Dänemarks und Schleswigholsteins*; Lornsen, *Über das Verfassungswerk in Schleswigholstein*; Manfred Jessen-Klingenberg, *Standpunkte zur neueren Geschichte Schleswig-Holsteins*, 45–54; Lange, *Geschichte Schleswig-Holsteins*, 428.

28. Theodor Olshausen to Justus Olshausen, November 27, 1822; July 31, 1824; February 4, 1828; July 25, 1828; April 15, 1829; October 1829; in *Theodor Olshausen 1802–1869*, 11, 13–14, 36–37, 49, 80–82, 88–89, 95–97; Karl Lorentzen, "Theodore Olshausen," in Allgemeine Deutsche Biographie, 24:330.

29. Ernst-Erich Marhencke, *Hans Reimer Claussen*, 25; Nikolaus Schmidt, "Hans Reimer Claussen," 3–4; Gerd Stolz, *Hans Reimer Claussen*, 7.

30. Rudolph M. Schleiden, *Jugenderinnerungen eines Schleswig-Holsteiners*, 120–123. Schleiden then worked for the German American Mining Company of Elberfeld, in Mexico. The Prussian minister in Washington (1846–1871), Friedrich Joseph Karl von Gerolt, joined the Deutsch-Amerikanischen Bergwerksverein Ebersfeld from 1824 to 1827 and worked in Mexico at the same time that Christian Schleiden was with the Verein in Mexico. Schleiden died in Mexico in November 1833.

31. István Deák, *The Lawful Revolution*, 1, 3–4, 41–44, 47–53; Laszlo Deme, *The Radical Left in the Hungarian Revolution of 1848*, 1, 4–5.

32. István Széchenyi and Joseph Vojdisek, *Ueber den Credit nebst einem Anhange enthaltend Ammerkungen und Zusätze von einem ungarischen Patrioten*, 273; Deák, *Lawful Revolution*, 16–17; Deme, *Radical Left*, 6–7; Andreas Oplatka, "Einführung: István Széchenyi-Der größte Ungar," in István Fazekas, Stefan Malfèr, and Péter Tusor, eds., *Széchenyi, Kossuth, Batthyány, Deák*, 13, 15; István Széchenyi and Michael Paziazi, *Licht oder aufhellende Bruchstücke zur Berichtigung einiger Irrthümer und Vorurtheile*, 248.

33. Henry W. DePuy, *Kossuth and His Generals*, 122.

34. Deák, *Lawful Revolution*, 20–21, 24–30, 33, 35; Zoltán Fónagy, "Einführung: Lajos Kossuth-Ein biographischer Überblick," in Fazekas, Malfèr, and Tusor, *Széchenyi, Kossuth, Batthyány, Deák*, 63–64.

35. Stephen Beszedits, "Alexander Asboth"; István K. Vida, *Hungarian Émigrés in the American Civil War*, 80, 89.

36. "Major Zagonyi," *Frank Leslie's Illustrated Newspaper*, November 28, 1861.

37. DePuy, *Kossuth and His Generals*, 346; Vida, *Hungarian Émigrés in the American Civil War*, 18–20.

38. Thomas Jefferson to William Smith, April 22, 1820, in John W. Bell and William Smith, *Memoirs of Governor William Smith, of Virginia*, 385; Joseph R. Stromberg, "Republicanism, Federalism, and Secession in the South, 1790–1865," in David Gordon, ed., *Secession, State, and Liberty*, 113.

39. Jeremy Black, *The War of 1812 in the Age of Napoleon*; Jon Latimer, *1812: War with America*; Thomas J. DiLorenzo, "Yankee Confederates: New England Secession Movements Prior to the War Between the States," in Gordon, *Secession, State, and Liberty*, 146–147; Alan Taylor, *The Civil War of 1812*.

40. Thomas Jefferson to John Holmes, April 22, 1820, in Ezra B. Chase, *Teachings of Patriots and Statesmen*, 367; Jon Meacham, *American Lion*, 53–54; Sean Wilentz, *Andrew Jackson*, 45.

41. William W. Freehling, *The Road to Disunion*, 1:213–215; James H. Hammond diary, December 27, 1850, quoted in William M. Meigs, *The Life of John Caldwell Calhoun*, 1:55, note 10; Manisha Sinha, *The Counterrevolution of Slavery*, 10–11.

42. Freehling, *Road to Disunion*, 1:255–257; Sinha, *Counterrevolution of Slavery*, 16–17.

43. John Calhoun, "South Carolina Exposition and Protest," in *The Papers of John C. Calhoun*, 10:533; Freehling, *Road to Disunion*, 1:257–258; Sinha, *Counterrevolution of Slavery*, 23.

44. Freehling, *Road to Disunion*, 273–275; Robert Tinkler, *James Hamilton of South Carolina*, 121.

45. Freehling, *Road to Disunion*, 276–277; Sinha, *Counterrevolution of Slavery*, 40, 43, 51.

46. Freehling, *Road to Disunion*, 278–279, 281.

47. Freehling, *Road to Disunion*, 282–284.

48. *Proceedings and Debates of the Virginia State Convention of 1829–1830*, 158–159; Freehling, *Road to Disunion*, 162–177.

49. *Proceedings and Debates*, 88.

50. Freehling, *Road to Disunion*, 285.

CHAPTER TWO

1. Adam J. Czajkowski, quoted in Robert Allen Berry, "Czartoryski and the Balkan Policies of the Hôtel Lambert, 1832–1847," 66.

2. For examples of this geographically limited approach, see Peter Jones, *The 1848 Revolutions*; Roger Price, *The Revolutions of 1848*. Among the better works is Dieter Dowe et al., *Europe in 1848*. The only Atlantic study of the Revolution of 1848 is Guy Thomson, ed., *The European Revolutions of 1848 and the Americas*. A good example is the Frankfurt Parliament in the German states, with its many political groupings. For works on the Frankfurt Parliament, see Frank Eyck, *The Frankfurt Parliament, 1848–49*; Brian E. Vick, *Defining Germany*. Some early historians of 1848 have presented a Marxist, economic history in which industrialization uprooted people and caused an unbearable environment. However, only in Great Britain, and arguably in Belgium, did there exist a fully developed and self-conscious working class. France and the Prussian Rhineland continued to lag behind in industrial development. See Priscilla Robertson, *Revolutions of 1848*; Jonathan Sperber, *Rhineland Radicals*.

3. Hans H. Hahn, "The Polish Nation in the Revolution of 1846–49," in Dieter et al., *Europe in 1848*, 170–174.

4. Mark F. Bielski, *Sons of the White Eagle in the American Civil War*, 114, 157; Hahn, "Polish Nation," 175–177. Little is known about the role of Kargé and Krzyżanowski in the course of 1848. Also see James S. Pula, *For Liberty and Justice*, 4–8.

5. Hans Reimer Claussen, "Die Norderdithmarsische Landesverfassung betreffend," *Dithmarsische Zeitung*, June 28, 1834, July 5, 1834, July 19, 1834, July 26, 1834, August 2, 1834; Ernst-Erich Marhencke, *Hans Reimer Claussen*, 32–35; Nikolaus Schmidt, "Hans Reimer Claussen," 5–7, 11, 13, 16–18.

6. *Correspondenz-Blatt* May 25, 1839; June 19, 1839; June 26, 1839.

7. Patent of the King of Denmark, July 8, 1846; FO 22/153, National Archive, Kew Gardens, United Kingdom; *Correspondenz-Blatt* May 4, 1839; Rudolph M. Schleiden, *Erinnerungen eines Schleswig-Holsteiners*, 93–95, 105–107; Claus Bjørn, *1848*, 53–54.

8. Schleiden, *Erinnerungen*, 243, 247, 249–250, 252.

9. Schleiden, *Erinnerungen*, 258–259, 261–262; Marhencke, *Hans Reimer Claussen*, 137–139.

10. Provisional government proclamation, March 24, 1848, in Rudolph M. Schleiden, ed., *Aktenstücke zur neuesten Schleswig-Holsteinischen Geschichte*, 2:1–2; Schleiden, *Erinnerungen*, 265–266, 268, 277–281; Ulrich Lange, *Geschichte Schleswig-Holsteins*, 442.

11. Danish King to Holstein Deputation, March 24, 1848, Fasc. 6, Nachlass Schleiden, Christian Albrecht Universität, Kiel, Germany.

12. Schleiden, *Aktenstücke*, 2:131-146.

13. Schleiden to provisional government, March 29, 1848; March 30, 1848, Fasc. 1, Nachlass Schleiden, Christian Albrecht Universität; Rudolph M. Schleiden, *Schleswig-Holsteins erste Erhebung, 1848-1849*, 6-8; Dr. Jucho, *Verhandlungen des Deutschen Parlaments*, 1:30-31; protocol of March 28, 1848, in Schleiden, *Aktenstücke*, 2:44-46.

14. Franz Wigard, *Stenographischer Bericht über die Verhandlungen der Deutschen Constituirenden Nationalversammlung zu Frankfurt am Main*, 1:445-448; Marhencke, *Hans Reimer Claussen*, 148-150, 190-191, 193-195; Schmidt, "Hans Reimer Claussen," 31-33, 36, 38.

15. Friedrich Graf von Reventlou and Wilhelm Hartwig Beseler to Schleiden, April 15, 1848, Fasc. 4, Nachlass Schleiden, Christian Albrecht Universität; Schleiden to provisional government, June 20, 1848, in Schleiden, *Aktenstücke*, 2:114, 321-322; Schleiden, *Schleswig-Holsteins erste Erhebung*, 42, 58, 86-88; Henry Wynn to Lord John Palmerston, May 8, 1848; May 20, 1848, FO 22/162, National Archives, Kew Gardens; Nick Svendsen, *The First Schleswig-Holstein War, 1848-1850*, 46-67. Svendsen's book is highly problematic, since the author cites such online encyclopedias as Wikipedia.

16. Friedrich Hedde, *Kein schimpflicher Vertrag mit Dänemark*.

17. Marhencke, *Hans Reimer Claussen*, 156-158; Schmidt, "Hans Reimer Claussen," 42.

18. Schleiden, *Schleswig-Holsteins erste Erhebung*, 349, 352-360; Rudolph M. Schleiden, *Schleswig-Holstein im zweiten Kriegsjahre, 1849-1850*, 2, 54, 144-145; Gerd Stolz, *Die Schleswig-Holsteinische Erhebung: Die Nationale Auseinandersetzung in und um Schleswig-Holstein von 1848/51*; Svendsen, *First Schleswig-Holstein War*, 83-103.

19. July 25, 1850, page 61; July 27, 1850, page 64; January 6, 1851, page 200-201, book 13, Schleswig-Holsteinische Landesbibliothek, Kiel, Germany; Wilhelm von Thümen and Alexander Graf von Mensdorff to Statthalter, January 3, 1851; protocol of January 6, 1851, in Schleiden, *Aktenstücke*, 1:9, 11-13; Schleiden, *Schleswig-Holstein im zweiten Kriegsjahre*, 228-229, 266-267, 360-362, 378-379; Svendsen, *First Schleswig-Holstein War*, 107-114, 116-121.

20. Statthalter to Staatsrat, January 8, 1851; proclamation of February 1, 1851, in Schleiden, *Aktenstücke*, 1:33, 113.

21. István Deák, *The Lawful Revolution*, 66-67; Henry W. DePuy, *Kossuth and His Generals*, xvii.

22. Deák, *Lawful Revolution*, 70-72, 76; Laszlo Deme, *The Radical Left in the Hungarian Revolution*, 16-17.

23. Deák, *Lawful Revolution*, 85-86; Deme, *Radical Left*, 26-37.

24. Deák, *Lawful Revolution*, 79, 110, 120; Deme, *Radical Left*, 49, 51-52, 56.

25. Deák, *Lawful Revolution*, 126-130.

26. DePuy, *Kossuth and His Generals*, 140-149.

27. DePuy, *Kossuth and His Generals*, 149-152.

28. Deák, *Lawful Revolution*, 135-137, 150; Deme, *Radical Left*, 58-61.

29. Deák, *Lawful Revolution*, 155-156, 159; DePuy, *Kossuth and His Generals*, 153-155.

30. Deák, *Lawful Revolution*, 153, 159, 165; DePuy, *Kossuth and His Generals*, 161-163.

31. Deák, *Lawful Revolution*, 161, 164, 167, 169, 180-181; Deme, *Radical Left*, 99, 117.

32. "Major Zagonyi," *Frank Leslie's Illustrated Newspaper*, November 28, 1861; István K. Vida, *Hungarian Émigrés in the American Civil War,* 89; Deák, *Lawful Revolution,* 208–212, 214, 224, 238–239, 248–249; Beke László et al., eds., *Nemzeti Évfordulóink 2010,* 11.

33. Deák, *Lawful Revolution,* 252–255; DePuy, *Kossuth and His Generals,* 199–200; László et al., *Nemzeti Évfordulóink,* 11.

34. Deák, *Lawful Revolution,* 261; DePuy, *Kossuth and His Generals,* 203–204.

35. DePuy, *Kossuth and His Generals,* 204–205.

36. DePuy, *Kossuth and His Generals,* 206–207, 211, 214, 217, 223–224.

37. Deák, *Lawful Revolution,* 267, 279, 284–285, 302, 306–307; DePuy, *Kossuth and His Generals,* 249; László et al., *Nemzeti Évfordulóink,* 11.

38. Deák, *Lawful Revolution,* 316–317; DePuy, *Kossuth and His Generals,* 253–254

39. Deák, *Lawful Revolution,* 323–327, 329–331; DePuy, *Kossuth and His Generals,* 259, 261–262.

40. Stephen Beszedits, "Alexander Asboth"; Deák, *Lawful Revolution,* 327; DePuy, *Kossuth and His Generals,* 285–288.

41. Aidan Hegarty, *John Mitchel,* 26–28; Robert Sloan, *William Smith O'Brien and the Young Ireland Rebellion of 1848,* 44–47.

42. John Mitchel, *The Crusade of the Period,* 97–98, 100–101.

43. Mitchel, *Crusade of the Period,* 128–130, 137, 149; Sloan, *William Smith O'Brien,* 89; Craig L. Symonds, *Stonewall of the West,* 18.

44. Mitchel, *Crusade of the Period,* 122–123; Sloan, *William Smith O'Brien,* 111, 122, 133–134, 146.

45. Symonds, *Stonewall of the West,* 17, 20–21; Howell Purdue and Elizabeth Purdue, *Pat Cleburne, Confederate General,* 8–9.

46. Michael Cavanagh, *Memoirs of General Thomas Francis Meagher,* 49–50.

47. Mitchel, *Crusade of the Period,* 160, 165; James Quinn, *John Mitchel,* 10; Sloan, *William Smith O'Brien,* 157.

48. Thomas Francis Meagher, February 16, 1846; March 2, 1846; June 15, 1846, in *Speeches on the Legislative Independence of Ireland,* 12, 31–32, 70.

49. Meagher, February 16, 1846; March 2, 1846; April 6, 1846, in *Speeches,* 12, 15, 29, 30–31, 33, 40.

50. Sloan, *William Smith O'Brien,* 158, 161; Hegarty, *John Mitchel,* 42–43; Quinn, *John Mitchel,* 13–14.

51. Meagher, July 28, 1846, in *Speeches,* 81–90.

52. Cavanagh, *Memoirs of General Thomas Francis Meagher,* 66; Hegarty, *John Mitchel,* 42–43; Sloan, *William Smith O'Brien,* 162; Quinn, *John Mitchel,* 14.

53. Hegarty, *John Mitchel,* 33–35; Mitchel, *Crusade of the Period,* 187–189; Sloan, *William Smith O'Brien,* 182.

54. Meagher, January 13, 1847, in *Speeches,* 98–102, 104, 111; Cavanagh, *Memoirs of General Thomas Francis Meagher,* 76–77; Hegarty, *John Mitchel,* 44; Sloan, *William Smith O'Brien,* 180.

55. Meagher, February 4, 1848, in *Speeches,* 212–213, 215, 217–218.

56. Meagher, April 7, 1847, in *Speeches,* 127–131, 134, 137.

57. John Mitchel, "To the Right Hon. The Earl of Clarendon," *United Irishman,* March 25, 1848; Hegarty, *John Mitchel,* 54–55, 59; Mitchel, *Crusade of the Period,* 259, 261, 264; Quinn, *John Mitchel,* 22–23, 27–28, 34–35.

58. Cavanagh, *Memoirs of General Thomas Francis Meagher,* 106, 109.

59. Meagher, March 15, 1848, in *Speeches,* 247, 252–254; Sloan, *William Smith O'Brien,* 218–219.

60. Meagher, April 14, 1848, in *Speeches,* 263.

61. Cavanagh, *Memoirs of General Thomas Francis Meagher,* 151–158; Sloan, *William Smith O'Brien,* 221–223.

62. Cavanagh, *Memoirs of General Thomas Francis Meagher,* 99, 202–203; Hegarty, *John Mitchel,* 63, 65–67; Mitchel, *Crusade of the Period,* 286–287; Sloan, *William Smith O'Brien,* 225, 229.

63. Meagher, June 6, 1848, in *Speeches,* 274, 276, 280; Cavanagh, *Memoirs of General Thomas Francis Meagher,* 206; Sloan, *William Smith O'Brien,* 235.

64. Cavanagh, *Memoirs of General Thomas Francis Meagher,* 238–239; Sloan, *William Smith O'Brien,* 246–247, 250, 253, 256–258, 267.

65. Sloan, *William Smith O'Brien,* 270, 276–278.

66. Cavanagh, *Memoirs of General Thomas Francis Meagher,* 291–292; Mitchel, *Crusade of the Period,* 305–309; Sloan, *William Smith O'Brien,* 281, 296–298.

67. Mitchel, *Crusade of the Period,* 317, 322–323.

68. "The Wilmot Proviso's Exclusion," *DeBow's Review* 4 (December 1847), 557; Sean Wilentz, *The Rise of American Democracy,* 595–599.

69. *Congressional Globe,* House of Representatives, Thirtieth Congress, 2nd Session, 519–520.

70. Walter R. Houghton, *Conspectus of the History of Political Parties and the Federal Government,* 41–42.

71. John C. Calhoun, "Resolutions on the Slave Questions," February 19, 1847, in Richard K. Crallé, ed., *Speeches of John C. Calhoun,* 347–348.

72. This work will refer to "fire-eaters," avoiding the often used term "radicals." Especially in light of the inclusion of Europeans, who supported radical ideas like democracy or communism, calling the fire-eaters radical seems misplaced. They were reactionary in political views, given that they desired to restore an older political order. See Eric H. Walther, *The Fire-Eaters*; Walther, *William Lowndes Yancey and the Coming of the Civil War*; Herman Vandenburg Ames, *John C. Calhoun and the Secession Movement of 1850,* 23–25; Merrill D. Peterson, *The Great Triumvirate,* 426–427.

73. Daniel W. Howe, *What Hath God Wrought*; Wilentz, *Rise of American Democracy,* 618, 625.

74. Holman Hamilton, *Prologue to Conflict*; Michael A. Morrison, *Slavery and the American West,* 96–131.

75. Avery Craven, *The Growth of Southern Nationalism, 1848–1861,* chapter 4; Elizabeth R. Varon, *Disunion!,* 223–231.

CHAPTER THREE

1. James M. Bergquist, *Daily Life in Immigrant America, 1820–1870*, xvi–xvii, 3–7, 11–14, 15–16.

2. John Mitchel, *Jail Journal*, 37, 62, 86, 127–129, 145, 155–156, 190, 230, 237–240, 261–269.

3. "Meagher Demonstration," *Daily Herald* (Cleveland, OH), June 10, 1852; *Savannah* (GA) *Morning News*, June 5, 1852; Michael Cavanagh, *Memoirs of General Thomas Francis Meagher*, 307–309.

4. "Thomas F. Meagher," *Semi-Weekly Ohio Statesman* (Columbus), August 10, 1852; "Thomas Francis Meagher," *Weekly Herald* (New York), June 12, 1852; Cavanagh, *Memoirs of General Thomas Francis Meagher*, 309–310, 314, 321–322, 324.

5. *Daily Herald* (Cleveland, OH), December 5, 1853; Mitchel, *Jail Journal*, 318–319, 325, 331–332, 339, 345–346, 349, 356, 370.

6. Craig L. Symonds, *Stonewall of the West*, 24, 26–27; Howell Purdue and Elizabeth Purdue, *Pat Cleburne, Confederate General*, 23–26.

7. István Deák, *The Lawful Revolution*, 338–341; István Fazekas, Stefan Malfèr, and Péter Tusor, eds., *Széchenyi, Kossuth, Batthyány, Deák*, 67–77.

8. Deák, *Lawful Revolution*, 341; Stephen Beszedits, "Alexander Asboth." Alexander Sándor Asbóth was among the group of close followers of Lajos Kossuth who were housed at this prison.

9. Henry W. DePuy, *Kossuth and His Generals*, 317–343.

10. Beszedits, "Alexander Asboth"; Deák, *Lawful Revolution*, 342; István K. Vida, *Hungarian Émigrés in the American Civil War*, 8–10, 12–13.

11. Eugene Pivány, *Hungarians in the American Civil War*, 8; Vida, *Hungarian Émigrés*, 21–22, 27, 29–34. Bela Estvàn is frequently mentioned among the Hungarian Forty-Eighter migrants. Historians like Ella Lonn, Dean Mahin, and Stephen Beszedits have described Estvàn as a Hungarian migrant of a variety of complex and perplexing identities. The problems with Estvàn begin with his claim that he left Hungary for the United States, settling in Richmond, Virginia, and had served in the Crimean War. Yet he could not have resided in the United States for thirteen years when the Civil War started and also have served in the Crimean War. A close examination of Estvàn by István K. Vida indicates that Estvàn's entire identity seems false and that Estvàn was, in reality, an Austrian. There is no agreement yet among historians about whether Estvàn was genuine or a con artist. See Stephen Beszedits, "Bela Estvàn: A Hungarian Officer of the Confederate Army," *Vasvary Collection Newsletter* 37 (2007); Ella Lonn, *Foreigners in the Confederacy*, 175; Vida, *Hungarian Émigrés*, 100–109.

12. Vida, *Hungarian Émigrés*, 34–35, 37, 40–41, 44, 47, 49, 80, 89. There is some indication that during the 1850s, after marrying Amanda Schweiger, Charles Zagonyi might have worked as a tailor.

13. Florian Stasik, *Polish Political Emigrés in the United States of America, 1831–1864*, vii, x; Lois Eugenia Rodgers, "Count Adam Gurowski," 18–30.

14. "Tochman Kacper," in Rafał Gerber, *Studenci Uniwersytetu Warszawskiego 1808–1831*, 219.

15. Mark F. Bielski, *Sons of the White Eagle in the American Civil War*, 65–66.

16. Bielski, *Sons of the White Eagle*, 159; Mirosława Kruszewska, "*Pierwsi Polacy w Ameryce*" [The First Poles in America], 10–11; Stasik, *Polish Political Emigrés*, 115

17. "Lettres Patentes du Roi de Danemarc, concernant l'Amnistie pour les Duches de Slesvig et de Holstein," March 29, 1852, British and Foreign State Papers, 41:1059–1060.

18. Theodor Olshausen to Justus Olshausen, June 14, 1851; July 12, 1851; November 16, 1851; T. Olshausen to Zoe Olshausen, April 20, 1855, in *Theodor Olshausen 1802–1869*, 140–146, 179. While the letter to his brother indicated his departure to New Orleans, likely in an effort to confuse potential prying eyes, historian Joachim Reppmann has claimed that Olshausen had arrived in New York instead. For a study of Germans in Saint Louis, see Kristen Layne Anderson, *Abolitionizing Missouri*.

19. T. Olshausen to J. Olshausen, November 16, 1851, in *Theodor Olshausen 1802–1869*, 141–146; H. R. Claussen to Wilhelm Hans Ahlmann, September 17, 1852, in Holger Andersen, *Idstedt und Danach*, 82, 87. For other secondary source assessments of the letters, see Ernst-Erich Marhencke, *Hans Reimer Claussen*, 278–284, 291; Nikolaus Schmidt, "Hans Reimer Claussen," 52–55; Gerd Stolz, *Hans Reimer Claussen*, 14.

20. H. R. Claussen to Ahlmann, September 20, 1852, in Andersen, *Idstedt und Danach*, 90–91.

21. Nachlass Dr. Rudolph M. Schleiden, December 29, 1850, book 13, 191–192; January 3, 1853, book 15, 172; March 11, 1853, book 15, 201; June 22, 1853, book 15, 275–278; June 30, 1853, book 15, 285–286, Schleswig-Holsteinische Landesbibliothek; Rudolph M. Schleiden, *Schleswig-Holsteins erste Erhebung, 1848–1849*, 11.

CHAPTER FOUR

1. John C. Calhoun, March 4, 1850, in *The Papers of John C. Calhoun*, 27:199.

2. Theodor Olshausen to Justus Olshausen, November 16, 1851, in *Theodor Olshausen 1802–1869*, 141–146; Lajos Kossuth, December 27, 1851; February 7, 1852, in *Select Speeches of Kossuth*, 131, 218; Donald S. Spencer, *Louis Kossuth and Young America*.

3. Kossuth, April 3, 1852, in *Select Speeches of Kossuth*, 296.

4. Michael Cavanagh, *Memoirs of General Thomas Francis Meagher*, 326, 329.

5. T. Olshausen to J. Olshausen, November 5, 1855, in *Theodor Olshausen 1802–1869*, 189; Cavanagh, *Memoirs of General Thomas Francis Meagher*, 367; Howell Purdue and Elizabeth Purdue, *Pat Cleburne, Confederate General*, 44; James Quinn, *John Mitchel*, 55–56; Craig L. Symonds, *Stonewall of the West*, 35–36, 38.

6. W. Barksdale, March 29, 1854; A. Harlan, May 19, 1854; House of Representatives, Thirty-Third Congress, 1st Session, *Congressional Globe*, 472, 1002; Michael A. Morrison, *Slavery and the American West*, 142–148; David M. Potter, *The Impending Crisis, 1848–1861*, 154–167.

7. While the Germans have been given credit in assisting the formation of the Republican Party, their role in Iowa remains elusive. See lack of reference in William E. Gienapp, *The Origins of the Republican Party, 1852–1856*. For German support for the free soil ideology, see Mischa Honeck, *We Are the Revolutionists*, 32–33, 67–68, 109; Bruce Levine, "Immigrants, Class, and Politics: German-American Working People and the Fight Against Slavery," in Charlotte L. Brancaforte, ed., *The German Forty-Eighters in the United States*, 119–140.

8. "John Mitchel's Proclamation to the Irish," *Weekly Herald* (New York), April 1, 1854; Quinn, *John Mitchel*, 54; Cavanagh, *Memoirs of General Thomas Francis Meagher*, 344. For works on the Crimean War, see Orlando Figes, *The Crimean War: A History*; Andrew Lambert, *The Crimean War*; Werner E. Mosse, *The Rise and Fall of the Crimean System, 1855–71*; Paul W. Schroeder, *Austria, Great Britain, and the Crimean War*.

9. Adam Gurowski, *Russia and Its People*, 11–12, 17, 56, 81, 91, 111, 113, 230; Lois Eugenia Rodgers, "Count Adam Gurowski," 26–27.

10. Gurowski, *Russia and Its People*, 236, 254, 260, 315.

11. Adam Gurowski, *The Turkish Question*, 7; Gurowski, *Russia and Its People*, 286, 292.

12. John Mitchel, *Jail Journal*, 358–359, 361–362. For works on the southern desire to expand into the Caribbean, see Robert E. May, *The Southern Dream of a Caribbean Empire, 1854–1861*; May, *Manifest Destiny's Underworld*.

13. Cavanagh, *Memoirs of General Thomas Francis Meagher*, 343, 347.

14. Eugene Pivány, *Hungarians in the American Civil War*, 9; Louis A. Schlesinger, "Personal Narrative of Louis Schlesinger of Adventures in Cuba and Ceuta," *United States Magazine and Democratic Review* (September 1852), 210; István K. Vida, *Hungarian Émigrés in the American Civil War*, 117, 162, 181.

15. T. Olshausen to J. Olshausen, May 12, 1856, in *Theodor Olshausen 1802–1869*, 187–189; Aidan Hegarty, *John Mitchel*, 87. For an introduction to Civil War–era print culture in the United States, see David W. Bulla and Gregory A. Borchard, *Journalism in the Civil War Era*.

16. "John Mitchel's Views on American Slavery," *The Liberator* (Boston), February 3, 1854; Hegarty, *John Mitchel*, 80, 88–89; Quinn, *John Mitchel*, 56.

17. Purdue and Purdue, *Pat Cleburne*, 55; Symonds, *Stonewall of the West*, 32–34, 42.

18. Mark F. Bielski, *Sons of the White Eagle*, 66.

19. Mitchel, *Jail Journal*, 170.

20. Hegarty, *John Mitchel*, 89; Quinn, *John Mitchel*, 57–58.

21. "John Mitchell and Slavery," *The Ohio Observer* (Hudson), January 25, 1854; "John Mitchel," *The Liberator*, January 27, 1854.

22. "John Mitchel, the Slave-Holder and Slave-Breeder," *The Liberator*, February 3, 1854.

23. Hegarty, *John Mitchel*, 90–91; Quinn, *John Mitchel*, 59.

24. "John Mitchel," *Daily South Carolinian*, May 31, 1854; "The South," *Hinds County Gazette* (Raymond, MS), October 14, 1857; Hegarty, *John Mitchel*, 92–94; Quinn, *John Mitchel*, 57–58, 61, 64, 66.

25. "The Renegade John Mitchel," *The Liberator,* September 18, 1857; "Letters from John Mitchel," *The Mississippian,* March 5, 1858.

26. Hegarty, *John Mitchel,* 93, 98–99; Quinn, *John Mitchel,* 64, 68.

27. Nachlass Dr. Rudolph M. Schleiden, April 2, 1858; April 30, 1858, book 18, 150, Schleswig-Holsteinische Landesbibliothek; Ernst-Erich Marhencke, *Hans Reimer Claussen,* 312–313; Honeck, *We Are the Revolutionists,* 20–21, 143–147; Bruce Levine, *The Spirit of 1848,* 239–253; Carl Wittke, *Refugees of Revolution,* 177–189; Gienapp, *Origins of the Republican Party;* Alice F. Tyler, *Freedom's Ferment.*

28. T. Olshausen to J. Olshausen, July 30, 1853, in *Theodor Olshausen 1802–1869,* 164–165; Theodor Olshausen, *Das Mississippi Thal,* 24–39.

29. T. Olshausen to J. Olshausen, July 30, 1853; April 20, 1855; November 5, 1855, in *Theodor Olshausen 1802–1869,* 164–165, 175–176, 185–186.

30. Adam Gurowski, *Slavery in History,* vii–xii, 23, 44, 57, 61–62, 171; Rodgers, "Count Adam Gurowski," 19–20.

31. Gurowski, *Slavery in History,* 67, 103, 106, 108–109, 111, 141.

32. Gurowski, *Slavery in History,* 219, 252–253, 255–256.

33. George Fitzhugh, "Wealth and Poverty-Luxury and Economy," *DeBow's Review,* April 30, 1861, 400–401.

34. William Yancey; D. H. Hamilton, quoted in Quigley, *Shifting Grounds,* 64, 104; Daniel Wallace, *The Political Life and Services of the Hon. R. Barnwell Rhett, of South Carolina,* 42.

35. Bryan P. McGovern, *John Mitchel,* 127; Eric H. Walther, *The Fire-Eaters,* 29, 31, 87, 189; Stephanie McCurry, *Confederate Reckoning.* McCurry makes a strong argument that the Confederate States were an experiment of "a modern proslavery and antidemocratic state" (1). Her case for "antidemocratic" relies in part on the exclusion of enslaved people and women, neither of whom could vote in other parts of the world.

36. A. Roane, "The South—In the Union or Out of It," *DeBow's Review* 29 (October 1860), 448–449.

CHAPTER FIVE

1. Nachlass Dr. Rudolph M. Schleiden, December 31, 1859, book 19, 47, Schleswig-Holsteinische Landesbibliothek; Rudolph Schleiden to Senats-Commission für die auswärtigen Angelegenheiten, December 16, 1859, 2-B.13.b.1.a.2.b.II, Staatsarchiv Bremen.

2. Theodor Olshausen to Justus Olshausen, March 18, 1860, in *Theodor Olshausen 1802–1869,* 198.

3. William W. Freehling, *The Road to Disunion,* 2:309–322; David M. Potter, *The Impending Crisis, 1848–1861,* 407–413.

4. Ernst-Erich Marhencke, *Hans Reimer Claussen,* 317–321, 323. Due to the awkward organization of Marhencke's book, it is unclear how the author can claim Hans Reimer Claussen's entry into politics in both 1856 and 1858. Marhencke also presents a rather one-sided narrative. For the German role in the Republican Party convention of

1860, see also James M. Bergquist, "The Forty-Eighters and the Republican Convention of 1860," in Charlotte L. Brancaforte, ed., *The German Forty-Eighters in the United States*, 141–156; Potter, *Impending Crisis*, 418–429.

5. Marhencke, *Hans Reimer Claussen*, 324. Marhencke here makes assumptions without solid evidence and it is therefore likely that he not only is mixing the chronology of the events in Davenport and Chicago but also is using hindsight to paint Lincoln as a candidate with earlier support. See Eric Foner, *Free Soil, Free Labor, Free Men*, 132–133; James M. McPherson, *Battle Cry of Freedom*, 220–21.

6. "To the Editors," *Daily National Intelligencer* (Washington, DC), June 23, 1860.

7. James L. Abrahamson, *The Men of Secession and Civil War, 1859–1861*, 94; Lawrence M. Anderson, *Federalism, Secession, and the American State*, 105–116.

8. Quotes from the South Carolina Declaration of Secession are taken from David Franklin Houston, *Ordinances of Secession and Other Documents, 1860–1861*, 3–9; Freehling, *Road to Disunion*, 2:346.

9. Quotes from the Georgia Declaration of Secession are taken from *Journal of the Public and Secret Proceedings of the Convention of the People of Georgia*, 349–361.

10. Quotes from the Mississippi Declaration of Secession are taken from *Journal of the State Convention, and Ordinances and Resolutions Adopted in March 1861*, 86–88.

11. Rudolph M. Schleiden, *Schleswig-Holsteins erste Erhebung, 1848–1849*, 1, 28; Lois Eugenia Rodgers, "Count Adam Gurowski," 47–48.

12. William J. Cooper Jr., *Jefferson Davis, American*; William C. Davis, *"A Government of Our Own"*; Mark E. Neely Jr., *Southern Rights*; George C. Rable, *The Confederate Republic*.

13. Howell Purdue and Elizabeth Purdue, *Pat Cleburne, Confederate General*, 68, 74–75; Craig L. Symonds, *Stonewall of the West*, 43, 46.

14. Mark F. Bielski, *Sons of the White Eagle*, 17, 49–50.

15. István K. Vida, *Hungarian Émigrés in the American Civil War*, 50–51.

16. Adam Gurowski, *Diary*, 1:13–14, 38; Russell McClintock, *Lincoln and the Decision for War*, chapter 7.

17. Gurowski, *Diary*, 1:20–21; Charles M. Hubbard, *The Burden of Confederate Diplomacy*, 9, 11–12; McClintock, *Lincoln and the Decision for War*, 207, 216.

18. Schleiden to Senats-Commission, March 26, 1861, 2-B.13.b.1.a.2.c.I, Staatsarchiv Bremen; Hubbard, *Burden of Confederate Diplomacy*, 9, 12; McClintock, *Lincoln and the Decision for War*, 205, 216, 238, 241.

19. David H. Donald, *Lincoln*, 285–302; Maury Klein, *Days of Defiance*; Ella Lonn, *Foreigners in the Confederacy*, 58; McClintock, *Lincoln and the Decision for War*, chapters 9–10; McPherson, *Battle Cry of Freedom*, 272–274.

20. Schleiden to Senats-Commission, April 22, 1861; April 24, 1861, 2-B.13.b.1.a.2.c.I, Staatsarchiv Bremen; Nachlass Dr. Rudolph M. Schleiden, May 4, 1858, book 18, 159, Schleswig-Holsteinische Landesbibliothek; Rudolph M. Schleiden, *Erinnerungen eines Schleswig-Holsteiners*, 266, 277.

21. Schleiden to Senats-Commission, April 24, 1861, evening letter, 2-B.13.b.1.a.2.c.I, Staatsarchiv Bremen.

22. Schleiden to Senats-Commission, April 24, 1861; May 2, 1861, 2-B.13.b.1.a.2.c.I, Staatsarchiv Bremen; Nachlass Dr. Rudolph M. Schleiden, April 27, 1861, book 19, 236, Schleswig-Holsteinische Landesbibliothek.

23. Schleiden to Senats-Commission, May 2, 1861, evening letter, 2-B.13.b.1.a.2.c.I, Staatsarchiv Bremen.

24. Nachlass Dr. Rudolph M. Schleiden, April 27, 1861, book 19, 237–238, Schleswig-Holsteinische Landesbibliothek; Alexander Stephens to Schleiden, April 28, 1861; Schleiden to Senats-Commission, May 2, 1861, 2-B.13.b.1.a.2.c.I, Staatsarchiv Bremen. Instead of recording the second conversation with Stephens, he only mentioned his cold, the meeting with a Mr. Garnett (likely Muscoe R. H. Garnett), Matthew Fontaine Maury, and Bremen's consul in Richmond Edward William de Voss, to whom he gave a few instructions about how the changed situation would influence commerce and international law.

25. Robert A. Toombs to William L. Yancey, Pierre A. Rost, A. Dudley Mann, March 16, 1861, in James D. Richardson, ed., *A Compilation of the Messages and Papers of the Confederacy*, 5; *Richmond Examiner*, October 3, 1861, quoted in Paul Quigley, *Shifting Grounds*, 134.

26. Andre M. Fleche, *The Revolution of 1861*, 43.

27. T. Olshausen to Zoe Olshausen, September 8, 1861, in *Theodor Olshausen 1802–1869*, 199–201. For a recent work on the divided German American community in Saint Louis and its views on slavery and racial equality, see Kristen Layne Anderson, *Abolitionizing Missouri*.

28. Gurowski, *Diary*, 1:84, 90, 181.

29. "Gen. Asboth and His Staff," *Frank Leslie's Illustrated Newspaper* (New York), April 5, 1862.

30. *New York Times*, May 3, 1861.

CHAPTER SIX

1. István K. Vida, *Hungarian Émigrés in the American Civil War*, 54.

2. Michael Cavanagh, *Memoirs of General Thomas Francis Meagher*, 369; Andre M. Fleche, *The Revolution of 1861*, 52.

3. "Call of Col. Asboth upon the Hungarians in America," *New York Herald*, May 3, 1861; "Colonel Asboth Organizing a Brigade," *New York Herald*, May 23, 1861. Frederick George D'Utassy was born on November 26, 1827, in Zala Nagy Kalirsa and had participated in the Hungarian uprising of 1848, leaving Hungary for the Ottoman Empire when the uprising failed. Cavanagh, *Memoirs of General Thomas Francis Meagher*, 374, 381; Vida, *Hungarian Émigrés*, 68.

4. "Thomas F. Meagher in Boston," *Daily National Intelligencer* (Washington, DC), October 2, 1861; Cavanagh, *Memoirs of General Thomas Francis Meagher*, 400, 404, 412.

5. Cavanagh, *Memoirs of General Thomas Francis Meagher*, 429, 432, 436.

6. Adam Gurowski, *Diary*, 1:70–71, 76, 106, 184, 214, 259.

7. Louis S. Gerteis, *Civil War St. Louis*, 89–100.

8. Fleche, *Revolution of 1861*, 46–47, 61, 94.

9. James McPherson, *Battle Cry of Freedom*, 290–292, 350.

10. "Major Zagonyi," *Frank Leslie's Illustrated Newspaper* (New York), November 28, 1861; *Daily National Intelligencer*, August 9, 1861; "Gen. Asboth and His Staff," *Frank Leslie's Illustrated Newspaper*, April 5, 1862; Stephen Beszedits, "Alexander Asboth"; Cavanagh, *Memoirs of General Thomas Francis Meagher*, 409; Ella Lonn, *Foreigners in the Confederacy*, 233; Eugene Pivány, *Hungarians in the American Civil War*, 21; Vida, *Hungarian Émigrés*, 55, 81, 90.

11. Theodor Olshausen to Zoe Olshausen, September 8, 1861, in *Theodor Olshausen 1802–1869*, 201–202; *Mississippi Blätter* (Saint Louis, MO), September 1, 1861; Ralf Bärner, "A Forty-Eighter Who Returned," in Charlotte L. Brancaforte, ed., *German Forty-Eighters in the United States*, 97–98; Gerteis, *Civil War St. Louis*, 147–148, 155–159.

12. *Der Demokrat* (Davenport, IA), September 28, 1861; Ernst-Erich Marhencke, *Hans Reimer Claussen*, 328.

13. Beszedits, "Alexander Asboth"; Pivány, *Hungarians in the American Civil War*, 28; Vida, *Hungarian Émigrés*, 81, 94–95.

14. Fleche, *Revolution of 1861*, 94–96.

15. "John Mitchel Among the Rebels," *New York Herald*, April 18, 1863; Aidan Hegarty, *John Mitchel*, 102–104; James Quinn, *John Mitchel*, 70–71.

16. Hegarty, *John Mitchel*, 106–110; Quinn, *John Mitchel*, 72.

17. Mark F. Bielski, *Sons of the White Eagle*, 52–54, 68; Lonn, *Foreigners in the Confederacy*, 160–161, 164.

18. Bielski, *Sons of the White Eagle*, 52; Lonn, *Foreigners in the Confederacy*, 162.

19. Craig L. Symonds, *Stonewall of the West*, 116–117, 121–123, 155.

20. Michael S. Green, *Freedom, Union, and Power*; Melinda Lawson, *Patriot Fires*; Mark E. Neely Jr., *The Fate of Liberty*; Adam I. P. Smith, *No Party Now*.

21. Ernst W. Heemann and Theodor Olshausen to Lincoln, September 8, 1862; Theodor Olshausen, Emil Preetorius, and R. E. Rombauer to James Taussig, May 16, 1863, Abraham Lincoln Papers, Library of Congress, Washington, DC; Gurowski, *Diary*, 1:38–39; Bärner, "A Forty-Eighter Who Returned," 98; Gerteis, *Civil War St. Louis*, 172–177.

22. T. Olshausen to Z. Olshausen, April 18, 1864, in *Theodor Olshausen 1802–1869*, 206; Allen C. Guelzo, *Lincoln's Emancipation Proclamation*; David E. Long, *The Jewel of Liberty*; Mark E. Neely Jr., *The Union Divided*.

23. Gurowski, *Diary*, 1:67, 149–150, 166, 187–188; Lois Eugenia Rodgers, "Count Adam Gurowski," 55–57.

24. Gurowski, *Diary*, 1:113, 246, 256, 277–278. Emphasis in original.

25. Patrick Cleburne, "Negro Enlistment Proposal," January 2, 1864, *The War of the Rebellion: A Compilation of the Official Records of the Union and Confederate Armies*, 52.2:586–592; Symonds, *Stonewall of the West*, chapter 10.

26. Edward B. Rugemer, *The Problem of Emancipation*.

27. "Gen. Meagher on Negro Suffrage," *Freedom's Champion* (Atchison, KS), August 24, 1865; *Daily Citizen and News* (Lowell, MA), August 14, 1865. Meagher illus-

trates a growing trend among Forty-Eighters to look into equal rights for African Americans, with the promised freedom a reality. Kristen Layne Anderson, *Abolitionizing Missouri,* chapters 5–6.

28. "The Irish Brigade," *Daily National Intelligencer,* May 15, 1863; Cavanagh, *Memoirs of General Thomas Francis Meagher,* 477, 483–485.

29. "Dinner to General Meagher," *New York Herald,* June 19, 1863.

30. Gurowski, *Diary,* 2:218–219, 223, 270–271. Emphasis in original.

31. Gurowski, *Diary,* 3:85.

32. Quinn, *John Mitchel,* 74; Rodgers, "Count Adam Gurowski," 66–67.

33. T. Olshausen to Z. Olshausen, April 18, 1864, in *Theodor Olshausen 1802–1869,* 206; Bärner, "A Forty-Eighter Who Returned," 98; Mischa Honeck, *We Are the Revolutionists,* 164.

34. *Der Demokrat,* February 18, 1864; February 25, 1864; Marhencke, *Hans Reimer Claussen,* 332–33.

35. Bärner, "A Forty-Eighter Who Returned," 99; Honeck, *We Are the Revolutionists,* 164–167; Jörg Nagler, *Fremont contra Lincoln,* 111, 213, 215–216.

36. *Der Demokrat,* October 27, 1864; Marhencke, *Hans Reimer Claussen,* 338; Nagler, *Fremont contra Lincoln,* 234, 248.

37. T. Olshausen to Z. Olshausen, January 23, 1865, in *Theodor Olshausen 1802–1869,* 208; Gurowski, *Diary,* 1:173, 3:382–383; John C. Waugh, *Reelecting Lincoln.*

38. Beszedits, "Alexander Asboth."

39. *New York Times,* November 26, 1864. See also Cavanagh, *Memoirs of General Thomas Francis Meagher,* 492; Vida, *Hungarian Émigrés,* 82–83.

CHAPTER SEVEN

1. Michael Cavanagh, *Memoirs of General Thomas Francis Meagher,* 361; Aidan Hegarty, *John Mitchel,* 96, 99; John Mitchel, *An Apology for the British Government in Ireland,* 3, 9, 34. For the literature on the Fenians and the Irish Republican Brotherhood, see R. V. Comerford, *The Fenians in Context*; Brian Jenkins, *Fenians and Anglo-American Relations During Reconstruction*; Jenkins, *The Fenian Problem*; Desmond Ryan, *The Fenian Chief*; Mabel G. Walker, *The Fenian Movement.*

2. "The Arrest of John Mitchel," *Boston* (MA) *Daily Advertiser,* June 16, 1865; Hegarty, *John Mitchel,* 111, 115–116, 123, 130–133; Robert Kee, *The Green Flag,* 351–363; James Quinn, *John Mitchel,* 77–81, 84–86.

3. Samuel Ricker to Lewis Cass, March 4, 1861, in Despatches from U.S. Consul in Frankfurt am Main, Germany, 1829–1906, M161, Diplomatic Records, National Archives; Alexander Gustav Adolf Graf von Schleinitz to Thérémin, March 11, 1861, in Christian Friese, ed., *Die auswärtige Politik Preussens 1858–1871,* chapter 7.

4. Adam Gurowski, *Diary,* 2:204; Stefan Kieniewicz, *Powstanie Styczniowe,* 340–341; Franciszka Ramotowska, *Rząd Narodowy Polski w Latach 1863–1864,* 14–21.

5. Gurowski, *Diary,* 3:301; Kieniewicz, *Powstanie Styczniowe.*

6. Mark F. Bielski, *Sons of the White Eagle*, 55; Stefan Kieniewicz, *Warszawa w Powstaniu Stycziowym*, 197–201.

7. A. Paget to Lord Russell, January 31, 1861, *British and Foreign State Papers*, 51:830–832; Keith A. P. Sandiford, *Great Britain and the Schleswig-Holstein Question, 1848–64*, 36–39.

8. Promemoria des Auswärtigen Amtes, December 6, 1862; Graf Alajos Karolyi to Johann Bernhard Graf von Rechberg, June 5, 1863; Promemoria des Auswärtigen Amtes, June 27, 1863; Albrecht Graf von Bernstorff to Otto von Bismarck, November 16, 1863; Bismarck to Hermann Ludwig von Balan, January 13, 1864; Andrew Buchanan to Bismarck, February 23, 1864; Karolyi to Bismarck, February 15, 1864; Robert Heinrich Ludwig Graf von der Goltz to Bismarck, April 17, 1864, in *Die auswärtige Politik Preussens*, 3:104–105, 606–607; 4:158–160, 427–428, 553, 597, 735; Rudolph Schleiden to Theodor Curtius, February 15, 1864, 7,116–2–7, Staatsarchiv Bremen.

9. Schleiden to Heinrich Smidt, May 27, 1864; August 19, 1864, 2-B.13.b.1.a.2.c.II, Staatsarchiv Bremen; Schleiden to Oscar Wydenbrugk, August 17, 1864, Fasc. 33, Christian Albrecht Universität; Schleiden to Johannes Rösing, September 8, 1864, in Rudolph Schleiden, Johannes Rösing, and Clara von Ammon, *Rheinromantik und Civil War im Diplomatischen Dienst in den Vereinigten Staaten*, 107; Theodor Olshausen to Justus Olshausen, April 18, 1864, in *Theodor Olshausen 1802–1869*, 205.

10. Schleiden to Rösing, June 6, 1862, in Schleiden, Rösing, and von Ammon, *Rheinromantik und Civil War*, 5; Schleiden to C. H. Merck, June 20, 1866; July 19, 1866, 7,116-1-2, Staatsarchiv Bremen.

11. February 13, 1867, book 21, 285, Schleswig-Holsteinische Landesbibliothek; Schleiden to Rösing, June 6, 1862, in Schleiden, Rösing, and von Ammon, *Rheinromantik und Civil War*, 5; *Stenographische Berichte über die Verhandlungen des Reichstages des Norddeutschen Bundes* (1867), 1:492, 3:434–437; (1868), 1:40–46, 244–246, 248–249, 576; *Stenographische Berichte über die Verhandlungen des Deutschen Reichstages* (1872), 2:643.

12. Schleiden to Rösing, January 15, 1874, in Schleiden, Rösing, and von Ammon, *Rheinromantik und Civil War*, 200–201.

13. Arnold Blumberg, "Russian Policy and the Franco-Austrian War of 1859," 137–153; Robert J. W. Evans, *Austria, Hungary, and the Habsburgs*, 286; Paul W. Schroeder, *Austria, Great Britain, and the Crimean War*.

14. Edward Crankshaw, *The Fall of the House of Habsburg*, 200–205; Béla K. Király, *Ferenc Deák*, 159–161.

15. Gyula Andrássy, *Ungarns Ausgleich mit Österreich vom Jahre 1867*; Crankshaw, *Fall of the House of Habsburg*, 238–240.

16. István K. Vida, *Hungarian Émigrés in the American Civil War*, 122.

17. Stephen Beszedits, "Alexander Asboth."

18. Eric Foner, *Reconstruction*, 183–184, 291–307.

19. *Montgomery Advertiser*, February 8, 1866, quoted in Michael Perman, *Reunion Without Compromise*, 155; Throckmorton speech, in Perman, 274.

20. George C. Rable, *But There Was No Peace*.

21. Foner, *Reconstruction*, 564–587.

22. Leon F. Litwack, *Trouble in Mind*; Donald G. Nieman, *African Americans and the Emergence of Segregation, 1865–1900*; Michael Perman, *Struggle for Mastery*; Howard N. Rabinowitz, *Race Relations in the Urban South, 1865–1890*.

CONCLUSION

1. William Ewart Gladstone, "Irish Home Rule Speech," House of Commons Debate, June 7, 1886, *Hansard Parliamentary Debates*, 306:1223.

2. Timothy Healy, June 7, 1886, *Hansard Parliamentary Debates*, 306:1245.

BIBLIOGRAPHY

PRIMARY SOURCES

Manuscript Collections

Library of Congress
Abraham Lincoln Papers
National Archives, Washington, DC
Despatches from U.S. Consuls in Frankfurt am Main, Germany, M161
Schleswig-Holsteinische Landesbibliothek Kiel
Nachlass Dr. Rudolph M. Schleiden
Staatsarchiv Bremen
Rudolf [Rudolph] Schleiden, Ministerresident, 1853
Nachlass Dr. Rudolf [Rudolph] M. Schleiden
The National Archives (formerly Public Record Office), London (Kew Gardens)
Foreign Office (FO) 22, Denmark
Universitätsbibliothek, Christian Albrecht Universität, Kiel
Nachlass Dr. Rudolf [Rudolph] M. Schleiden

Newspapers

Boston (MA) *Daily Advertiser*
Congressional Globe (Washington, DC)
Correspondenz-Blatt (Kiel, Germany)
Daily Citizen and News (Lowell, MA)
Daily Herald (Cleveland, OH)
Daily National Intelligencer (Washington, DC)
Daily South Carolinian (Columbia)
DeBow's Review (New Orleans)
Der Demokrat (Davenport, IA)
Dithmarsische Zeitung (Heide, Germany)

Frank Leslie's Illustrated Newspaper (New York)
Frederick Douglass' Paper (Rochester, NY)
Freedom's Champion (Atchison, KS)
Hinds County Gazette (Raymond, MS)
The Liberator (Boston)
Mississippi Blätter (Saint Louis, MO)
The Mississippian (Vicksburg)
New York Herald
New York Times
The Ohio Observer (Hudson)
Savannah (GA) *Morning News*
Semi-Weekly Ohio Statesman (Columbus)
The Times (London)
United Irishman (Dublin)
United States Magazine and Democratic Review (Washington, DC)
Weekly Herald (New York)

Primary Books, Articles, and Essays

Bell, John W., and William Smith. *Memoirs of Governor William Smith, of Virginia: His Political, Military, and Personal History.* New York: Moss Engraving, 1891.

Beszedits, Stephen. *The Libby Prison Diary of Colonel Emeric Szabad.* Toronto: B and L Information Services, 1999.

Calhoun, John C. *The Papers of John C. Calhoun.* Edited by Robert Lee Meriwether, William Edwin Hemphill, and Clyde Norman Wilson. 28 vols. Columbia: University of South Carolina Press, 1959–2003.

Chase, Ezra B. *Teachings of Patriots and Statesmen; Or, The "Founders of the Republic" on Slavery.* Philadelphia: J. W. Bradley, 1860.

Chesnut, Mary Boykin Miller. *Mary Chesnut's Civil War.* Edited by C. Vann Woodward. New Haven, CT: Yale University Press, 1981.

Claussen, Hans Reimer. "Die Norderdithmarsische Landesverfassung betreffend." *Dithmarsische Zeitung*, June 28, July 5, July 19, July 26, August 2, 1834.

Claussen, Hans Reimer. *Vertheidigungsschrift für den Eisnbahndirector, Deputierten, Bürger und Redacteur Theodor Olshausen.* Kiel: Schröder, 1847.

Cobb, Howell. "Letter . . . to the People of Georgia." In *Southern Pamphlets on Secession, November 1860–April 1861.* Edited by Jon L. Wakelyn, 99–100. Chapel Hill: University of North Carolina Press, 1996.

Crallé, Richard K., ed. *Speeches of John C. Calhoun.* New York: D. Appleton, 1851.

DePuy, Henry W. *Kossuth and His Generals: With a Brief History of Hungary.* Buffalo, NY: Phinney, 1852.

Dr. Jucho. *Verhandlungen des Deutschen Parlaments.* Frankfurt: J. D. Sauerländer's Verlag, 1848.

Fichte, Johann Gottlieb. *Addresses to the German Nation.* Translated by R. F. Jones and G. H. Turnbull. Chicago: University of Chicago Press, 1922.

Fichte, Johann Gottlieb. *Reden an die deutsche Nation.* Leipzig: F. U. Brockhaus, 1871.

Friese, Christian, ed. *Die auswärtige Politik Preussens, 1858–1871.* 10 vols. Oldenburg: Gerhard Stalling Verlarg, 1935–1945.

Great Britain Foreign Office. *British and Foreign State Papers.* London: William Ridgway, 1868–1870.

Gurowski, Adam. *Diary.* 2 vols. New York: Carleton, 1864.

Gurowski, Adam. *Russia and Its People.* London: T. Nelson and Sons, 1854.

Gurowski, Adam. *Russia as It Is.* New York: D. Appleton, 1854.

Gurowski, Adam. *Slavery in History.* New York: A. B. Burdick, 1860.

Gurowski, Adam. *The Turkish Question.* New York: William Taylor, 1854.

Harring, Harro. *Memoiren über Polen unter russischer Herrschaft.* Leipzig: Literarisches Museum, 1831.

Harring, Harro. *Poland Under the Dominion of Russia.* Boston: I. S. Szymanski, 1834.

Hedde, Friedrich. *Kein schimpflicher Vertrag mit Dänemark.* Kiel: J. G. Raeck, 1848.

Hegel, Georg Wilhelm Friedrich. *Phänomenologie des Geistes.* Leipzig: Felix Meiner, 1907.

Houghton, Walter R. *Conspectus of the History of Political Parties and the Federal Government.* Indianapolis, IN: Granger, Davis, 1880.

Houston, David Franklin. *Ordinances of Secession and Other Documents, 1860–1861.* New York: A. Lovell, 1896.

Jottrand, Lucien Leopold. *Louis de Potter.* Brussels: A. Decq, 1860.

Journal of the Public and Secret Proceedings of the Convention of the People of Georgia, Held in Milledgeville and Savannah in 1861. Together with the Ordinances Adopted. Milledgeville, GA: Boughton, Nisbet and Barnes, 1861.

Journal of the State Convention, and Ordinances and Resolutions Adopted in March 1861. Jackson, MS: E. Barksdale, 1861.

Kossuth, Lajos. *Select Speeches of Kossuth.* Edited by Francis William Newman. New York: C. S. Francis, 1854.

Lelewel, Joachim. *Geschichte Polens*. Leipzig: W. Jurany, 1847.

Lornsen, Jens U. *Die Unions-Verfassung Dänemarks und Schleswigholsteins*. Edited by Georg Beseler. Jena: Friedrich Frommann, 1841.

Lornsen, Jens U. *Über das Verfassungswerk in Schleswigholstein*. Kiel: C. F. Mohr, 1839.

Madison, James, and Thomas Jefferson. *Resolutions of Virginia and Kentucky*. Richmond, VA: R. I. Smith, 1835.

Mazzini, Giuseppe. *A Cosmopolitanism of Nations: Giuseppe Mazzini's Writings on Democracy, Nation Building, and International Relations*. Edited by Stefano Recchia and Nadia Urbinati. Translated by Stefano Recchia. Princeton, NJ: Princeton University Press, 2009.

Mazzini, Giuseppe. *Selected Writings*. Edited by Nagendranath Gangulee. London: L. Drummond, 1945.

Meagher, Thomas Francis. *Speeches on the Legislative Independence of Ireland: With Introductory Notes*. New York: Redfield, 1853.

Metternich, Klemens von. *Memoirs of Prince Metternich, 1815–1829*. Edited by Prince Richard Metternich. 1881. New York: Howard Fertig, 1970.

Mitchel, John. *An Apology for the British Government in Ireland*. Dublin: O'Donoghue, 1905.

Mitchel, John. *The Crusade of the Period: And Last Conquest of Ireland (Perhaps)*. New York: Lynch, Cole and Meehan, 1878.

Mitchel, John. *Jail Journal; or, Five Years in British Prisons*. New York: The *Citizen*, 1854.

Mitchel, John. "To the Right Hon. The Earl of Clarendon." *United Irishman*, March 25, 1848.

O'Connell, Daniel, and John O'Connell. *Life and Speeches of Daniel O'Connell, M.P.* Dublin: J. Duffy, 1846.

Olshausen, Theodor. *Das Mississippi Thal*. Kiel: Akademische Buchhandlung, 1854.

Olshausen, Theodor. *Theodor Olshausen 1802–1869: Briefe an den Bruder Justus*. Edited by Joachim Reppmann. Wyk: Verlag für Amerikanistik, 2003.

Pincus, Steven C. A., ed. *England's Glorious Revolution, 1688–1689: A Brief History with Documents*. New York: Palgrave Macmillan, 2006.

Proceedings and Debates of the Virginia State Convention of 1829–1830. Richmond, VA: S. Shepherd, 1830.

Reinhart, Joseph R., ed. *August Willich's Gallant Dutchmen: Civil War Letters from the 32nd Indiana Infranty*. Kent, OH: Kent State University Press, 2006.

Richardson, James D. *A Compilation of the Messages and Papers of the Confederacy*. 2 vols. Nashville, TN: United States Publishing Company, 1905.

Schleiden, Rudolph M., ed., *Aktenstücke zur neuesten Schleswig-Holsteinischen Geschichte*. 3 vols. Leipzig: Verlag von Wilhelm Engelmann, 1851.

Schleiden, Rudolph M. *Erinnerungen eines Schleswig-Holsteiners*. Wiesbaden: Verlag von J. F. Bergmann, 1890.

Schleiden, Rudolph M. *Jugenderinnerungen eines Schleswig-Holsteiners*. Wiesbaden, Germany: Verlag von J. F. Bergmann, 1886.

Schleiden, Rudolph M. *Reise Erinnerungen aus den Vereinigten Staaten von Amerika*. New York: E. Steiger, 1873.

Schleiden, Rudolph M. *Schleswig-Holsteins erste Erhebung, 1848–1849*. Wiesbaden: Verlag von J. F. Bergmann, 1891.

Schleiden, Rudolph M. *Schleswig-Holstein im zweiten Kriegsjahre, 1849–1850*. Wiesbaden: Verlag von J. F. Bergmann, 1894.

Schleiden, Rudolph, Johannes Rösing, and Clara von Ammon. *Rheinromantik und Civil War im Diplomatischen Dienst in den Vereinigten Staaten*. Edited by Norbert Klatt. Göttingen: Norbert Klatt Verlag, 2003.

Springer, Anton. *Friedrich Christoph Dahlmann*. 2 vols. Leipzig: Verlag von S. Hirzel, 1870.

Stenographische Berichte über die Verhandlungen des Deutschen Reichstages. Berlin: Verlag der Buchdruckerei der Norddeutschen Allgemeinen Zeitung, 1871–1873.

Stenographische Berichte über die Verhandlungen des Reichstages des Norddeutschen Bundes. Berlin: Verlag der Buchdruckerei der Norddeutschen Allgemeinen Zeitung, 1867–1870.

Széchenyi, István, and Michael Paziazi. *Licht oder aufhellende Bruchstücke zur Berichtigung einiger Irrthümer und Vorurtheile*. Pesth: Wigand, 1832.

Széchenyi, István, and Joseph Vojdisek. *Ueber den Credit nebst einem Anhange enthaltend Ammerkungen und Zusätze von einem ungarischen Patrioten*. Leipzig: Wigand, 1830.

Tone, Theobald Wolfe. *Memoirs of Theobald Wolfe Tone*. Edited by William Theobald Wolfe Tone. London: H. Colburn, 1827.

United Kingdom. *Hansard Parliamentary Debates*. 1886.

United States War Department. *The War of the Rebellion: A Compilation of the Official Records of the Union and Confederate Armies*. 128 vols. Washington, DC: Government Printing Office, 1880–1901.

Wallace, Daniel. *The Political Life and Services of the Hon. R. Barnwell Rhett, of South Carolina*. 1859.

Wigard, Franz. *Stenographischer Bericht über die Verhandlungen der Deutschen Constituirenden Nationalversammlung zu Frankfurt am Main*. 9 vols. Frankfurt: Johann David Sauerländer, 1848.

SECONDARY SOURCES

Abrahamson, James L. *The Men of Secession and Civil War, 1859–1861.* Wilmington, DE: SR Books, 2000.

Adams, Charles. *Slavery, Secession, and Civil War: Views from the United Kingdom and Europe, 1856–1865.* Lanham, MD: Scarecrow, 2007.

Ames, Herman Vandenburg. *John C. Calhoun and the Secession Movement of 1850.* Freeport, NY: Books for Libraries, 1971.

Andersen, Holger. *Idstedt und Danach: Schleswig-Holstein in den USA.* Plön: Hermann Sönksen Verlag, 1987.

Anderson, Benedict. *Imagined Communities: Reflection on the Origin and Spread of Nationalism.* London: Verso, 1983.

Anderson, Kristen Layne. *Abolitionizing Missouri: German Immigrants and Racial Ideology in Nineteenth-Century America.* Baton Rouge: Louisiana State University Press, 2016.

Anderson, Lawrence M. *Federalism, Secession, and the American State: Divided, We Secede.* New York: Routledge, 2012.

Andrássy, Gyula. *Ungarns Ausgleich mit Österreich vom Jahre 1867.* Leipzig: Duncker and Humblot, 1897.

Arenson, Adam. *The Great Heart of the Republic: St. Louis and the Cultural Civil War.* Columbia: University of Missouri Press, 2011.

Auge, Oliver, and Burkhard Büsing, eds. *Der Vertrag von Ripen 1460 und die Anfänge der politischen Partizipation in Schleswig-Holstein, im Reich und in Nordeuropa.* Ostfildern: Jan Thorbecke Verlag, 2012.

Banning, Lance. *The Jeffersonian Persuasion: Evolution of a Party Ideology.* Ithaca, NY: Cornell University Press, 1978.

Barnes, L. Diane, Brian Schoen, and Frank Towers, eds. *The Old South's Modern Worlds: Slavery, Region, and Nation in the Age of Progress.* New York: Oxford University Press, 2011.

Baycroft, Timothy, and Mark Hewitson, eds. *What Is a Nation? Europe, 1789–1914.* Oxford: Oxford University Press, 2006.

Bayly, Christopher A. *The Birth of the Modern World, 1780–1914: Global Connections and Comparisons.* Malden, MA: Blackwell, 2004.

Bender, Thomas. *A Nation Among Nations: America's Place in World History.* New York: Hill and Wang, 2006.

Bensel, Richard Franklin. *Yankee Leviathan: The Origins of Central State Authority in America, 1859–1877.* Cambridge: Cambridge University Press, 1990.

Bergquist, James M. *Daily Life in Immigrant America, 1820–1870.* Westport, CT: Greenwood, 2008.

Berry, Robert Allen. "Czartoryski and the Balkan Policies of the Hôtel Lambert, 1832–1847." PhD diss., Indiana University, 1974.

Berthoff, Rowland. *Republic of the Dispossessed: The Exceptional Old-European Consensus in America.* Columbia: University of Missouri Press, 1997.

Beszedits, Stephen. "Alexander Asboth: Hungarian Patriot, Union General and American Diplomat." *Vasvary Collection Newsletter* 38 (2007).

Beszedits, Stephen. "Bela Estvàn: A Hungarian Officer of the Confederate Army." *Vasvary Collection Newsletter* 37 (2007).

Betley, J. A. *Belgium and Poland in International Relations, 1830–1831.* The Hague: Mouton, 1960.

Bielski, Mark F. *Sons of the White Eagle in the American Civil War: Divided Poles in a Divided Nation.* Philadelphia: Casemate, 2016.

Bjørn, Claus. *1848: Borgerkrig og Revolution.* Copenhagen: Gyldendal, 1998.

Black, Jeremy. *The War of 1812 in the Age of Napoleon.* Norman: University of Oklahoma Press, 2009.

Blumberg, Arnold. "Russian Policy and the Franco-Austrian War of 1859." *Journal of Modern History* 26 (June 1954): 137–153.

Boren, Mark Edelman. *Student Resistance: A History of the Unruly Subject.* New York: Routledge, 2001.

Bowen, Wayne H. *Spain and the American Civil War.* Columbia: University of Missouri Press, 2011.

Bowman, Shearer Davis. *Masters and Lords: Mid-19th Century U.S. Planters and Prussian Junkers.* New York: Oxford University Press, 1993.

Brancaforte, Charlotte L., ed. *The German Forty-Eighters in the United States.* New York: Peter Lang, 1989.

Brandt, Hartwig. *Europe, 1815–1850: Reaktion-Konstitution-Revolution.* Stuttgart: W. Kohlhammer, 2002.

Brewer, David. *The Greek War of Independence: The Struggle for Freedom from Ottoman Oppression and the Birth of the Modern Greek Nation.* Woodstock, NY: Overlook, 2001.

Bulla, David W., and Gregory A. Borchard. *Journalism in the Civil War Era.* New York: Peter Lang, 2010.

Cabestan, Jean-Pierre, and Aleksandar Pavković. *Secessionism and Separatism in Europe and Asia: To Have a State of One's Own.* New York: Routledge, 2012.

Camboni, Marina, ed. *Translating America: The Circulation of Narratives, Commodities, and Ideas Between Italy, Europe, and the United States.* Bern: Peter Lang, 2011.

Canny, Nicholas P. *Making Ireland British, 1580–1650.* Oxford: Oxford University Press, 2001.

Carr, William. *The Origins of the Wars of German Unification*. London: Longman, 1991.

Cavanagh, Michael. *Memoirs of General Thomas Francis Meagher: Comprising the Leading Events of His Career Chronologically Arranged*. Worcester, MA: Messenger, 1892.

Clogg, Richard, ed. *The Movement for Greek Independence, 1770–1821: A Collection of Documents*. New York: Barnes and Noble, 1976.

Comerford, R. V. *The Fenians in Context: Irish Politics and Society, 1848–82*. Dublin: Wolfhound Press, 1985.

Cooper, William J., Jr. *Jefferson Davis, American*. New York: Vintage, 2000.

Cortada, James W. "Spain and the American Civil War: Relations at Mid-Century, 1855–1868." *Transactions of the American Philosophical Society* 70 (July 1980): 1–121.

Crankshaw, Edward. *The Fall of the House of Habsburg*. New York: Penguin, 1983.

Craven, Avery. *The Growth of Southern Nationalism, 1848–1861*. Baton Rouge: Louisiana State University Press, 1953.

Crofts, Daniel W. *Lincoln and the Politics of Slavery: The Other Thirteenth Amendment and the Struggle to Save the Union*. Chapel Hill: University of North Carolina Press, 2016.

Dakin, Douglas. *The Greek Struggle for Independence, 1821–1833*. Berkeley: University of California Press, 1978.

Dal Lago, Enrico. *William Lloyd Garrison and Giuseppe Mazzini: Abolition, Democracy, and Radical Reform*. Baton Rouge: Louisiana State University Press, 2013.

Davis, Richard P. *The Young Ireland Movement*. Dublin: Gill and Macmillan, 1988.

Davis, William C. *"A Government of Our Own": The Making of the Confederacy*. Baton Rouge, Louisiana State University Press, 1994.

Deák, István. *The Lawful Revolution: Louis Kossuth and the Hungarians, 1848–1849*. New York: Columbia University Press, 1979.

Deme, Laszlo. *The Radical Left in the Hungarian Revolution of 1848*. Boulder, CO: East European Quarterly, 1976.

Demoulin, Robert. *La Révolution de 1830*. Brussels: La Renaissance du Livre, 1950.

Donald, David H. *Lincoln*. New York: Simon and Schuster, 1995.

Dowe, Dieter, Heinz-Gerhard Haupt, Dieter Langewiesche, and Jonathan Sperber. *Europe in 1848: Revolution and Reform*. Translated by David Higgins. New York: Berghahn, 2001.

Doyle, Don H., ed. *American Civil Wars: The United States, Latin America, Europe, and the Crisis of the 1860s.* Chapel Hill: University of North Carolina Press, 2017.

Doyle, Don H. *The Cause of All Nations: An International History of the American Civil War.* New York: Basic, 2015.

Doyle, Don H., ed. *Secession as an International Phenomenon: From America's Civil War to Contemporary Separatist Movements.* Athens: University of Georgia Press, 2010.

Doyle, Don H., and Marco A. Pamplona, eds. *Nationalism in the New World.* Athens: University of Georgia Press, 2006.

Droz, Jacques. *Europe Between Revolutions, 1815–1848.* Translated by Robert Baldick. New York: Harper and Row, 1967.

Durden, Robert Franklin. *The Self-Inflicted Wound: Southern Politics in the Nineteenth Century.* Lexington: University Press of Kentucky, 1985.

Egan, Timothy. *The Immortal Irishman: The Irish Revolutionary Who Became an American Hero.* Boston: Houghton Mifflin Harcourt, 2016.

Eimers, Enno. *Preussen und die USA 1850 bis 1867.* Berlin: Duncker and Humblot, 2004.

Elliott, Marianne. *Wolfe Tone: Prophet of Irish Independence.* New Haven, CT: Yale University Press, 1989.

Ellis, Steven G. *Ireland in the Age of the Tudors, 1447–1603: English Expansion and the End of Gaelic Rule.* London: Longman, 1998.

Evans, Robert J. W. *Austria, Hungary, and the Habsburgs: Central Europe, c. 1683–1867.* Oxford: Oxford University Press, 2006.

Eyck, Frank. *The Frankfurt Parliament, 1848–49.* London: Macmillan, 1968.

Fahrmeir, Andreas. *Citizenship: The Rise and Fall of a Modern Concept.* New Haven, CT: Yale University Press, 2007.

Fazekas, István, Stefan Malfèr, and Péter Tusor, eds. *Széchenyi, Kossuth, Batthyány, Deák: Studien zu den ungarischen Reformpolitikern des 19. Jahrhunderts und ihren Beziehungen zu Österreich.* Vienna: Institute für Ungarische Geschichteforschung, 2011.

Figes, Orlando. *The Crimean War: A History.* New York: Picador, 2010.

Fleche, Andre M. *The Revolution of 1861: The American Civil War in the Age of Nationalist Conflict.* Chapel Hill: University of North Carolina Press, 2012.

Foner, Eric. *Free Soil, Free Labor, Free Men: The Ideology of the Republican Party Before the Civil War.* New York: Oxford University Press, 1970.

Foner, Eric. *Reconstruction: America's Unfinished Revolution, 1863–1877.* New York: Perennial Classics, 2002.

Freehling, William W. *Prelude to Civil War: The Nullification Controversy in South Carolina, 1816–1836*. New York: Oxford University Press, 1966.

Freehling, William W. *The Road to Disunion*. 2 vols. New York: Oxford University Press, 1990, 2007.

Freitag, Sabine. *Friedrich Hecker: Biographie eines Republikaners*. Stuttgart: Franz Steiner Verlag, 1998.

Fröhlich, Helgard, Margarete Grandner, and Michael Weinzierl, eds. *1848 im europäischen Kontext*. Vienna: Turia und Kant, 1999.

Gerber, Rafał. *Studenci Uniwersytetu Warszawskiego 1808–1831*. Wrocław: Zakład Narodowy Imienia Ossolińskich, 1977.

Gerteis, Louis S. *Civil War St. Louis*. Lawrence: University Press of Kansas, 2001.

Gienapp, William E. *The Origins of the Republican Party, 1852–1856*. New York: Oxford University Press, 1987.

Gläser, Elisabeth, and Hermann Wellenreuther, eds. *Bridging the Atlantic: The Question of American Exceptionalism in Perspective*. Washington, DC: German Historical Institute, 2002.

Gordon, David, ed. *Secession, State, and Liberty*. New Brunswick, NJ: Transaction, 1998.

Goujon, Bertrand. *Monarchies Postrévolutionnaires, 1814–1848*. Paris, France: Éditions du Seuil, 2012.

Green, Michael S. *Freedom, Union, and Power: Lincoln and His Party During the Civil War*. New York: Fordham University Press, 2004.

Guelzo, Allen C. *Lincoln's Emancipation Proclamation: The End of Slavery in America*. New York: Simon and Schuster, 2004.

Hamilton, Holman. *Prologue to Conflict: The Crisis and Compromise of 1850*. Lexington: University of Kentucky Press, 1964.

Hammen, Oscar J. *The Red '48ers: Karl Marx and Friedrich Engels*. New York: Charles Scribner's Sons, 1969.

Hearne, John M., and Rory T. Cornish, eds. *Thomas Francis Meagher: The Making of an Irish American*. Dublin: Irish Academic Press, 2005.

Hegarty, Aidan. *John Mitchel: A Cause Too Many*. Belfast: Camlane, 2005.

Helo, Ari, and Peter S. Onuf. "Jefferson, Morality, and the Problem of Slavery." *The William and Mary Quarterly* 60 (July 2003): 583–614.

Hobsbawm, Eric. *The Age of Capital, 1848–1875*. New York: Vintage, 1996.

Honeck, Mischa. *We Are the Revolutionists: German-Speaking Immigrants and American Abolitionists After 1848*. Athens: University of Georgia Press, 2011.

Houston, David Franklin. *A Critical Study of Nullification in South Carolina*. New York: Russell and Russell, 1967.

Howe, Daniel W. *What Hath God Wrought: The Transformation of America, 1815–1848*. New York: Oxford University Press, 2007.

Hubbard, Charles M. *The Burden of Confederate Diplomacy.* Knoxville: University of Tennessee Press, 1998.

Huzzey, Richard. *Freedom Burning: Anti-Slavery and Empire in Victorian Britain.* Ithaca, NY: Cornell University Press, 2016.

Janes, Henry L. "The Black Warrior Affair." *American Historical Review* 12 (January 1907): 280–298.

Jenkins, Brian. *The Fenian Problem: Insurgency and Terrorism in a Liberal State, 1858–1874.* Montreal: McGill-Queen's University Press, 2008.

Jenkins, Brian. *Fenians and Anglo-American Relations During Reconstruction.* Ithaca, NY: Cornell University Press, 1969.

Jessen-Klingenberg, Manfred. *Standpunkte zur neueren Geschichte Schleswig-Holsteins.* Malente: Schleswig-Holsteinischer Geschichtsverlag, 1998.

Jones, Peter. *The 1848 Revolutions.* London: Longman, 1991.

Kammen, Michael. "The Problem of American Exceptionalism: A Reconsideration." *American Quarterly* 45 (March 1993): 1–43.

Karp, Matthew. *This Vast Southern Empire: Slaveholders at the Helm of American Foreign Policy.* Cambridge, MA: Harvard University Press, 2016.

Kee, Robert. *The Green Flag: A History of Irish Nationalism.* London: Quartet, 1972.

Kenny, Kevin. *The American Irish: A History.* Harlow: Pearson Education, 2000.

Kieniewicz, Stefan. *Powstanie Styczniowe* [The January Uprising]. Warsaw: Państwowe Wydawn Naukowe, 1972.

Kieniewicz, Stefan. *Warszawa w Powstaniu Stycziowym* [Warsaw in the January Uprising]. Warsaw: Wiedza Powszechna, 1983.

Király, Béla K. *Ferenc Deák.* Boston: Twayne, 1975.

Klein, Maury. *Days of Defiance: Sumter, Secession, and the Coming of the Civil War.* New York: Vintage, 1999.

Körner, Axel. *America in Italy: The United States in the Political Thought and Imagination of the Risorgimento, 1763–1865.* Princeton, NJ: Princeton University Press, 2017.

Körner Axel, Nicola Miller, and Adam I. P. Smith, eds. *America Imagined: Explaining the United States in Nineteenth-Century Europe and Latin America.* New York: Palgrave Macmillan, 2012.

Kramer, Lloyd S. *Nationalism in Europe and America: Politics, Cultures, and Identities Since 1775.* Chapel Hill: University of North Carolina Press, 2011.

Kruszewska, Mirosława. "Pierwsi Polacy w Ameryce, Zapomniany bohater" [The First Poles in America: A Forgotten Hero]. *Gwiazda Polarna* 102 (November 5, 2011): 10–11.

Lambert, Andrew. *The Crimean War: British Grand Strategy Against Russia, 1853–56.* Surrey: Ashgate, 2011.

Lange, Ulrich, ed. *Geschichte Schleswig-Holsteins: Von den Anfängen bis zur Gegenwart*. Neumünster: Wachholz Verlag, 1996.

Langewiesche, Dieter. *Europa zwischen Restauration und Revolution, 1815–1849*. Munich: R. Oldenbourg Verlag, 1989.

László, Beke, Gazda István, Szász Zoltán, and Szörényi László, eds. *Nemzeti Évfordulóink 2010*. Budapest: Balassi Intézet, 2009.

Latimer, Jon. *1812: War with America*. Cambridge, MA: Belknap, 2007.

Lawson, Melinda. *Patriot Fires: Forging a New American Nationalism in the Civil War North*. Lawrence: University Press of Kansas, 2002.

Lenihan, Pádraig. *Consolidating Conquest: Ireland 1603–1727*. Harlow: Longman, 2008.

Leslie, R. F. *Polish Politics and the Revolution of November 1830*. London: Athlone, 1956.

Levine, Bruce. *The Spirit of 1848: German Immigrants, Labor Conflict, and the Coming of the Civil War*. Urbana: University of Illinois Press, 1992.

Lichtheim, George. *Marxism: An Historical and Critical Study*. New York: Praeger, 1965.

Litwack, Leon F. *Trouble in Mind: Black Southerners in the Age of Jim Crow*. New York: Knopf, 1998.

Long, David E. *The Jewel of Liberty: Abraham Lincoln's Re-election and the End of Slavery*. Mechanicsburg, PA: Stackpole, 1994.

Lonn, Ella. *Foreigners in the Confederacy*. Chapel Hill: University of North Carolina Press, 1940.

Lorentzen, Karl. "Theodore Olshausen." *Allgemeine Deutsche Biographie*. 45 vols. Munich: Duncker und Humblot, 1875–1900.

Lucas-Dubreton, J. *The Restoration and the July Monarchy*. Translated by E. F. Buckley. New York: G. P. Putman's Sons, 1929.

Mahin, Dean B. *The Blessed Place of Freedom: Europeans in Civil War America*. Dulles, VA: Brassey's, 2002.

Mann, Michael. *The Sources of Social Power: The Rise of Classes and Nation-States, 1760–1914*. Cambridge: Cambridge University Press, 1986.

Marhencke, Ernst-Erich. *Hans Reimer Claussen: Kämpfer für Freiheit und Recht in zwei Welten*. Frankfurt: Peter Lang, 1999.

May, Robert E. *Manifest Destiny's Underworld: Filibustering in Antebellum America*. Chapel Hill: University of North Carolina Press, 2002.

May, Robert E. *Slavery, Race, and Conquest in the Tropics: Lincoln, Douglas, and the Future of Latin America*. New York: Cambridge University Press, 2013.

May, Robert E. *The Southern Dream of a Caribbean Empire, 1854–1861*. Gainesville: University of Florida Press, 2002.

McClintock, Russell. *Lincoln and the Decision for War: The Northern Response to Secession.* Chapel Hill: University of North Carolina Press, 2008.

McCurry, Stephanie. *Confederate Reckoning: Power and Politics in the Civil War South.* Cambridge, MA: Harvard University Press, 2010.

McDaniel, W. Caleb. *The Problem of Democracy in the Age of Slavery: Garrisonian Abolitionists and Transatlantic Reform.* Baton Rouge: Louisiana State University Press, 2013.

McGovern, Bryan P. *John Mitchel: Irish Nationalist, Southern Secessionist.* Knoxville: University of Tennessee Press, 2009.

McGurk, John. *The Elizabethan Conquest of Ireland: The 1590s Crisis.* Manchester: Manchester University Press, 1997.

McPherson, James. "Antebellum Southern Exceptionalism: A New Look at an Old Question." *Civil War History* 29 (September 1983): 230–244.

McPherson, James M. *Battle Cry of Freedom: The Civil War Era.* Oxford: Oxford University Press, 2003.

Meacham, Jon. *American Lion: Andrew Jackson in the White House.* New York: Random House, 2008.

Mehrländer, Andrea. *The Germans of Charleston, Richmond and New Orleans During the Civil War Period, 1850–1870: A Study and Research Compendium.* Berlin: Walter de Gruyter, 2011.

Meigs, William M. *The Life of John Caldwell Calhoun.* New York: Neale, 1917.

Minnen, Cornelis Abraham Van, and Manfred Berg, eds. *The US South and Europe: Transatlantic Relations in the Nineteenth and Twentieth Centuries.* Lexington: University Press of Kentucky, 2013.

Morgan, Edmond S. *American Slavery, American Freedom: The Ordeal of Colonial Virginia.* New York: W. W. Norton, 2003.

Morrison, Michael A. *Slavery and the American West: The Eclipse of Manifest Destiny and the Coming of the Civil War.* Chapel Hill: University of North Carolina Press, 1997.

Mosse, Werner E. *The Rise and Fall of the Crimean System, 1855–71: The Story of a Peace Settlement.* London: Macmillan, 1963.

Murphy, Angela F. *American Slavery, Irish Freedom: Abolition, Immigrant Citizenship, and the Transatlantic Movement for Irish Repeal.* Baton Rouge: Louisiana State University Press, 2010.

Murphy, Thomas K. *A Land Without Castles: The Changing Image of America in Europe, 1780–1830.* Lanham, MD: Lexington, 2001.

Nagel, Daniel. *Von republikanischen Deutschen zu deutsch-amerikanischen Republikanern: Ein Beitrag zum Identitätswandel der deutschen Achtundvierziger in den Vereinigten Staaten, 1850–1861.* St. Ingbert: Röhrig Universitätsverlag, 2012.

Nagler, Jörg. *Fremont contra Lincoln: Die deutsch-amerikanische Opposition in der Republikanischen Partei während des amerikanischen Bürgerkrieges.* Frankfurt: Peter Lang, 1984.

Nagler, Jörg, Don H. Doyle, and Marcus Gräser, eds. *The Transnational Significance of the American Civil War.* Cham: Palgrave Macmillan, 2016.

Neely, Mark E., Jr. *The Fate of Liberty: Abraham Lincoln and Civil Liberties.* New York: Oxford University Press, 1991.

Neely, Mark E., Jr. *Southern Rights: Political Prisoners and the Myth of Confederate Constitutionalism.* Charlottesville: University Press of Virginia, 1999.

Neely, Mark E., Jr. *The Union Divided: Party Conflict in the Civil War North.* Cambridge, MA: Harvard University Press, 2002.

Nelson, Bruce. *Irish Nationalists and the Making of the Irish Race.* Princeton, NJ: Princeton University Press, 2012.

Nieman, Donald G. *African Americans and the Emergence of Segregation, 1865–1900.* New York: Garland, 1994.

Norman, Wayne J. *Negotiating Nationalism: Nation-Building, Federalism, and Secession in the Multinational State.* Oxford: Oxford University Press, 2006.

O'Connor, Peter. *American Sectionalism in the British Mind, 1832–1863.* Baton Rouge: Louisiana State University Press, 2017.

O'Neill, Peter D. *Famine Irish and the American Racial State.* New York: Routledge, 2017.

Öfele, Martin W. *True Sons of the Republic: European Immigrants in the Union Army.* Westport, CT: Praeger, 2008.

Onuf, Nicholas Greenwood, and Peter S. Onuf. *Nations, Markets, and War: Modern History and the American Civil War.* Charlottesville: University of Virginia Press, 2006.

Osterhammel, Jürgen. *Die Verwandlung der Welt: Eine Geschichte des 19. Jahrhunderts.* Munich: C. H. Beck, 2011.

Pavković, Aleksandar, and Peter Radan, eds. *The Ashgate Research Companion to Secession.* Farnham: Ashgate, 2011.

Peart, Daniel, and Adam I. P. Smith, eds. *Practicing Democracy: Popular Politics in the United States from the Constitution to the Civil War.* Charlottesville: University of Virginia Press, 2015.

Perman, Michael. *Reunion Without Compromise: The South and Reconstruction, 1865–1868.* New York: Cambridge University Press, 1973.

Perman, Michael. *Struggle for Mastery: Disfranchisement in the South, 1888–1908.* Chapel Hill: University of North Carolina Press, 2001.

Peterson, Merrill D. *The Great Triumvirate: Webster, Clay, and Calhoun.* New York: Oxford University Press, 1987.

Piványi, Eugene. *Hungarians in the American Civil War.* Cleveland, OH: Dongo, 1913.

Potter, David M. *The Impending Crisis, 1848–1861.* New York: Harper Perennial, 1976.

Price, Roger. *The Revolutions of 1848.* Atlantic Highlands, NJ: Humanities Press International, 1988.

Pula, James S. *For Liberty and Justice: A Biography of Brigadier General Włodzimierz B. Krzyżanowski, 1824–1887.* Utica, NY: Ethnic Heritage Studies Center, 2008.

Purdue, Howell, and Elizabeth Purdue. *Pat Cleburne, Confederate General: A Definitive Biography.* Hillsboro, TX: Hill Jr. College Press, 1973.

Quigley, Paul. *Shifting Grounds: Nationalism and the American South, 1848–1865.* New York: Oxford University Press, 2012.

Quinn, James. *John Mitchel.* Dublin: University College Dublin Press, 2008.

Rabinowitz, Howard N. *Race Relations in the Urban South, 1865–1890.* New York: Oxford University Press, 1978.

Rable, George C. *But There Was No Peace: The Role of Violence in the Politics of Reconstruction.* Athens: University of Georgia Press, 1984.

Rable, George C. *The Confederate Republic: A Revolution Against Politics.* Chapel Hill: University of North Carolina Press, 1994.

Ramotowska, Franciszka. *Rząd Narodowy Polski w Latach 1863–1864: Skład, Organizacja, Kancelaria* [Polish National Government in the Years 1863–1864]. Łódź: Państwowe Wydawn Naukowe, 1978.

Ramotowska, Franciszka. *Tajemne Państwo Polskie w Powstaniu Styczniowym 1863–1864: Struktura Organizacyjna* [Secret Polish State in the January Uprising, 1863–1864: Organizational Structure]. 2 vols. Warsaw: Wydawn DiG, 1999.

Randers-Pehrson, Justine Davis. *Adolf Douai, 1819–1888: The Turbulent Life of a German Forty-Eighter in the Homeland and in the United States.* New York: Peter Lang, 2000.

Reppmann, Joachim. *"Freedom, Education, and Well-Being for All!" Forty-Eighters from Schleswig-Holstein in the USA, 1847–1860* (Wyk: Verlag für Amerikanistik, 1999).

Reppmann, Joachim. Program for "Legacy of 1848: German-American History Conference." Wartburg College, October 20–22, 2013.

Reynolds, David S. *John Brown, Abolitionists: The Man Who Killed Slavery, Sparked the Civil War, and Seeded Civil Rights.* New York: Vintage, 2005.

Robertson, Priscilla. *Revolutions of 1848: A Social History.* Princeton, NJ: Princeton University Press, 1952.

Rodgers, Lois Eugenia. "Count Adam Gurowski." Master's thesis, University of Wisconsin, Madison, 1945.

Rüegg, Walter. *A History of the University in Europe.* 4 vols. Cambridge: Cambridge University Press, 1992.

Rugemer, Edward B. *The Problem of Emancipation: The Caribbean Roots of the American Civil War.* Baton Rouge: Louisiana State University Press, 2008.

Ryan, Desmond. *The Fenian Chief: A Biography of James Stephens.* Coral Gables, FL: University of Miami Press, 1967.

Sandiford, Keith A. P. *Great Britain and the Schleswig-Holstein Question, 1848–64: A Study in Diplomacy, Politics, and Public Opinion.* Toronto: University of Toronto Press, 1975.

Schmidt, Nikolaus. "Hans Reimer Claussen: Ein 'Achtundvierziger' in Amerika, 1804–1873." Master's thesis, Ruprecht-Karls-Universität, Heidelberg, 1989.

Schroeder, Paul W. *Austria, Great Britain, and the Crimean War: The Destruction of the European Concert.* Ithaca, NY: Cornell University Press, 1972.

Sheehan-Dean, Aaron Charles. *Struggle for a Vast Future.* Oxford: Osprey, 2006.

Siemann, Wolfram. *Die Deutsche Revolution von 1848/49.* Frankfurt: Suhrkamp, 1985.

Sim, David. *A Union Forever: The Irish Question and U.S. Foreign Relations in the Victorian Age.* Ithaca, NY: Cornell University Press, 2013.

Sinha, Manisha. *The Counterrevolution of Slavery: Politics and Ideology in Antebellum South Carolina.* Chapel Hill: University of North Carolina Press, 2000.

Sloan, Robert. *William Smith O'Brien and the Young Ireland Rebellion of 1848.* Dublin: Four Courts Press, 2000.

Slottman, William B. *Ferenc II Rákóczi and the Great Powers.* Boulder, CO: East European Monographs, 1997.

Smith, Adam I. P. *No Party Now: Politics in the Civil War North.* New York: Oxford University Press, 2006.

Smith, Jon, and Deborah N. Cohn, eds. *Look Away!: The U.S. South in New World Studies.* Durham, NC: Duke University Press, 2004.

Smyth, Jim. *The Men of No Property: Irish Radicals and Popular Politics in the Late Eighteenth Century.* New York: St. Martin's, 1992.

Spain, August O. *The Political Theory of John C. Calhoun.* New York: Bookman, 1951.

Spencer, Donald S. *Louis Kossuth and Young America: A Study of Sectionalism and Foreign Policy, 1848–1852.* Columbia: University of Missouri Press, 1977.

Spencer, Metta, ed. *Separatism: Democracy and Disintegration.* Lanham, MD: Rowman and Littlefield, 1998.

Sperber, Jonathan. *The European Revolutions, 1848–1851.* Cambridge: Cambridge University Press, 2005.

Sperber, Jonathan. *Rhineland Radicals: The Democratic Movement and the Revolution of 1848–1849.* Princeton, NJ: Princeton University Press, 1991.

Stasik, Florian. *Polish Political Emigrés in the United States of America, 1831–1864.* Edited by James S. Pula. Translated by Eugene Podraza. Boulder, CO: East European Monographs, 2002.

Steinwascher, Gerd. *Die Oldenburger: Die Geschichte einer Europäischen Dynastie.* Stuttgart: Kohlhammer, 2011.

Stevenson, Louise L. *Lincoln in the Atlantic World.* New York: Cambridge University Press, 2015.

Stolz, Gerd. *Die Schleswig-Holsteinische Erhebung: Die Nationale Auseinandersetzung in und um Schleswig-Holstein von 1848/51.* Husum: Idstedt-Stiftung, 1996.

Stolz, Gerd. *Hans Reimer Claussen: Der vergessene Revolutionär aus Dithmarschen, 1804–1894.* Fedderingen: Self-published, 1994.

Summerhill, Thomas, and James C. Scott, eds. *Transatlantic Rebels: Agrarian Radicalism in Comparative Context.* East Lansing: Michigan State University Press, 2004.

Svendsen, Nick. *The First Schleswig-Holstein War, 1848–1850.* Solihull: Helion, 2007.

Symonds, Craig L. *Stonewall of the West: Patrick Cleburne and the Civil War.* Lawrence: University Press of Kansas, 1997.

Taylor, Alan. *The Civil War of 1812: American Citizens, British Subjects, Irish Rebels, and Indian Allies.* New York: Vintage, 2010.

Thomson, Guy, ed. *The European Revolutions of 1848 and the Americas.* London: Institute of Latin American Studies, 2002.

Tinkler, Robert. *James Hamilton of South Carolina.* Baton Rouge: Louisiana State University Press, 2004.

Trefousse, Hans L. *Carl Schurz: A Biography.* Knoxville: University of Tennessee Press, 1982.

Tyler, Alice F. *Freedom's Ferment: Phases of American Social History to 1860.* Minneapolis: University of Minnesota Press, 1944.

Tyrrell, Ian. "American Exceptionalism in an Age of International History." *American Historical Review* 96 (October 1991): 1031–1055.

Tyrrell, Ian. *Transnational Nation: United States History in Global Perspective Since 1789.* London: Palgrave, 2007.

Tyrrell, Ian. "What Is American Exceptionalism?" March 4, 2008. https://iantyrrell.wordpress.com/papers-and-comments.

Varon, Elizabeth R. *Disunion! The Coming of the American Civil War, 1789–1859*. Chapel Hill: University of North Carolina Press, 2008.

Vick, Brian E. *Defining Germany: The 1848 Frankfurt Parliamentarians and National Identity*. Cambridge, MA: Harvard University Press, 2002.

Vida, István K. *Hungarian Émigrés in the American Civil War: A History and Biographical Dictionary*. Jefferson, NC: McFarland, 2012.

Wakelyn, Jon L., ed. *Southern Pamphlets on Secession, November 1860–April 1861*. Chapel Hill: University of North Carolina Press, 1996.

Walker, Mabel G. *The Fenian Movement*. Colorado Springs, CO: Ralph Myers, 1969.

Walther, Eric H. *The Fire-Eaters*. Baton Rouge: Louisiana State University Press, 1992.

Walther, Eric H. *William Lowndes Yancey and the Coming of the Civil War*. Chapel Hill: University of North Carolina Press, 2006.

Ward, Lee. *The Politics of Liberty in England and Revolutionary America*. Cambridge: Cambridge University Press, 2004.

Waugh, John C. *Reelecting Lincoln: The Battle for the 1864 Presidency*. New York: Crown, 1997.

Wegner, Matthias. *Hanseaten: Von stolzen Bürgern und schönen Legenden*. Berlin: Siedler, 1999.

Whelan, Kevin. *The Tree of Liberty: Radicalism, Catholicism, and the Construction of Irish Identity, 1760–1830*. Notre Dame, IN: University of Notre Dame Press, 1996.

Wilentz, Sean. *Andrew Jackson*. New York: Times Books, 2005.

Wilentz, Sean. *The Rise of American Democracy: Jefferson to Lincoln*. New York: W. W. Norton, 2005.

Wittke, Carl. *Refugees of Revolution: The German Forty-Eighters in America*. Philadelphia: University of Pennsylvania Press, 1952.

Wood, Gordon S. *Empire of Liberty: A History of the Early Republic, 1789–1815*. New York: Oxford University Press, 2009.

Wylie, Paul R. *The Irish General: Thomas Francis Meagher*. Norman: University of Oklahoma Press, 2007.

Zucker, Adolph E., ed. *The Forty-Eighters: Political Refugees of the German Revolution of 1848*. New York: Columbia University Press, 1950.

INDEX

CPSIA information can be obtained
at www.ICGtesting.com
Printed in the USA
LVHW091301101019
633792LV00004B/12/P